simply in season

Also by Tony de Luca
Recipes from Wine Country

simply in

season

12 months of wine country cooking

by TONY DE LUCA

whitecap

Whitecap Books is known for its expertise in the cookbook market, and has produced some of the most innovative and familiar titles found in kitchens across North America. Visit our website at www.whitecap.ca.

EDITED BY Julia Aitken
DESIGN BY Mauve Pagé
PHOTOGRAPHY BY Anna D'Agrosa, except pages 24–25 (orchard) ©iStockphoto.com/Jeff Chevrier; 46–47 (onions) ©iStockphoto.com/ Vladimir Vladimirov; 62–63 (halibut) ©iStockphoto.com/Carol Gering; 88–89 (asparagus) ©iStockphoto.com/Tyler Stalman; 236–37 (oysters) ©iStockphoto.com/Susanna Fieramosca Naranjo; and personal photos throughout (courtesy of the author).
FOOD STYLING BY Tony de Luca

Printed in China

Poetry by Maria Giuliani reprinted with permission of the author.

Library and Archives Canada Cataloguing in Publication

De Luca, Tony
    Simply in season : 12 months of wine country cooking / Tony de Luca.

ISBN 978-1-55285-951-3

    1. Cookery—Ontario—Niagara Peninsula. 2. Cookery, Canadian—Ontario style. I. Title.

TX907.5.C22N52 2010   641.59713'38   C2009-906423-5

The publisher acknowledges the financial support of the Government of Canada through the Canada Book Fund (CBF) and the Province of British Columbia through the Book Publishing Tax Credit.

10 11 12 13 14 5 4 3 2 1

de Luca's
RESTAURANT

contents

foreword

IN HIS LATEST BOOK, *Simply in Season*, Tony relates how he learned his trade as a chef in a variety of great restaurants in southern Ontario and abroad. As he shares the many interesting stories from the kitchens of those famed restaurants, you'll have the feeling you were actually there with him. What's more, these stories amply demonstrate how Tony gained his love of Niagara cuisine.

From the start of his adventure, in his family kitchen at the young age of 12, he began developing a great instinct for Mediterranean cuisine—fresh, wholesome, creative, vibrant, and local, all made with a passion that he obviously inherited from his family.

Tony takes you through the months of the year by creating dishes that combine and enhance all the ingredients of those seasons. His dedication to letting the "terroir" shine through is obvious; he goes to great lengths to maintain and nurture the essence of each ingredient. As Tony himself puts it, he truly "lets the recipes write themselves."

The Niagara region is a wonderful four-season destination and a great area to discover and experience regional food and wine at their best. Its trademark cuisine exhibits an original culinary style, one that reflects the land and its people. Chefs like Tony de Luca make regular pilgrimages to the Niagara countryside to stock their kitchens with fruits and vegetables, the product of fine harvests.

It's little wonder Tony is so passionate about the region: the success of the entire Niagara food and wine industry has much to do with the land itself. The Niagara Peninsula, a small, geographically distinct parcel of land, is sheltered on the north by Lake Ontario, on the south by Lake Erie, on the east by the Niagara River, and on the west by the height of the Niagara Escarpment. A myriad of vegetables, greens, and fruits, including peaches, cherries, and apricots, thrives on the farmlands here. Most notably, the area favours the growing of Vitis vinifera varieties of grapes such as Pinot Noir, Riesling, and Chardonnay. Considered a cool-climate viticultural area, the region fosters the ideal conditions for producing high-quality, mature grapes in summer. Blessed with cold winters, it also furnishes the perfect setting for crafting internationally renowned VQA icewines that have become Canadian icons. Tony uses these icewines in several creative recipes in the February chapter, which is of course most appropriate.

Enjoy the book and challenge yourself by preparing one of Tony's recipes. Tony's passion is infectious, and comes through in his recipes. I urge you to try a recipe and see for yourself!

Donald J. P. Ziraldo, CM, LLD
An accomplished vintner, Donald is a co-founder of Inniskillin Wines and a member of L'Académie Internationale du Vin.

introduction

SIMPLY IN SEASON. Having a Mediterranean heritage has given me an intuitive understanding of what those three words mean. There is beauty in simplicity. There is beauty in the seasons. It's really not that difficult to put the two together. Each season has wonderful nuances pulsing through it, and all we need to do is tune our senses to the music of the earth. Mother Nature demands respect, and could there be anything more satisfying than offering that respect?

I am blessed with the good fortune of living and cooking in a country with distinctive seasons, and the gentle rhythm of those seasons is my creative inspiration. At different times of the year countless rhythms of nature are played out for our gastronomic enjoyment.

How does this translate to a professional kitchen? Anticipating the next crop of fruits or vegetables creates an incredible buildup of excitement. There's a certain anxiety in the kitchen, a creative "cooking by the seat of our pants" mentality. You can see it in each cook's eyes. And, it contributes in a very real way to making the food fresh, vibrant, and meaningful.

From the light and delicate flavours of summer to the warm and comforting foods of winter, every season is a symphony of colours, tastes, and textures. Planning each month's menu begins with the expectation of the harvest to come. It's like experiencing a child's anticipation of Christmas morning every month—indeed, several times a month. And the rhythm of the seasons can yield surprises, both good and bad. Sometimes, just as a new menu is ready to be introduced, one of our farmer friends will call and tell us not to expect this or that, due to some weather or soil condition. (Luckily, they're always ready with a substitute.)

My cooks often hear me say, "Let the recipes write themselves." By this I mean that no one can improve on Mother Nature. The best dishes allow the natural integrity and quality of each ingredient to shine through. Our creative and artistic energy must concentrate on "leaving well enough alone." Although, admittedly, it's a challenge to cook interesting recipes while still respecting the nuances of each of their components.

One of my favourite ways to spend a Saturday morning, before heading into the kitchens of my restaurants, is to visit our magnificent farmers' market here in Niagara-on-the-Lake. It could be the season for Betty Smith's heirloom tomatoes, or for the sweetest corn you've ever tasted from Maureen MacSween of Quiet Acres Farm. I love spending time with the farmers and growers. The passion they exhibit for working the land is admirable. Truly, my success here in Niagara is directly the result of their labour. And I feel just a bit jealous of them for being able to spend their days with their hands in the cool, dark earth.

I'm lucky to live in a region that respects those who farm our land. Driving to work is like travelling through a veritable Garden of Eden, with bounty in every kilometre. What makes living here more special is that over the years the farmers who supply my restaurants have also become my friends. I often bump into them at a kids' soccer game, or at the movies. It's a true network of growers, chefs, winemakers, and neighbours—the human side of terroir. And this network defines the nuances of my food. Finding the quickest way from earth to plate: that is my "fast food."

The farm-to-table food movement that's trendy here in North America has existed in Italy forever, and Italians are amused that we should have just "discovered" this way of thinking. When I immigrated to Canada in 1970 (at the age of four), I was part of the last wave of Italian migration, which had begun earlier in the century. As a young boy here in Canada, I was raised in very typical immigrant fashion, and many of the traditions of the Old World found their way into our new lives. Like many European immigrants, we had a huge vegetable garden in the backyard, and we raised livestock such as goats, rabbits, and chickens. To many Canadians back then, this way of life must have seemed very strange. Can you imagine Ward Cleaver cutting the head off a live chicken while June cooks fresh beans from the garden, and out back Wally and the Beaver skin rabbits and pluck chickens?

Where and When It All Began: L'Altro Mondo Restaurant, 1978

AFTER EMIGRATING FROM STURNO (in the province of Avellino in southern Italy) in 1970, it took my parents a few years to realize their dream of entrepreneurship. In 1978, they moved the family to a small town north of Toronto called Oak Ridges and opened a little 35-seat restaurant called L'Altro Mondo. It was in a humble two-storey building that had been a women's hair salon. My dad and uncles renovated the space, put in a tiny kitchen, slapped on some paint, and opened the doors.

At first we lived above the restaurant in a small apartment. The restaurant's grand opening coincided with the start of the school year, and I had no idea that would be the day that changed my life forever, sending me on a path that after 32 years is still full of surprises. I was 12. Coming home from school on the bus that day, I remember noticing how slow the bus was. My friend observed we were in some kind of traffic jam, a ridiculous idea as there were not enough cars in our neighbourhood to create one. But sure enough, peering through the front window of the bus, I noticed a procession of slow-moving cars ahead of us. I asked the driver if I could walk the rest of the way home as it was the street I lived on. And off I went.

As I approached the restaurant, I felt a strange mixture of wonder and anxiety as I realized all the cars were trying to get into our parking lot. It was a chaotic scene with honking horns and general confusion. Outside the restaurant, there was a lineup of people. I remember wondering what the hell was going on, and why all these people were waiting outside my home. It never occurred to me that they were trying to get in to

TONY AND HIS BROTHER, DAN, AT L'ALTRO MONDO, THE ONLY PICTURE OF THAT AUSPICIOUS BEGINNING

eat. I just assumed, since we lived upstairs, that they were all coming to visit us.

I walked around to the back of the building to the kitchen entrance and went through the door. I've relived the scene in my mind a thousand times. There, laid out before me, was my future. And it was pandemonium. What I remember most was the authoritative yet terrified look in my mother's eyes as she turned and, not expecting to see me nor really knowing at whom she was yelling, shouted at me to go and make six Caesar salads. "What's a Caesar salad?" I cried.

There were people in various levels of distress, confusion, terror, and exhaustion working frantically to my mother's orders. It was a frightening yet beautiful sight for someone totally ignorant of what was going on. I felt an adrenalin rush: my first high! They say you never forget your first time. I'm sure that's not supposed to refer to working in a restaurant kitchen, but that day has stayed with me forever.

My first service, my first Caesar salad, my first burn, my first cut, my first enormous pile of dishes and pots to wash (in those days, we didn't have a mechanical dishwasher but washed every pot, pan, utensil, bowl, dish, glass, and piece of cutlery by hand)—I experienced it all by the end of the night. The initial hours of my 32-year restaurant career were more intense and memorable than the first time I had sex. That night

after school, I worked a seven-hour shift. By the end, I was exhausted but extremely happy. We had done well. We had served 80 customers in a 35-seat restaurant, and people had raved about the food. Needless to say, not much of my homework got done that night, or many other nights after that. I was hooked.

So much of how I cook today was absorbed during those formative years working beside my mom, both at home and in the restaurant. Of course, as a young man whose focus was squarely on the future, I never appreciated those influences at the time. I never really stopped to acknowledge them at all. In fact, I spent much of my early culinary life ignoring those very things. But I came to realize that I grew up with great food. It was a part of my life. Being the eldest son in a family with deep culinary roots in our region of Italy afforded me the kind of exposure most chefs learn only in books or on the Internet. I lived it every day.

The meaning of this really hit home one spring, sometime in the late '80s, when my parents and I visited cousins in Long Island, New York, in the city of Glen Cove. I went to an espresso bar that, at the end of the 19th century, had been a restaurant owned by my great-grandfather and great-uncle. The realization that members of my family had made the same career choice 100 years ago had a profound effect on me. When I got back home, I decided to embrace my roots and incorporate the many beautiful elements of the Mediterranean palate into my cuisine. The recipes in this book are the latest manifestation of that creative burst, a snapshot of a particular place that has taken a lifetime to bring into focus.

The Windsor Arms Hotel, 1987

WHEN I WAS 22, I got a job at the famous Windsor Arms Hotel on St. Thomas Street, Toronto. In 1987, the Windsor Arms was the crown jewel of a large company owned by Harry Minden—a company that, at its peak, operated The Millcroft Inn in Alton, Ontario, and several popular Toronto restaurants, such as the Bay Street Car and Noodles. Many well-known, creative chefs have worked at one time or another at the Windsor Arms. (Anyone familiar with the Toronto dining scene will recognize the names of Suzanne Baby, Michael Blackie, Michael Bonacini, Robert Buchanan, Robert Clark, Michael Ewing, Sam Glass, Gary Hoyer, Jamie Kennedy, (the late) Freddy Lo Cicero, Lorenzo Loseto, Dante Rota, Herbert Sonzogni, Fredy Stamm, Marc Thuet, Anthony Walsh, and Peter Zambri.) It's a veritable who's who of Canadian chefs.

Since the late '60s the Windsor Arms had been an iconic symbol of all that was fine in dining and service. For many people, it was the destination of choice for special occasions, for romantic retreats, or for the latest in culinary innovation. In its day, the Windsor Arms hosted famous guests as diverse as Liberace, Suzanne Somers, Sophia Loren, The Rolling Stones, and Led Zeppelin.

How I even got the job at Windsor Arms is a story of extraordinary luck, which once prompted a colleague to remark that I must have horseshoes stuck up my butt. (I like to think it was more a consequence of my charming personality and engaging demeanour . . .) I was working at Eaton Hall, a catering facility in King City (a town near my home in Oak Ridges), which had advertised at my college for apprentice chefs to help with the banqueting. There I was befriended by an Asian chef named Long who had a roommate, Tan, who was a sous-chef at the Windsor Arms. When he mentioned that Tan was looking for apprentice chefs, I jumped at the chance.

My interview was on Saturday, June 10, 1987, at 3 p.m. with the executive chef, Michael Bonacini. Apart from the date, I don't remember much about the inter-view, but I must have made a good impression because I started at the hotel the following Monday.

During those days at the Windsor Arms we worked hard but partied with equal rigour. They were heady times. It was just before it became fashionable to be a chef, but we all knew the "celebrity chef" cult was coming, and we were all jostling to reap any rewards.

Having worked in my mother's kitchen from such an early age, I soon gained a reputation with my superiors for being a very hard worker with passion, dedication, and enough perseverance to succeed at any tasks thrown my way. My time at the Windsor Arms was invaluable. I felt blessed and extremely fortunate to have landed at such a prestigious address and humbled by the great chefs working alongside me at the time. It was a period of development that exposed me to an incredible array of food, cooking techniques, management styles, and adventures.

The Fire and the Idiot

AS APPRENTICES AT WINDSOR ARMS, we were expected to work long hours and in all departments. It was crucial to our development as future chefs to experience everything to do with the hotel kitchen. Typically, a new employee would begin with the breakfast shift. It was a horrible experience. I started work at 6 a.m.,

TONY IN ACTION

which meant getting up at 3:30 a.m. to make it in on time from my home in Oak Ridges.

Luckily I was on that shift for only a month or so. I think executive chef Bonacini took pity on me because of this one particular morning when I helped prevent the hotel from burning down.

That day, as the veteran on the breakfast shift, I was instructed to train a new recruit. He was a stubborn little fellow. I was having a difficult time making him understand that executive chef Bonacini liked things done a specific way and if he wanted to make the right impression, he should pay attention to me.

Every morning, one of the first tasks was to clarify butter for the hollandaise sauce. I clearly explained to the new guy that you simply melt the butter in a big pot over low heat and simmer it gently. The idiot ignored everything I said, and the butter overflowed over the entire bank of ovens, causing a huge fire about 12 feet long and 3 feet deep.

Did I mention that one of the skills I learned at this juncture involved *grace under pressure*? In a desperate attempt to put out the flames, I shouted to my trainee to push the fire-suppression button. He must have spotted the terror in my eyes because he promptly removed his apron and calmly walked out of the kitchen, never to be seen again.

Meanwhile, I had a huge fire on my hands so I rushed downstairs in a panic and knocked on executive chef Bonacini's office door.

"Excuse me, Chef, there seems to be a serious problem upstairs."

"Oh really, Tony, what could be so serious?"

"Well, Chef, it seems my trainee has left."

"Really, what do you mean, left? Was it something you said?"

"No, Chef, it was because he set the entire kitchen line on fire with your delicious clarified butter."

"Shit."

At that point, the fear in my eyes was reflected in the eyes of my chef and he literally leaped over his desk and blew by me. When I caught up with him, the fire suppression had been activated, and miraculously, the hotel did not burn down. Mind you, I was late getting the breakfast out that morning, and my eggs weren't the best they could have been.

The Bloody Nose

AFTER MY TIME spent in the hotel's Courtyard Café, I was transferred downstairs to the main kitchen to work the butcher station. Here, I learned the many ways to butcher just about any meat. Typically when you move to a new station of a hotel restaurant, you shadow the trainer while you get a hang of things. I had the good fortune to shadow and work with a very capable chef and butcher named Peter Brookes. His expertise and confidence with a boning knife was something to marvel at. We didn't spend much time working together in the butcher department, but it was long enough to pick up few good pointers, all of which have stayed with me.

When Peter was transferred to the Three Small Rooms, the formal dining room in the Windsor Arms, this was cause for celebration since it was every apprentice's goal to cook on that line one day. The Three Small Rooms was the finishing school of your apprenticeship. The chefs there were the real deal. All were veterans who had gone through the wringer.

But, it was well known that at Three Small Rooms, there was no room for mistakes, like walking on hot coals. You kept your mouth shut. You learned quickly that no quarter was given. You worked extremely hard, utilizing all the skills you'd learned in the other areas of the hotel. You were expected to be subservient. It was not a place where you would freely discuss the culinary ideas and ideals of the day. (Actually, now that I think of it, you didn't discuss anything.) It was intimidating, but when Peter made it in there, I felt happy for him and resolved to follow him soon.

I spent about six months in the butcher department, and by the end, I thought I was destined to become a vegetarian, with all the cutting and portioning of animal flesh. Sometimes I felt like Lady Macbeth, unable to scrub the imagined blood off my hands. Dogs loved me. They'd make a beeline for me and lick my hands like they were two large bowls of Alpo.

Peter was also the central character of one of the most brutal incidents I ever witnessed. A restaurant kitchen can be an intense, and sometimes violent, place. During one particular nasty service, I heard shouting and noises that sounded like pots and pans being thrown around. The chef of the Three Small Rooms had lost it! There was profanity followed by more pot and pan throwing. I was working at the butcher counter in the back of the kitchen. My head was down concentrating on my work when I looked up to see Peter standing in front of me. His face was a mess. Blood spilling from his nose and mouth covered the front of his white chef tunic.

"Peter, what the hell . . . ?"

"Shut the fuck up and give me the veal," he replied.

"But, you're covered in blood," I said.

"Don't worry your ass, just give me the meat or he'll take out the rest of my teeth," he screamed.

"He" was the chef of the Three Small Rooms, who'd smashed a frying pan into Peter's face, resulting in a broken nose, a broken tooth, and a cut lip. For Peter Brookes, that was the price of admission to the Three Small Rooms.

Chewton Glen, 1988

MY TIME IN THE THREE SMALL ROOMS was the most memorable period of cooking I have ever experienced, and I enjoyed every moment of it. Looking back on that time, I feel really fortunate to have worked with such a serious, talented team of culinarians. Despite the intensity, which often manifested itself in various forms of abuse and violence, we all felt lucky to be part of it.

But, after six months or so, I felt I needed a change. I was thinking for a while about working abroad, in Europe—and since England was English speaking I thought this would be the easiest transition for me. I asked my executive chef Michael Bonacini if he would recommend me for a position in that country. I was amazed at how he immediately picked up the phone and called the Chewton Glen hotel in New Milton, in southern England. It was almost as if Chef Bonacini was happy to have me leave his kitchen!

Just a couple of weeks later I was headed across the Atlantic. Since I had never been to England before, I decided to travel for a few weeks prior to starting at the Glen and bum around the countryside capturing the flavour and culture of my new home. After exploring some charming historic towns I felt rested and revitalized, ready for the next stop on my culinary journey.

Regrettably, having run out of money, I had to spend the last few nights before I was expected at the hotel sleeping on a park bench outside of town. On the day

I was due to arrive at the Glen, I was a mess. I walked into the swanky, prestigious, Michelin-starred, Relais & Chateaux hotel without having shaved, bathed, or eaten for two days. When I asked at reception for Geoffrey Bray Cotton, who was Michael Bonacini's contact at the hotel, I felt the up-and-down stares of staff and guests alike. Luckily, Geoffrey was an enlightened employer, took it all in stride, and quickly ushered me to his office.

After exchanging brief pleasantries, Geoffrey kindly asked if I would like tea. "That would be nice," I answered. Soon after, an Italian waiter in a tux brought three trays loaded with cookies, pastries, little sandwiches, and fruit tarts. When Geoffrey excused himself to find the sous-chef, who was to give me a tour of the kitchen, I proceeded to eat the entire contents of the trays and satisfactorily did justice to my very first English tea.

Having experienced the rigours of working at the Windsor Arms, it was a good thing that I felt prepared for my new position as commis chef at Chewton Glen. The chef, Pierre, was a maniac. A short man

with a large Napoleon complex, he was the first—and only—chef I'd seen climb up onto the pass (the area where the chef calls out the orders to the cooks in the kitchen) during service and, with fists clenched, jump up and down and scream at his staff. Pierre had also perfected the art of throwing plates of food at incompetent wait staff. Many an evening saw me ducking flying crockery aimed not at my head but at that of some hapless waiter who'd raised the chef's ire.

It was a very international environment where French was the primary language. I worked with chefs from France, England, the United States, Australia, South America, and Italy. Although the kitchen seemed very disorganized, it was remarkable for the quality of the products it used and the complicated composition of its recipes. Fresh black truffles, foie gras, and beluga caviar were used with abandon. It was food as I'd never seen it before. I remember once having to hang 70 pheasants in the larder after a very sophisticated man in a thick tweed jacket and ascot had us unload them from the back of his Range Rover. I also remember coming into the larder one morning some days later to the smell of rotting pheasant flesh and having to discard half of them because of a maggot infestation.

In the grand scheme of things, Chewton Glen was mostly about the association and great friendship I

TONY'S DAD, BROTHER DANNY,
AND SISTER-IN-LAW ASHLEIGH

developed with Geoffrey. He has been a constant in my career from the day I met him, and truly a trusted friend. He let me crash at his apartment in England and introduced me to his wife, Barbara (who's also become a great friend), and newborn daughter Zoë. Always dressed in a bow tie, Geoffrey was the consummate professional, yet was just as much at home flying a kite off the cliffs at Christchurch (a small town near Chewton Glen) or riding around town on his little scooter.

When Geoffrey left Chewton Glen to become the first manager of Langdon Hall Country House Hotel, a Relais & Chateaux property in Cambridge, Ontario, I had a motive to move back to Canada. So in 1989, I joined the opening team at Langdon Hall as *chef de partie*.

Oliver's Bakery, 1989

AFTER I LANDED BACK in Canada and prior to starting at Langdon Hall, I decided that it was time for me to learn the basics of pastry and baking. I took a job as a pastry cook at Peter Oliver's famous Oliver's Bakery in Toronto and worked with pastry chef Ian Gallagher and his sous-chef Catherine O'Donnell. Even though I only spent three months in that kitchen, it was an important time. Not only did I learn the fundamentals of pastry, I also found I hated it. It was tedious and boring always to be weighing out flour, sugar, and eggs.

Those three months were significant for another reason because it was at Oliver's Bakery that I met Christine Weiss. Christine was a German pastry cook who had come to Canada to learn English and gain experience working with chef Gallagher, who was quite renowned at the time. Christine and I soon became a couple, and as our relationship grew, we decided that she would follow me to Langdon Hall.

Langdon Hall Country House Hotel, 1989

RECENTLY I RECEIVED A CALL from William Bennett, the owner of Langdon Hall, inviting me to the hotel's 20th anniversary celebrations. It's hard to believe that so many years have passed since Langdon Hall opened. I think back with affection on those days in the late '80s because my time there coincided with my realization that, in the kitchen at least, I knew what I was doing.

I felt a real passion for my profession and realized the time I had invested working at the Windsor Arms and Chewton Glen had not been wasted. The countless unpaid hours spent grinding it out, day in, day out, in the intense atmospheres of those very prestigious kitchens were paying off. At Langdon, I felt I was coming into my own. Most of my fond memories focus on the wonderful and interesting personalities I met there, many of whom are still very good friends of mine.

I remember the first time I laid eyes on Langdon Hall. Through its unassuming entrance, a long, winding driveway led through thickly forested grounds until, round the last bend, the hotel appeared majestically as if out of nowhere. The building was an awesome sight, and I felt really intimidated. I still get goose pimples when I go there.

The inside of the building was another story, however. On that first rainy day, Geoffrey met me and gave me a tour. The house was empty, and entire sections of floor were missing so that, in some places, you could see straight up to the roof and right down to the basement. It was damp, cold, and smelly, and in my wildest imagination, I could never have believed how beautiful and functional the finished hotel would turn out to be.

One of my favourite parts of Langdon Hall was the gardens. I loved working in a place where we harvested so many of the vegetables and fruits we used in the kitchen. We grew haricots verts, tomatoes, carrots, potatoes, green peppers, eggplants, zucchini, lettuce, strawberries, raspberries, and so much more. We were challenged to keep up with Mother Nature in those days.

Perhaps I always had a great attachment to Langdon Hall because, at the very start, I was more labourer than chef. When I started, I had already left my job at Oliver's Bakery. Many of us had left our jobs expecting to begin at Langdon, but there were the inevitable construction delays. Since we didn't want to sit around and wait for the kitchen to be ready, we volunteered to work with the construction crew—to help speed things up, and to make some money! Mostly we helped with the cleanup and sweeping, and we got to know the property pretty intimately.

For instance, the beautiful shallow lily pond outside the dining room windows had actually been the swimming pool of the original house and wasn't really so shallow. I remember helping to put in the pond's false bottom with Todd Clarmo, and crawling underneath to clean out leaves and other debris before the last slab of concrete was put in place. I also worked on insulating many of the bedrooms in the main house, and installed the bedroom furniture in the cloisters.

I also fondly remember our tightly knit kitchen brigade. Our fearless leader was executive chef Nigel Didcock. In the kitchen, chef Nigel was the consummate professional, but he did love his practical jokes. During my time at Langdon Hall, I was a regular jogger and usually went for a brisk run during my afternoon break. One day I got back from my run a bit late and, after a quick shower before changing into clean chef whites, I couldn't find my underwear. In my haste, I decided to go "alfresco" as it were, and got on the line in the kitchen just in time. The restaurant was full that night and the kitchen busy. In the middle of this mayhem, chef Nigel yelled at me to get the beef sauce that I'd prepared that morning. When I couldn't find it (a real problem since the beef would get cold and maybe have to be made again), he screamed at me to

TONY AND CHEF NIGEL AFTER GATHERING MOREL MUSHROOMS ON THE GROUNDS OF LANGDON HALL, 1989

get the backup sauce from my fridge and warm that instead. In my haste, I didn't notice that what I poured out into the saucepan to heat up was not the backup beef sauce but my underwear. As the brigade broke out laughing and I noticed the smell of burning elastic, I realized that chef Nigel had snuck down to the shower and stolen my briefs while I was jogging and had put one over on me real good!

Nigel lived on the property, and I always appreciated how he would make us feel like family by having Christmas presents for all of us, and with his wife, Catherine, hosting a holiday celebration in his apartment. The first Christmas after his underwear heist, he presented me with a framed pair of briefs with my name written on them in cocoa. That was Nigel.

Chef Nigel always went out of his way to help us professionally as well. It was he who arranged my stage in Washington, D.C., in 1989 with the late, great Jean-Louis Palladin, whose small restaurant, Jean-Louis at the Watergate, underneath the Watergate Hotel, was a beacon of the new Franco-American food movement of the time. Chef Palladin was a two-Michelin-star chef in France, and wrote the cookbook *Cooking with the Seasons*, which continues to be a huge inspiration to me.

In 1991, I followed Christine to Munich, Germany. While our relationship did not flourish there, I loved living in Germany. Not only did I meet some exceptional people, but I also landed great jobs with Michelin-starred chefs like Otto Koch at Le Gourmet, and at the Hotel Bayerischer Hof in Munich. Although working in these kitchens solidified my culinary skills, the experience was incredibly difficult as I couldn't speak a word of German. Regrettably, when my relationship with Christine came to an end, so did my time working in Germany, and I came home.

Millcroft Inn & Spa, 1992

AS I DROVE UP Highway 10 to the Millcroft Inn in Alton, Ontario, just north of Toronto, I really had no ambition to become a head chef. I was working with executive chef Susan Weaver at the Four Seasons Hotel in Yorkville and had just met two colleagues—Lynn Crawford and Lino Collevecchio—whom I very much enjoyed working with. (Lynn has since gone on to have a wonderful career. She's appeared on many Food Network TV shows and is currently working as the executive chef at the Four Seasons Hotel in Manhattan. We remain close and, while we don't see each other often, when we do it seems as if barely a day has gone by since we last met. Lino is the most creative and hard-working of chefs, and is now the very successful executive chef of Via Allegro, one of the Greater Toronto Area's best restaurants.)

I had joined the Four Seasons at a very good time, as the hotel was in the process of reopening the beautiful Studio Café, plus the chef of the property's fine dining restaurant, Truffles, was none other than Patrick Lin, a true culinary master. Patrick was extraordinary. He was the first chef I'd met who drew pictures of his menu items. His remarkably detailed sketches included a legend indicating what his shorthand meant—a star might be a julienne of carrots, an asterisk, glazed pearl onions. I copied chef Patrick's technique and, while I'm not as accomplished an artist as he, the technique of drawing the recipes before actually plating them has become a very worthwhile training tool for me and my current staff of cooks.

Meanwhile, back on Highway 10, I'd heard through the culinary grapevine that the long-time chef of the Millcroft Inn, Fredy Stamm, was moving on, and I thought it would be good for me to get a bit more interview experience. I knew about the Millcroft because it had been the sister property of the Windsor Arms. Like many other beautiful Relais & Chateaux

TONY AT MILLCROFT INN, 1992

properties, the Millcroft Inn sits in spectacular grounds, complete with a waterfall, pond, and 100 acres of unspoiled natural beauty. When I arrived that cold January day, the waterfall had frozen creating a beautiful dome of icicles. It was one of the most stunning things I'd ever seen.

My interview with general manager Peter Culp went well, and I really enjoyed the tour of the hotel. I fell in love with the kitchen, which was spacious and extremely well lit, with large windows overlooking the garden. One odd aspect of that day was that I spent a good deal of time being interviewed by outgoing chef Stamm. When I was about to leave, Mr. Culp offered me the job, and on the drive home, I replayed the entire experience, not really believing I had just secured my first executive chef position. I was just 26 years old.

Back at the Four Seasons, I went into chef Weaver's office in tears to resign—the first (and last) time I've ever actually cried at work. To the chef's credit, she took it all in stride, saying that, although she was sorry to see me go, the move to the Millcroft Inn would be a good challenge for me.

I started my job as executive chef of the Millcroft Inn on a cold February day and was fortunate to have some great chefs working for me, which made my first management experience a very positive one. My staff included Robert Buchanan, who had worked with me at the Windsor Arms; Paul Boehmer, whom I knew from Langdon Hall; and Reinhard Scheer-Hennings, who was the acting sous-chef left by Fredy Stamm. The four of us worked our tails off, and I owe much of my initial success as a chef to those guys.

When I speak to young culinarians now I often tell them about the early years of my career. I explain the sense of commitment, which meant I often slept in my office overnight so I could approve everything that left my kitchen. I relate the sacrifices I had to make while working the breakfast, lunch, and dinner shifts seven days a week. And I describe the passion and love I had for our craft (I think my menus during that time where probably the most inspired of my life).

Regrettably, the Millcroft Inn was also where one of the sorriest episodes of my career occurred. I had started working at the inn during the winter when things were a little slower, so I was a bit unprepared when summer came and business went through the roof. On one of the first busy Saturday evenings of the season, the restaurant manager, who shall remain nameless, came to the pass and told me that a guest was complaining about the "slow" kitchen. As I was explaining that we were very busy and were backed up, the manager turned on his heel and said, "You just don't care."

Since I'd been working around the clock for the past few months, that was the worst thing he could have said. I flew into a rage and started channelling Chewton Glen's chef Pierre. I flung every plate I could

reach in the restaurant manager's direction. He could not believe what was happening, and I was just barely aware of it myself. In my anger, I couldn't stop myself and he just froze in the line of fire. Beef tenderloin, lobster, pasta, chicken, shrimp—all were tossed at the poor man. He was a mess. His clothes destroyed, his hair covered in gravy, he was close to tears, and all because of a little miscommunication. Needless to say, in no incident since have I had a worse tantrum or been more of a jerk.

Hillebrand Winery, 1996

IT WAS WHILE WORKING at the Four Seasons Hotel that I met my future wife, Kaleen. So I spent the next few years learning to be a good husband, then a good father when my first child Matthew was born in 1995.

After I left the Millcroft Inn, I was working at a little Italian restaurant called Colori on Toronto's Danforth Avenue when I got a phone call from my good friend Robert Buchanan, who was now the chef and owner of Acqua restaurant in BCE Place in Toronto. He told me a very persistent headhunter named Leo Lecours wanted Rob to submit his name as a candidate for executive chef of a new winery restaurant in Niagara-on-the-Lake. Robert had no interest in moving there so asked me if I'd be interested. Having never been to Niagara, I had no notion of what was going on there at the time, but something about the move appealed to me.

I had never considered myself a city boy so had been dreaming for a while about leaving the hustle and bustle of Toronto behind. Also, having a newborn baby and an adventurous wife made me think that the rural life might be for us. I told Robert he could suggest my name to Leo, and things began happening rather quickly. After I met Leo, I was very keen to go and see the project. During the week while I waited to be called for an interview, unbeknownst to me, I was feeding the hiring committee from Hillebrand Winery, who had been dining regularly at Colori.

Kaleen and I packed up Matthew on a cold January day and drove to Niagara-on-the-Lake. The long interview process involved a mock television appearance. After a tour of the winery, it was love at first sight for me. Back at work the following day, I got a call from Leo, who said they had offered me the position. When I went home, Kaleen and I celebrated with the bottle of bubbly that we had bought at Hillebrand the day before.

On February 5, 1996, I started working at Hillebrand and was there almost ten years. I was blessed to work with some very special people, not the least of which were Greg Berti and Bob Davis, David Black and Robert Stanley, Ross Midgley, Mark Torrance, Sherry Lockwood, Alison Zalepa, Isa Diorio, Shelly Brown, Cathy Kvas, Audrey Davis, Susan Julien, Grant Moore, and of course John and Dianne Peller, and J-L Groux, winemaker extraordinaire, who may have the best palate in the world. Wine tasting with J-L was such a great learning experience, and it changed forever my perception of wine and wine tasting.

Some of the highlights of my time at the winery include two visits as guest chef to the Epcot International Food & Wine Festival at Walt Disney World in Florida, being featured as guest Canadian chef at the Kempinski Hotel in Beijing, and perhaps my greatest achievement of all, the publication of my first cookbook, *Recipes from Wine Country*.

It was one hell of a ride.

ICEWINE JELLY
by Maria Giuliani

Something sultry on my tongue
Bites me
Like the dry cold air of a hundred days of brevity
Tempered briefly by this small wafer in my hand
Oozing over and drunk with a light decadence.
Something shimmering and sweet
Reminds me
Of something else
Something golden,
Now preserved under glass
Something stolen
From a season that has passed.
And as my taste buds twirl
Over and around
Each voluminous curve,
As a slow sigh escapes into a frosty mist
I think,
This—
This must be the sun.

January Hard frozen earth. Cold wind blowing through the icicled branches. Frostbitten fingers. Wanting to stay in your warm, snuggly bed. Rutabagas and more rutabagas. No other month hides its potential more than the first month of the year. Shouldn't we have the option of skipping from December straight though to April?

It's hard to be inspired by January. The month is like a long hangover. By its very nature, January is a big letdown. The festive buildup reaches a frenzied state over Christmas and just getting to New Year's Eve requires such a burst of enthusiasm, both creative and physical, that you lay all your culinary cards on the table. And suddenly it's the big night.

The busboys run through the dining room. In the kitchen, cooks and servers dance around each other. It's adrenalin time, a great culinary surge. Cooking on New Year's Eve has always been one of my great professional pleasures. Your guests must be impressed, sure, but you get to enjoy yourself, too, with the occasional glass of bubbly. Or two. Or three. Then New Year's Day comes, and comes too quickly.

Like a great novel after the exciting ending has been revealed, January often feels to me like the finish of a story, an anticlimax. Menus that flow with pleasure and ease the rest of the year become challenging. Recipes that normally write themselves feel contrived.

Nothing comes in the back door but a big snowdrift.

How do you avoid the doldrums caused by January's cold-hearted nature? With fire, just like our ancestors did, that's how. But, in my kitchen, the fire's in the pizza oven! The smell of the wood smoke infuses the restaurant with a fulfilling sense of warmth. The sound of the wood crackling perks us up. The flames, as they get higher, get hotter, their heat radiating and filling the restaurant with a sense of conviviality. It makes you think there's hope.

There is always hope, my friends. For instance, I hope the icewine gets made. The golden elixir so closely related to the very identity of our terroir here in Niagara, needs cold, cold winters. Icewine makes the gloom of the season worthwhile.

Back in the kitchen, let's add another log to the fire. Feel the heat as you reach in to position it, the gentle smoke enveloping your arm. You'll still smell that smoke hours later. Isn't it amazing how comfortable you're feeling? Now we're getting hungry. Let's see what's in the fridge and pantry. There's the bison Arden Vaughn delivered from Lake Land Meats in St. Catharines. We could wrap it in some pancetta and roast it. And what about those tiny, new Brussels sprouts that just came in? We could team those with some fresh chestnuts. We could poach some lovely, ripe pears in a hearty wine like winemaker J-L Groux's Stratus Red. I love his wines, so full of flavour with just the right amount of oak. Can you imagine how good that would taste? Now we're cooking!

It's January, we have wine, we have fire. Now if I could only shovel out that snowdrift at the back door . . .

I can't resist including a chicken liver pâté recipe in this book. Perhaps because I had to make pâté so often at the Windsor Arms, a collection of recipes without it seems a bit soulless. Although

Chicken Liver Pâté with Pickled Eggplant and Roasted Garlic–Onion Jam

a chicken liver pâté recipe appeared in my first cookbook, this one is slightly different. The livers are seared first in olive oil to give them a more defined, less subtle flavour. At any rate, a pâté seems a good way to start a cookbook, especially one in which the first chapter is all about January. A creamy, rich, and satisfying pâté, paired with the lively flavours of pickled eggplant, will go a long way to warming you up . . . from the inside out!

SERVES 6

CHICKEN LIVER PÂTÉ

½ cup (125 mL) olive oil, divided

3 lb (1.5 kg) chicken livers, cleaned of all sinew

¼ cup (60 mL) unsalted butter

1 onion, chopped

4 cloves garlic, minced

4 sprigs thyme, leaves picked off from stems and finely chopped

2 sprigs rosemary, leaves picked off from stems and finely chopped

½ cup (125 mL) brandy

½ cup (125 mL) Madeira

1 cup (250 mL) 35% cream

7 eggs

2 Tbsp (30 mL) granulated sugar

2 Tbsp (30 mL) kosher salt

1 Tbsp (15 mL) cracked black peppercorns

PREHEAT THE OVEN to 300°F (150°C).

Heat a large skillet over medium-high heat and add ¼ cup (60 mL) of the olive oil. When the oil just begins to smoke, add the chicken livers and sauté, stirring frequently, for about 10 minutes or until browned on all sides and no longer pink in the centre. Transfer to a plate lined with paper towels and set aside.

In the same skillet, heat the remaining oil and the butter over medium heat. When the butter foams, add the onion and garlic and sauté, stirring frequently, until the onion is golden brown. Add the herbs and stir well. Add the brandy and Madeira and, standing well back, ignite carefully. When the flames die away, simmer until the liquid has reduced by half. Remove the skillet from the heat and let the onion mixture cool to room temperature.

Recipe continued . . .

Transfer the onion mixture to a food processor or blender. Add the seared chicken livers, cream, eggs, sugar, salt, and peppercorns. Process until the mixture is quite smooth.

Transfer the chicken liver mixture to a 10-cup (2.5 L) ovenproof dish and cover first with strong plastic wrap, then with aluminum foil. Bake for 1½ hours or until the pâté has set and an instant-read thermometer inserted into the centre of the pâté registers 160°F (71°C).

Let the pâté cool to room temperature then refrigerate it overnight.

PICKLED EGGPLANT

2 medium eggplants
4 Tbsp (60 mL) kosher salt, divided
1¼ cups (310 mL) plus 1 Tbsp (15 mL) olive oil
1 cup (250 mL) cider vinegar

1 bunch Italian parsley
1 Tbsp (15 mL) honey
½ tsp (2 mL) black pepper
3 bay leaves
5 cloves garlic, minced

BRING A VERY LARGE POT of water to a boil. Cut the eggplant into ½-inch (1 cm) dice but do not peel. Add 3 Tbsp (45 mL) of the salt to the pot of water, then add the eggplant and simmer for 5 minutes. Using a large skimmer or a slotted spoon, remove the eggplant and place it in a colander set in the sink. Allow to drain.

In a large skillet, heat 1¼ cups (310 mL) of the olive oil over medium-high heat. Sauté the simmered eggplant, in batches if necessary, for about 6 minutes or until golden brown on all sides. Remove the eggplant from the skillet and set aside.

In a large saucepan, combine 2 cups (500 mL) water, the vinegar, parsley, honey, pepper, bay leaves, and remaining salt. Bring to a boil over high heat, then boil for 3 minutes. Remove the saucepan from the heat and set aside.

Meanwhile, in a small skillet, heat the remaining oil over medium heat. Add the garlic and sauté for about 1 minute or until fragrant.

Pour the vinegar mixture into a large non-reactive container and add the sautéed eggplant and garlic. Cover and refrigerate for at least 24 hours before serving.

ROASTED GARLIC–ONION JAM

¼ cup (60 mL) grapeseed oil

¼ cup (60 mL) unsalted butter

2 cups (500 mL) diced onions

1 Tbsp (15 mL) roasted garlic (page 257)

1 cup (250 mL) dry white wine

1 Tbsp (15 mL) grated lemon zest

1 bay leaf

2 Tbsp (30 mL) packed brown sugar

1 Tbsp (15 mL) ground fennel seed
    (optional)

1 tsp (5 mL) kosher salt

HEAT A MEDIUM SAUCEPAN over medium heat, then add the grapeseed oil and butter. When the butter foams, add the onions and garlic. Sauté, stirring frequently, until the onions and garlic are golden brown.

Add the wine, lemon zest, and bay leaf. Simmer until the wine has completely evaporated. Stir in the brown sugar, fennel seed (if using), and salt and cook for an additional 5 minutes. Remove the saucepan from the heat and set aside until ready to serve.

TO SERVE

baby salad greens for garnish

PLACE A GENEROUS spoonful of roasted garlic–onion jam in the centre of each of 6 chilled dinner plates. Using the back of a spoon, spread out the jam so it forms a thin circular layer on the plate. Drain the pickling liquid from the pickled eggplant and scatter the eggplant cubes around the plate. Using 2 warm dinner spoons, form the pâté into nice barrel shapes and place on the jam. Garnish each plate with a small bouquet of salad greens.

Chestnuts are one of my favourite winter ingredients, and their aroma can instantly snap me back to my childhood.

With this recipe, I honour the late

Purée of Chestnut Soup with Quail Confit and Sautéed Shiitake Mushrooms

Jean-Louis Palladin, the Washington, D.C., chef in whose restaurant, Jean-Louis at the Watergate, I worked in 1989. Chef Palladin treated the soup course with the same passion and maniacal attention to detail as he did all the other courses of a meal. He showed me that soup should never be an afterthought but should be prepared slowly and intentionally, and garnished with complementary ingredients prepared with equal reverence.

Ask your butcher to bone the quail, but keeping the skin on and the leg bones intact.

SERVES 6

QUAIL CONFIT

2 cups (500 mL) duck fat	kosher salt and black pepper
2 cloves garlic, crushed	to taste
4 black peppercorns	3 sprigs thyme
1 bay leaf	1 large sprig rosemary
3 boneless quail	3 lemon quarters

IN A MEDIUM SAUCEPAN, heat the duck fat over low heat until it liquefies. Add the garlic, peppercorns, and bay leaf. Adjust the heat so the duck fat remains just under simmering point.

Meanwhile, season the quail on both sides with salt and pepper. Place 1 sprig of the thyme, one-third of the rosemary, and 1 lemon quarter on the meaty side of each quail. Fold each quail over to enclose the flavourings and tie with butcher twine.

Submerge the quail in the duck fat. Cover and cook gently (the duck fat should barely simmer) for about 1 hour or until an instant-read thermometer inserted into the meaty part of the quails' thighs registers 160°F (71°C).

Remove the quail from the duck fat (reserve 2 Tbsp/30 mL of the fat for the shiitake mushrooms) and set aside until cool enough to handle. Snip the twine around each quail and discard the flavourings. Cut each quail in half lengthwise and keep warm until ready to serve.

PURÉE OF CHESTNUT SOUP

¼ cup (60 mL) unsalted butter

¼ cup (60 mL) olive oil

2 cups (500 mL) sweet chestnuts,
  peeled (see sidebar) and chopped

1 large onion, chopped

1 potato, peeled and chopped

2 stalks celery, chopped

2 small cloves garlic, minced

6 cups (1.5 L) vegetable stock
  (page 255) or water

3 sprigs Italian parsley

2 whole cloves

1 bay leaf

2 Tbsp (30 mL) dry sherry

kosher salt and black pepper
  to taste

HEAT A LARGE SAUCEPAN over medium heat and add the butter and oil.
When the butter foams, add the chestnuts, onion, potato, celery, and garlic and cook, covered and stirring frequently, for about 15 minutes or until
the onion is softened but not browned.

Add the stock and bring to a boil, then simmer, uncovered, for 30 minutes or until the chestnuts and vegetables are soft enough to purée. Add
the parsley sprigs, cloves, and bay leaf and simmer for an additional 5 minutes. Remove the parsley sprigs, cloves, and bay leaf.

In a blender (not a food processor), purée the soup until very smooth.
Pour the soup back into the rinsed-out saucepan. Stir in the sherry and
season with salt and pepper to taste. Keep warm until ready to serve.

TO PEEL CHESTNUTS

With a sharp knife, cut an X in the shell of each chestnut. Arrange the chestnuts in a single layer on a baking sheet and broil them for about 10 minutes or until their skins are easy to peel off. Remove the chestnuts from the broiler and set aside until cool enough to handle, then remove the peel.

SAUTÉED SHIITAKE MUSHROOMS

2 Tbsp (30 mL) duck fat (reserved from the quail confit)

12 large shiitake mushrooms, cleaned and stems removed (reserve stems for another use)

IN A MEDIUM SKILLET, heat the duck fat over high heat. Add the shiitake mushrooms and sauté, stirring frequently, for 3 minutes on each side or until golden brown and crispy.

With a slotted spoon, remove the mushrooms from the skillet and drain on a plate lined with paper towels. Keep warm until ready to serve.

TO SERVE, ladle the soup into 6 warm soup bowls. Place 1 shiitake mushroom in the centre of each bowl of soup. Place 1 piece of quail on top of each shiitake and top with remaining shiitakes, effectively making a "sandwich" in the centre of the soup.

Confession time: I love Caesar salad, especially when it's made with clever twists like this one. The dressing recipe makes about 2 cups (500 mL), and you'll need only ½ cup (125 mL) for the

Hearts of Romaine Lettuce with Quail Eggs, Pancetta, and Caesar Dressing

salad, but the remainder can be stored in the fridge for up to three days.

SERVES 6

CAESAR DRESSING

3 egg yolks	1 tsp (5 mL) kosher salt
3 anchovy fillets, rinsed and coarsely chopped	1 tsp (5 mL) garlic powder
	¼ tsp (1 mL) Tabasco sauce
1 Tbsp (15 mL) Dijon mustard	¼ tsp (1 mL) Worcestershire sauce
1 cup (250 mL) grapeseed oil	3 Tbsp (45 mL) freshly grated Parmesan cheese
3 Tbsp (45 mL) lemon juice	
3 Tbsp (45 mL) white wine vinegar	kosher salt and black pepper to taste
2 Tbsp (30 mL) olive oil	

IN A FOOD PROCESSOR OR BLENDER, process the egg yolks, anchovies, and mustard until fairly smooth. With the motor running, add the grapeseed oil, lemon juice, vinegar, olive oil, salt, garlic powder, Tabasco sauce, and Worcestershire sauce. Process until well blended and creamy.

Scrape the dressing into a bowl and fold in the Parmesan. Season with pepper and more salt to taste. Cover and refrigerate until ready to serve.

SALAD

6 slices pancetta

12 quail eggs

3 romaine lettuce hearts

½ cup (125 mL) Caesar dressing

3 Tbsp (45 mL) freshly grated
   Parmesan cheese

2 Tbsp (30 mL) olive oil

PREHEAT the oven to 350°F (180°C).

Arrange the pancetta slices in a single layer on a rimmed baking sheet and bake for 25 minutes or until very crispy. Remove the pancetta from the oven and let cool on a plate lined with paper towels. Set aside until ready to serve.

Meanwhile, in a small saucepan of simmering water, cook the quail eggs for 4 minutes. Drain well and immediately cool under cold running water. Remove the shells and cut the eggs in half lengthwise. Set aside until ready to serve.

Discard any dark outer leaves from the romaine hearts then cut the hearts in half lengthwise. In a large bowl, toss the romaine hearts with the dressing and Parmesan.

TO SERVE, divide the romaine hearts among 6 salad plates (or spoon onto 1 large platter). Scatter the quail egg halves over the salads and drizzle evenly with the olive oil. Top each salad with a crispy pancetta slice.

Polenta is one of my favourite, heart-warming, belly-filling foods. I also love it for its versatility—it can be eaten either hot or cold, almost any flavourings can be folded into it, and, of

Sesame and Polenta Crusted Scallops with Chardonnay-Braised Red Cabbage and Ginger Beurre Blanc

course, leftovers can be warmed in the oven or even grilled under the broiler. Whichever way you serve it, polenta is the quintessential winter meal.

SERVES 6

SESAME POLENTA

3 Tbsp (45 mL) kosher salt

3 cups (750 mL) fine cornmeal

¼ cup (60 mL) freshly grated
   Parmesan cheese

3 Tbsp (45 mL) unsalted butter

1 cup (250 mL) sesame seeds

1 cup (250 mL) olive oil

IN A LARGE POT, bring 9 cups (2.2 L) water to a boil over high heat. Add the salt then reduce the heat until the water is simmering. Slowly pour the cornmeal into the simmering water, stirring vigorously as you do so. Cook, stirring constantly, for 30 to 45 minutes or until the polenta is thickened, smooth, and creamy.

Add the Parmesan and butter, stirring until well combined. The polenta will pull away from the sides of the pot when it's ready.

Pour the polenta onto a large, rimmed baking sheet. (Ungreased is fine.) With a wet spatula, smoothe into a uniform layer. Sprinkle the sesame seeds evenly over the top, and continue to smoothe out the polenta until you have an even, 1-inch-thick (2.5 cm) cake. Let cool to room temperature.

With a 2-inch (5 cm) cookie cutter, cut 18 discs from the polenta. In a large skillet, heat the oil over medium-high heat. Add the polenta discs sesame-seed side down (you may have to cook them in batches). Cook for 2 minutes or until golden brown. Turn the discs and cook on the other side until golden brown. Drain the discs, sesame-seed side up, on a plate lined with paper towels. Keep warm until ready to serve.

RAISIN-CAPER PURÉE

1 Tbsp (15 mL) unsalted butter

1 shallot, chopped

2 cloves garlic, minced

2 cups (500 mL) golden raisins

½ cup (125 mL) drained capers

½ cup (125 mL) grapeseed oil

lemon juice to taste

IN A MEDIUM SKILLET, heat the butter over medium heat. When the butter foams, add the shallot and garlic and sweat them until softened but not browned. Add the raisins and capers and cook, stirring frequently, just until they are heated through.

In a food processor or blender, process the raisin mixture until finely minced. With the motor running, gradually add the oil and lemon juice. Process until smooth. Set aside until ready to serve.

CHARDONNAY-BRAISED RED CABBAGE

2 slices bacon, diced

1 small onion, chopped

1 red cabbage, cored and
    finely chopped

½ cup (125 mL) Chardonnay

½ cup (125 mL) 35% cream

1 Tbsp (15 mL) cider vinegar

2 Tbsp (30 mL) finely chopped
    Italian parsley

kosher salt and black pepper to taste

IN A LARGE SKILLET, cook the bacon over medium heat for about 3 minutes or until cooked but not browned. With a slotted spoon, remove the bacon to a plate lined with paper towels. Pour off all but 1 Tbsp (15 mL) fat from the skillet.

Add the onion to the skillet and sauté, stirring frequently, for 5 minutes or until softened but not browned. Add the cabbage, Chardonnay, cream, and vinegar. Bring to a boil, then reduce heat to medium-low and cook, covered, for 15 minutes, stirring frequently, until cabbage is tender.

Remove the skillet from the heat. Stir in the reserved bacon, parsley, and salt and pepper to taste. Keep warm until ready to serve.

GINGER BEURRE BLANC

¼ cup (60 mL) Chardonnay
1 shallot, finely chopped
2 Tbsp (30 mL) grated fresh ginger
juice of 1 lemon

½ cup (125 mL) cold unsalted
   butter, cubed
2 Tbsp (30 mL) finely chopped chives
kosher salt and white pepper to taste

IN A SMALL SAUCEPAN, combine the Chardonnay, shallot, and ginger over medium heat, then simmer until the liquid has reduced to 1 Tbsp (15 mL). Stir in the lemon juice.

Reduce the heat to low and whisk in the butter a little at a time, allowing each addition to melt before you add the next, and whisking constantly to emulsify the sauce. Stir in the chives and salt and pepper to taste. Keep warm until ready to serve.

SEARED SCALLOPS

18 fresh large sea scallops
kosher salt and white pepper to taste

¼ cup (60 mL) grapeseed oil

PAT THE SCALLOPS DRY and sprinkle generously with salt and pepper. Heat a large skillet over medium heat and add the oil. When the oil is hot, add the scallops and sear them for about 5 minutes, turning once, until golden brown and just cooked through. Transfer the scallops to a warm plate and set aside.

TO SERVE, make 3 piles of cabbage on each of 6 warm dinner plates. Top each pile of cabbage with a scallop and top each scallop with a disk of polenta, sesame side up. Spoon a little raisin-caper purée between each pile of cabbage, and drizzle ginger beurre blanc around each plate.

One of my favourite techniques is to wrap very lean meat, such as bison, in cured meat. Here, the rich, porky fat of the pancetta adds moisture to the bison, and roasted together, the

Pancetta-Wrapped Bison Strip Loin with Chestnut and Brussels Sprout Sauté, Blue Cheese Clafoutis, and Mocha Sauce

crisp pancetta and the juicy bison are a formidable pair.

SERVES 4

MOCHA SAUCE

2 Tbsp (30 mL) unsalted butter

1 lb (500 g) bison bones and trimmings

½ cup (125 mL) chopped mushrooms

2 sprigs thyme

1 bay leaf

6 white peppercorns

1½ cups (375 mL) dry red wine

4 cups (1 L) chicken stock (page 255)

1 Tbsp (15 mL) chopped unsweetened chocolate

1 Tbsp (15 mL) crushed (not ground) espresso coffee beans

HEAT A LARGE STOCKPOT over medium heat and add the butter. When the butter foams, add the bison bones and trimmings, mushrooms, thyme, bay leaf, and peppercorns. Sauté, stirring frequently, until the bones, trimmings, and mushrooms are browned.

Add the wine and simmer until the liquid has reduced by three-quarters. Add the stock and simmer again until the liquid has reduced by three-quarters. Strain through a fine-mesh sieve into a clean saucepan, discarding the solids.

Simmer the reduced stock until it thickens enough to coat the back of a spoon. Stir in the chocolate until it has melted. Remove the saucepan from the heat and stir in the espresso beans. Let stand for 5 minutes to let the flavours develop. Strain through a fine-mesh sieve and keep warm until ready to serve.

PANCETTA-WRAPPED BISON STRIP LOIN

24 thin slices round pancetta	black pepper to taste
1½ lb (750 g) bison strip-loin fillet, cut into four 6 oz (175 g) pieces	¼ cup (60 mL) grapeseed oil

PREHEAT THE OVEN to 375°F (190°C).

Cut four 12-inch (30 cm) squares of plastic wrap. Across the centre of 1 piece of plastic wrap, arrange 6 slices of pancetta, overlapping the slices slightly. Centre 1 piece of bison on the pancetta. Lift the edges of the wrap and roll the bison so the pancetta wraps around to enclose it, pulling away and removing the plastic wrap as you roll. Repeat with the remaining plastic wrap, pancetta, and bison. Cover and refrigerate the pancetta-wrapped bison for 1 hour.

In a large ovenproof skillet, heat the oil over medium heat. Sprinkle the pancetta-wrapped bison with black pepper to taste. Add the bison to the skillet and immediately transfer the skillet to the oven. Roast for about 8 minutes, turning once, until an instant-read thermometer inserted into the centre of a piece of bison registers 130°F (54°C). Remove the bison to a board and let stand for 5 minutes before serving.

BLUE-CHEESE CLAFOUTIS

softened unsalted butter for greasing	½ cup (125 mL) loosely packed slivered basil leaves
⅓ cup (80 mL) crumbled blue cheese	½ cup (125 mL) freshly grated Parmesan cheese, divided
6 to 8 cherry tomatoes (depending on size)	¼ cup (60 mL) milk
4 eggs	kosher salt and black pepper to taste
2 Tbsp (30 mL) all-purpose flour	
¾ cup (185 mL) plain yogurt or sour cream	

PREHEAT THE OVEN to 350°F (180°C).

Lightly butter 6 muffin cups or individual custard cups. Sprinkle the blue cheese into the cups, dividing evenly. Halve the tomatoes, or quarter if large, and divide among the cups.

In a medium bowl, beat the eggs, then beat in the flour until smooth. Whisk in the yogurt, basil, ⅓ cup (80 mL) of the Parmesan, and the milk. Season lightly with salt and pepper.

Pour the batter into the prepared cups, dividing evenly. Sprinkle with the remaining Parmesan. Bake for 30 minutes or until the tops of the clafoutis are lightly golden and a knife inserted into the centre of one of them comes out clean. Let the clafoutis cool for 10 minutes in the cups, then loosen the edges with a knife and invert to release. Turn the clafoutis right side up and keep warm until ready to serve.

CHESTNUT AND BRUSSELS SPROUT SAUTÉ

½ cup (125 mL) chicken stock
  (page 255)
2 Tbsp (30 mL) unsalted butter
1 cup (250 mL) peeled (page 7) and
  chopped sweet chestnuts

1 cup (250 mL) lightly packed
  Brussels sprout leaves
kosher salt and black pepper
  to taste

IN A MEDIUM SAUCEPAN, bring the stock and butter to a boil over high heat. Add the chestnuts, reduce the heat to a simmer, and cook for about 5 minutes or until chestnuts are tender and can be easily pierced with the tip of a knife.

Add the Brussels sprout leaves. Continue cooking until the stock has completely evaporated. Season with salt and pepper to taste.

TO SERVE, spoon a small amount of the mocha sauce in the centre of each of 4 warm dinner plates. Cut the bison pieces crosswise into ½-inch (1 cm) slices and fan out over the sauce. Top each portion of bison with a blue-cheese clafoutis and scatter the chestnut and Brussels sprout sauté around each plate. Dot the edges of the plates with more mocha sauce.

When I worked at the Chewton Glen hotel in New Milton, southern England, I was billeted with a wonderful couple, John and Mariam Upjohn. I worked most evenings, but occasionally

Sticky Toffee Pudding with Hazelnut–Caramel Sauce

they would leave some dinner for me, which I'd invariably eat at one or two in the morning. This is one of Mrs. Upjohn's recipes, and it's still one of my favourite wintertime "puddin's."

SERVES 6

HAZELNUT-CARAMEL SAUCE

⅔ cup (160 mL) granulated sugar
¼ cup (60 mL) unsalted butter
1⅓ cups (330 mL) 35% cream

¼ cup (60 mL) toasted hazelnuts
(see sidebar), chopped

IN A SMALL SAUCEPAN, stir together the sugar and butter over low heat until melted and smooth. Continue cooking, stirring frequently, until the mixture is golden brown and bubbly.

Remove the saucepan from the heat and, standing back in case the mixture splatters, stir in the cream until smooth. Stir in the hazelnuts. Set aside. Warm the sauce over low heat just before serving.

TO TOAST AND SKIN HAZELNUTS

Preheat the oven to 350°F (180°C). Spread the hazelnuts out on a rimmed baking sheet and bake 6 to 8 minutes, stirring occasionally, until the hazelnuts are fragrant. Enclose the hazelnuts in a clean kitchen towel and rub vigorously to remove any loose skins.

STICKY TOFFEE PUDDING

non-stick baking spray

1 cup (250 mL) chopped pitted dates

1 tsp (5 mL) baking soda

¾ cup (185 mL) granulated sugar

¼ cup (60 mL) unsalted
   butter, softened

2 eggs

2 Tbsp (30 mL) dark rum

1¼ cups (310 mL) self-rising flour

PREHEAT THE OVEN to 350°F (180°C). Spray six ¾-cup (185 mL) ramekins with non-stick baking spray.

In a small saucepan, bring 1⅓ cups (330 mL) water to a boil over high heat. Remove the saucepan from the heat and stir in the dates and baking soda until well combined.

In the bowl of a stand mixer fitted with the wire whisk attachment, beat the sugar and butter on medium speed until light, creamy, and fluffy. Add the eggs, one at a time, beating well after adding each one. With the mixer on low speed, gradually add the date mixture and rum, then add the flour, one spoonful at a time, continuing to whisk on low speed until well combined.

Divide the batter among the prepared ramekins, filling them not quite full. Place the ramekins on a baking sheet and bake for 30 minutes or until a toothpick inserted in the centre of one of the puddings comes out clean. Remove the puddings from the oven and let cool slightly.

TO SERVE, loosen the edges of each pudding and invert the ramekins on 6 dessert plates, shaking slightly if necessary to release the puddings. Drizzle hazelnut-caramel sauce over and around each pudding.

Poached pears are another of my favourite cold-weather desserts, and are a staple of my winter menus. Served chilled on buttery greens as an appetizer, or warm for dessert, they're

Red Wine Poached Pears with Nutmeg Cookies

always tasty and gratifying. I've used a hearty red wine here but any type will work, so experiment with dry or sweet, red or white wine, or even for-tified wine such as port and sherry, if you're feeling adventurous!

SERVES 6

NUTMEG COOKIES

1¼ cups (310 mL) cake or pastry flour

1 tsp (5 mL) freshly grated nutmeg

½ tsp (2 mL) baking powder

½ tsp (2 mL) baking soda

pinch table salt

1 cup (250 mL) packed brown sugar

⅓ cup (80 mL) unsalted butter, softened

¼ cup (60 mL) sour cream

1 egg yolk

½ tsp (2 mL) vanilla

PREHEAT THE OVEN to 325°F (160°C). Line a large baking sheet with parchment paper.

In a large bowl, whisk together the flour, nutmeg, baking powder, baking soda, and salt. Set aside.

In the bowl of a stand mixer fitted with the wire whisk attachment, cream the sugar and butter on medium speed for about 8 minutes or until light, creamy, and fluffy.

With the mixer on low speed, gradually add the sour cream, egg yolk, and vanilla. Gradually add the flour mixture, one spoonful at a time, continuing to whisk on low speed until well combined.

Using a spoon dipped in hot water, drop 2 Tbsp (30 mL) portions of the batter onto the prepared baking sheet, spacing the cookies about 2 inches (5 cm) apart. Bake the cookies for 18 to 20 minutes or until they are just golden on the outside but still soft in the middle. Remove the cookies to a wire rack and let cool completely. Store in an airtight container until ready to serve.

RED WINE POACHED PEARS

6 ripe pears, peeled but stems left on

1 bottle (750 mL) robust red wine

2 cups (500 mL) simple syrup
  (see sidebar)

1 cup (250 mL) unsweetened
  cherry juice

juice of 2 lemons, plus zest removed
  with a vegetable peeler

juice of 2 limes, plus zest removed
  with a vegetable peeler

1 cinnamon stick

PUT THE PEARS in a large non-reactive bowl and add the remaining ingredients, making sure pears are completely submerged in the liquid. If they aren't, weigh them down with a small plate. Cover and let stand overnight.

Transfer the pears and liquid to a large non-reactive pot and bring to a simmer over medium heat. Simmer, covered, for about 10 minutes or until pears are tender but still slightly firm. Remove the pot from the heat and let cool to room temperature.

Use a melon baller to scoop the core from the bottom of each pear. Return the pears to the poaching liquid, cover, and refrigerate until ready to serve.

TO SERVE, divide the pears and some of their juices among 6 shallow bowls. Serve with the nutmeg cookies on the side.

SIMPLE SYRUP

Combine 2 cups (500 mL) granulated sugar and 2 cups (500 mL) water in a medium saucepan. Bring to a simmer over medium-high heat, stirring to dissolve the sugar completely. Remove from the heat and let cool to room temperature. Refrigerate in a sealed container until required. Makes about 3 cups (750 mL).

Winter is the time for comfort, for good food and warmth, for the touch of a friendly hand and for a talk beside the fire: it is the time for home.

(Edith Sitwell, English poet and novelist, 1887–1964)

February In the depths of winter, February brings us joy in the celebration of Valentine's Day. If you are lucky enough to be in love, you may decide to spend the evening in your favourite restaurant. Just the two of you, sitting face to face at a candlelit table, basking in the warmth of each other's affection. Soft music plays in the background and, as the meal progresses, you gaze into the other's eyes to see your own love reflected back at you. Sounds great, doesn't it?

I find it very significant that food is so closely associated with romance. If you have ever had the opportunity to prepare a meal for someone special, you'll know that the taste of the food is directly proportional to how fond you are of the person you're cooking for. "Cooking with love" is not just a cliché. When we cook for the ones we love, the meal can transcend the ordinary and create memories to cherish forever.

Romantic interludes notwithstanding, if you live in a cold climate, February is also the time of the year you may reach the point where you have had enough of the frigid, windy, snowy weather and are desperate to feel the warm embrace of the sun again. At this time of the year, a month removed from the excitement of New Year's and with weeks to go before the spring thaw, our palates yearn for something to reassure us the warm weather is on its way.

Often, when I'm thinking about new menu items in February, my mind wanders to Europe. The crystal-blue warm waters of the Mediterranean can inspire dishes like stuffed flounder with a saffron-scented mussel and clam ragout, while from southern France, a sunny citrus glaze brightens up rich pan-seared foie gras. Suddenly, spring doesn't seem as far away.

Cooking foie gras at home might seem a bit over-the-top, but I wanted to include this recipe because it often appears on my winter tasting menus. The richness of the foie gras combined

Pan-Seared Foie Gras with Blood-Orange Glaze and Toasted Pain d'Épices

with the tartness of the blood orange glaze is the business!

Working with foie gras can be a bit intimidating. It is a very expensive, luxurious ingredient but is well worth the cost, and perfect for a special dinner or an occasion like Valentine's Day. You can find foie gras in specialty butcher shops and gourmet grocery stores in most larger cities. If not, call your local store and have them order it. My favourite is the rich foie gras that comes to us from Quebec.

SERVES 6

PAIN D'ÉPICES

non-stick baking spray	2 tsp (10 mL) ground ginger
1 cup (250 mL) rye flour	¾ cup (185 mL) honey
1 cup (250 mL) all-purpose flour	½ cup (125 mL) whole milk
2½ tsp (12 mL) baking powder	3 eggs
2 tsp (10 mL) mix of ground spices–	3 Tbsp (45 mL) packed brown sugar
use a combination of nutmeg,	grated zest of ½ lemon
five-spice powder, cinnamon,	grated zest of ½ orange
and/or cloves	2 tsp (10 mL) vanilla

PREHEAT THE OVEN to 375°F (190°C). Spray a 9- × 5-inch (2 L) loaf pan with non-stick baking spray.

Whisk the rye and all-purpose flours, baking powder, and spices together in a large bowl. Set aside.

Warm the honey and milk in a small saucepan over low heat until the honey melts. Keep warm over low heat until needed.

In the bowl of a stand mixer fitted with the wire whisk attachment, whisk the eggs and sugar together for about 12 minutes or until very light and fluffy and the whisk leaves a trail. Remove the bowl from the mixer and stir in the warm honey mixture, citrus zest, and vanilla. Fold in the flour mixture until well combined.

Turn the dough out onto a lightly floured surface and knead for 15 minutes or until the dough is smooth and elastic. Form into a loaf shape and place in the prepared pan. Brush the top of the loaf with a little water. Bake for 30 minutes. Reduce the temperature to 300°F (150°C) and continue to bake for 1 hour longer, or until a skewer inserted into the centre of the loaf comes out clean. Let cool in the pan on a wire rack for 30 minutes. Turn out the loaf and let cool completely on the wire rack.

BLOOD-ORANGE GLAZE

1½ cups (375 mL) blood-orange
   juice (about 8 oranges)

2 cups (500 mL) chicken stock
   (page 255)

½ cup (125 mL) dry white wine

2 shallots, finely chopped

¼ cup (60 mL) red wine vinegar

1 Tbsp (15 mL) veal reduction
   (page 254)

½ cup (125 mL) olive oil

kosher salt and white pepper to taste

IN A SMALL SAUCEPAN, simmer the blood-orange juice over medium heat until it is reduced to ¼ cup (60 mL). Set aside and keep warm.

In a separate small saucepan, combine the chicken stock, wine, shallots, vinegar, and veal reduction. Simmer over medium heat until the liquid has reduced by half. Strain through a fine-mesh sieve, discarding the solids.

Put reduced chicken stock mixture in a blender (not a food processor). With the motor running on low speed, gradually add the olive oil and reduced blood-orange juice. Blend until smooth and creamy. Pour sauce into a small saucepan and season with salt and pepper to taste. Keep warm over low heat until ready to serve.

PAN-SEARED FOIE GRAS

1½ lb (750 g) foie gras, large veins
   removed and cut into 6 even-size
   medallions

kosher salt and black pepper
   to taste

SEASON THE PIECES OF FOIE GRAS on both sides with salt and pepper. Preheat a large, good-quality non-stick skillet over very high heat. Place the foie gras in the skillet and cook without moving them for 1 minute or until golden brown on the underside. Foie gras yields a lot of fat so don't be surprised to see it "swimming" in its own fat. Spoon out the excess fat while searing to prevent it from poaching in the fat.

Using a spatula or an egg lifter, carefully turn the foie gras over and continue cooking for 1 minute. Carefully touch the top of the foie gras in the centre with your index finger. It's done when you feel no resistance in the centre. It should be crispy on the outside and molten on the inside. Using a spatula or an egg lifter, carefully remove it from the skillet and transfer to a plate lined with paper towels to absorb the excess fat.

TO SERVE, cut 6 slices of pain d'épices and toast them lightly on both sides, then place on each of 6 warm dinner plates. Carefully place a piece of foie gras on top. Spoon the blood-orange glaze around each plate.

The Salt Spring Island Cheese Company is a famous West Coast dairy started by David Wood. His goat and sheep cheeses have been on my menu for close to 10 years and I do so cherish

Salt Spring Island Goat Cheese and Winter Mushroom Phyllo Turnovers with Roasted Shallot Vinaigrette

their smooth, rich, and very mildly capricious nature. They can be found in any of the excellent fromageries around the country.

These turnovers, paired with a sweet and sour vinaigrette, make great canapés to serve at the Super Bowl party your brother-in-law invites you to every year or, indeed, any mid-winter gathering. If you prefer, the recipe can be plated as an appetizer for six by tossing a selection of greens with the roasted shallot vinaigrette then topping each portion of salad with two turnovers.

SERVES 6

ROASTED SHALLOT VINAIGRETTE

4 shallots	1 Tbsp (15 mL) honey
2 whole heads garlic, separated into individual cloves	1 tsp (5 mL) finely chopped rosemary
	1 tsp (5 mL) finely chopped thyme
1 cup (250 mL) olive oil	1 tsp (5 mL) kosher salt
3 Tbsp (45 mL) aged balsamic vinegar	½ tsp (2 mL) black pepper

PREHEAT THE OVEN to 300°F (150°C).

Peel the shallots and garlic and place them in a small roasting pan. Pour the oil over the top so the shallots and garlic are completely submerged. Cover the pan with aluminum foil and roast for 2 to 3 hours or until the shallots and garlic are extremely soft and slightly golden brown. Remove the pan from the oven and let cool to room temperature.

Strain the roasted shallots and garlic, reserving the oil. In a blender or a food processor on low speed, purée the shallots, garlic, vinegar, honey, rosemary, thyme, salt, and pepper until fairly smooth. With the motor running, slowly pour in the reserved oil, then blend until the vinaigrette is smooth and creamy. Pour into an airtight container and refrigerate until ready to use. Let come to room temperature and whisk well before serving.

SALT SPRING ISLAND GOAT CHEESE AND WINTER MUSHROOM PHYLLO TURNOVERS

2 Tbsp (30 mL) olive oil

2 Tbsp (30 mL) unsalted butter

1 lb (500 g) mushrooms, coarsely chopped

3 shallots, finely chopped

2 Tbsp (30 mL) dry sherry

2 Tbsp (30 mL) aged sherry vinegar

4 sprigs thyme, leaves picked off from stems and finely chopped

½ cup (125 mL) Salt Spring Island goat cheese

¼ cup (60 mL) freshly grated Parmesan cheese

kosher salt and black pepper to taste

3 sheets phyllo pastry (each 14 × 9 inches/35 × 23 cm)

non-stick baking spray

HEAT A LARGE SKILLET over medium-high heat and add the oil and butter. When the butter foams, add the mushrooms and sauté, stirring frequently, for 5 minutes or until mushrooms have wilted slightly. Stir in the shallots. Add the sherry, vinegar, and thyme.

Simmer, stirring frequently, for about 5 minutes or until the liquid has almost all evaporated and the mushrooms are tender. Remove the skillet from the heat. Let the mushroom mixture cool to room temperature, then refrigerate for 1 hour.

Preheat oven to 400°F (200°C). Scrape the mushroom mixture into a bowl and stir in the goat cheese, Parmesan, and salt and pepper to taste.

Place 1 phyllo sheet on a work surface (cover the remaining dough with a damp cloth to keep it from drying out). Lightly spray the phyllo with baking spray. Cut the phyllo sheet lengthwise into four 3½-inch-wide (9 cm) strips.

With the shorter end facing you, spoon about 1 rounded Tbsp (15 mL+) mushroom mixture onto the bottom right-hand corner of 1 strip. Fold up the phyllo over the filling so that the bottom edge of the strip lies along the right side to form a right-angle triangle. Continue folding the strip up and over as if you were folding a flag, until you reach the end of the strip. Place, seam side down, on a baking sheet. Repeat with remaining strips, then repeat with remaining phyllo sheets and filling, spraying each sheet first with baking spray.

Lightly coat tops of turnovers with baking spray. Bake for 12 minutes or until golden brown and crisp.

TO SERVE, spoon the roasted shallot vinaigrette into a small ramekin and place in the centre of a large, round platter. Arrange the turnovers on the platter and use the vinaigrette as a dip.

We keep lobster carcasses in the restaurants' freezers, and when the mood strikes, we use them to prepare this richly flavoured soup. Sometimes we like to include soups on our tasting

Lobster Bisque with Niagara Gold Beignets

menus and serve them in little espresso or coffee cups—we call them "sips."

Using the milk of Guernsey cattle, the Upper Canada Cheese Company of Jordan Station, Ontario, crafts a variety of artisanal raw-milk cheese, of which "Niagara Gold" is my favourite. These beignets served with the bisque taste rather like a "reverse fondue." Two coatings, one of phyllo and one of batter, make them ultra-crisp outside with a lovely, gooey cheese centre. You can also use Gruyère if you wish.

SERVES 6 TO 8

LOBSTER BISQUE

4 to 6 lobster carcasses

¼ cup (60 mL) unsalted butter

2 Tbsp (30 mL) olive oil

3 carrots, chopped

2 onions, chopped

6 cloves garlic, crushed

½ cup (125 mL) tomato paste

½ cup (125 mL) brandy

4 tomatoes, chopped

1 cup (250 mL) dry white wine

8 sprigs thyme

kosher salt, white pepper,
    and cayenne to taste

4 cups (1 L) fish stock (page 255)

1 cup (250 mL) 35% cream

USING A HEAVY KNIFE or a cleaver, crush the lobster carcasses into small pieces. In a large heavy pot, heat the butter and olive oil over medium heat. When the butter foams, add the carrots, onions, and garlic, then cook, stirring frequently, until the onion is translucent but not browned. Add the lobster shells and stir well to combine. Stir in the tomato paste.

Add the brandy and, standing back, ignite carefully. When the flames die away, add the tomatoes, wine, thyme, and salt, pepper, and cayenne to taste. Add the stock. Bring to a boil and simmer until the liquid is reduced by one-quarter. Add the cream and simmer until the soup has reduced by another quarter, then remove the pot from the heat.

Pour the soup through a fine-mesh sieve into a clean saucepan, discarding the solids. Just before serving, return the bisque to a simmer and season with more salt and pepper to taste. Remove the saucepan from the heat and, using an immersion blender, blend the bisque until it is light and frothy. Keep warm until ready to serve.

NIAGARA GOLD BEIGNETS

¾ lb (375 g) Niagara Gold cheese, cut
    into 24 even-size fingers
1 Tbsp (15 mL) Dijon mustard
24 sage leaves
6 sheets phyllo pastry (each 14 × 9
    inches/35 × 23 cm), each cut into
    4 even-size pieces

¼ cup (60 mL) unsalted butter, melted
1 tsp (5 mL) active dry yeast
½ cup (125 mL) warm milk (approx.)
¾ cup (185 mL) cornstarch
kosher salt and white pepper
    to taste
vegetable oil for deep-frying

USING A SMALL PASTRY BRUSH, coat each piece of cheese with the Dijon mustard. Lay 1 sage leaf on each piece of cheese, pressing so the leaves stick to the cheese.

Brush 1 piece of phyllo with a little butter, then place a piece of prepared cheese on the phyllo. Fold in the sides of the phyllo and roll up like a spring roll. Place the wrapped cheese on a baking sheet. Repeat with remaining cheese, phyllo, and butter. Refrigerate the phyllo-wrapped cheese for 1 hour.

Place yeast in a medium bowl with ¼ cup (60 mL) of the warm milk. Stir to dissolve the yeast and let stand for 1 minute. Stir in the cornstarch, then add enough of the rest of the milk to make a smooth batter. Season with salt and pepper to taste.

Heat the oil in a deep pot until a candy thermometer registers 360°F (182°C), or use a deep fat fryer and follow the manufacturer's instructions. Working with 1 piece of phyllo-wrapped cheese at a time, drop it into the batter and turn to coat completely. As each piece is coated, remove it from the batter and place gently into the hot oil. Cook for 2 minutes or until golden brown and crisp. Remove the cheese beignets from the pot with tongs or a slotted spoon and drain on a plate lined with paper towels.

TO SERVE, ladle the lobster bisque into 6 to 8 warm coffee cups. Serve with the cheese beignets on the side.

This is one of my most popular dishes. People seem to like its playful nature as it's quite unlike any other "pasta" course. In fact, there is no pasta here at all but, rather, delicate crêpes into

Lobster Manicotti with Pan-Seared Sea Scallops and Tarragon-Icewine Butter Sauce

which the succulent scallop filling is stuffed. To make this the ultimate dish, serve with a cooked lobster claw. Rewarm the lobster claw in the sauce before serving.

SERVES 6

LOBSTER MANICOTTI

1 lb (500 g) fresh sea scallops

1¼ tsp (6 mL) kosher salt, divided

¼ tsp (1 mL) white pepper

¼ tsp (1 mL) granulated sugar

1 egg white

2 Tbsp (30 mL) olive oil

1 tsp (5 mL) cornstarch

½ cup (125 mL) 35% cream

1 cup (250 mL) diced cooked lobster meat (see sidebar next page)

1⅓ cups (330 mL) all-purpose flour

1½ cups (375 mL) milk

4 eggs

¼ cup (60 mL) melted unsalted butter

1 Tbsp (15 mL) finely chopped dill

non-stick baking spray

IN THE CHILLED BOWL of a food processor, purée the scallops, 1 tsp (5 mL) of the salt, the pepper, and the sugar until smooth.

In a separate bowl, whisk together the egg white, olive oil, and cornstarch. Add the egg white mixture to the scallops and purée until just combined. Add the cream and process until smooth.

Scrape the mixture into a bowl and stir in the lobster. Cover and refrigerate for 1 hour.

In a large bowl, whisk together the flour and remaining salt. In a separate bowl, whisk together the milk, eggs, and melted butter. Whisk the milk mixture into the flour and continue whisking until a smooth batter forms. Stir in the dill and season with more white pepper to taste. Cover and refrigerate the crêpe batter for 1 hour.

Remove the crêpe batter from the fridge and let come to room temperature. Spray a large skillet with non-stick baking spray and heat it over medium heat.

Pour ¼ cup (60 mL) crêpe batter into the skillet, swirling the skillet to spread the crêpe evenly to an 8-inch (20 cm) round. Cook for about

Recipe continued . . .

1 minute or until starting to turn golden on the underside. Flip the crêpe with a spatula, then cook for a further 30 seconds or until golden. Remove the crêpe to a wire rack and repeat with remaining batter to make 6 crêpes in all, stacking the crêpes on the wire rack as each one cooks. (Any left-over batter can be refrigerated for up to 2 days.)

Preheat the oven to 350°F (180°C).

To make the manicotti, lay the crêpes in a single layer on a work surface. Spoon the seafood filling onto the centre of each crêpe, dividing it evenly. Fold the sides of each crêpe over the filling to cover it completely. Carefully place the crêpes, seam side down, in a single layer on a large, non-stick baking sheet. Bake for 12 to 15 minutes or until the filling is set and an instant-read thermometer inserted into the filling registers 150°F (65°C). Keep the manicotti warm until ready to serve.

PAN-SEARED SEA SCALLOPS AND TARRAGON-ICEWINE BUTTER SAUCE

18 fresh large sea scallops	juice of 1 lemon
kosher salt and white pepper to taste	2 Tbsp (30 mL) Niagara icewine
⅔ cup (160 mL) cold unsalted butter, cubed	1 Tbsp (15 mL) finely chopped tarragon
¼ cup (60 mL) dry white wine	2 Tbsp (30 mL) finely chopped chives (optional)
¼ cup (60 mL) white wine vinegar	
2 Tbsp (30 mL) finely chopped shallots	

PAT THE SCALLOPS DRY and sprinkle generously with salt and pepper. Heat a large skillet over medium heat and add 1 Tbsp (15 mL) of the butter. When the butter foams, add the scallops and sear them for about 5 minutes, turning once, until golden brown and just cooked through. Transfer the scallops to a warm plate and set aside.

In a small saucepan, bring the dry white wine, vinegar, and shallots to a boil over medium-high heat. Add any juices that have seeped out of the scallops, then boil until the liquid has reduced to about ¼ cup (60 mL).

Reduce the heat to low and whisk in the remaining butter a little at a time, letting each piece melt before you add the next, then whisk until the sauce has a nice creamy consistency. Remove from the heat and stir in the lemon juice, icewine, tarragon, and more salt and pepper to taste.

TO SERVE, slice the scallops. Spoon some butter sauce on each of 6 warm dinner plates. Place 1 lobster manicotti on each plate, and nestle sliced scallops next to each manicotti. Garnish with chives if desired.

TO COOK LIVE LOBSTERS

Buying live lobsters and cooking them yourself is the only way to ensure the lobster meat is as fresh and sweet as Mother Nature intended. The following technique ensures you end up with perfect results every time.

Bring a pot of lobster court bouillon (page 256) to a rapid boil. Carefully add the lobster(s) to the pot, one at a time, and cover with a tight-fitting lid. Turn off the heat and let the lobster(s) cook for 8 minutes. Using a pair of tongs, carefully lift lobster(s) out of the pot and drain well.

When cool enough to handle, use kitchen scissors to cut along the underside of the tail shell of each lobster. Gently remove the tail meat and set aside. Using scissors or crackers, cut open or crack the claws and remove the meat.

Stuffed Pinwheel of Flounder with Saffron-Scented Ragout of Mussels and Clams

and Georgia, but it is most abundant from the Gulf of St. Lawrence to the Chesapeake Bay. It is often called lemon sole.

In this elegant recipe, the fish fillets are stuffed with shrimp mousse and rolled up into pinwheels and, against the sunny-coloured mussel and clam sauce, the effect is striking.

SERVES 6

SHRIMP MOUSSE

½ lb (250 g) black tiger shrimp	2 Tbsp (30 mL) olive oil
1 tsp (5 mL) kosher salt	1 tsp (5 mL) cornstarch
¼ tsp (1 mL) white pepper	½ cup (125 mL) 35% cream
¼ tsp (1 mL) granulated sugar	juice of 1 lemon
1 egg white	2 Tbsp (30 mL) finely chopped chives

IN THE CHILLED BOWL of a food processor, purée the shrimp, salt, pepper, and sugar until smooth.

In a separate bowl, whisk together the egg white, olive oil, and cornstarch. Add the egg white mixture to the shrimp mixture and purée until just combined. Add the cream and process until smooth.

Scrape the mixture into a bowl and stir in the lemon juice and chives. Cover and refrigerate for 1 hour.

STUFFED PINWHEEL OF FLOUNDER

18 flounder or sole fillets (3 lb/1.5 kg total weight)	Shrimp Mousse
	1 cup (250 mL) dry white wine
kosher salt and white pepper to taste	2 Tbsp (30 mL) unsalted butter, melted

PREHEAT THE OVEN to 400°F (200°C).

Dry the fillets well with paper towel. Working with 2 or 3 fillets at a time, arrange them skin side up and tails facing you on a cutting board and sprinkle with salt and pepper to taste. Spoon about 1 Tbsp (15 mL) shrimp mousse near the centre of the tail end of each fillet. Roll up each fillet from the tail end to enclose the filling. Stand the pinwheels on their ends in a shallow baking dish. Repeat with the remaining fillets and shrimp mousse.

Pour the wine and butter into the dish and cover with aluminum foil. Bake for about 12 minutes or until the fish feel firm to the touch and are cooked through. Keep warm until ready to serve.

SAFFRON-SCENTED RAGOUT OF MUSSELS AND CLAMS

2 Tbsp (30 mL) unsalted butter	1 cup (250 mL) tomato juice
2 Tbsp (30 mL) grapeseed oil	18 tightly closed fresh clams, scrubbed
2 leeks (white parts only), thinly sliced	18 tightly closed fresh mussels, scrubbed
2 small carrots, thinly sliced	2 Tbsp (30 mL) olive oil
2 shallots, chopped	kosher salt and white pepper to taste
2 cloves garlic, finely chopped	
1-inch (2.5 cm) piece fresh ginger, peeled and grated	2 Tbsp (30 mL) finely chopped tarragon
pinch saffron	
1 cup (250 mL) dry white wine	1 Tbsp (15 mL) finely chopped chives

HEAT A LARGE SKILLET over medium heat and add the butter and oil. When the butter foams, add the leeks, carrots, shallots, and garlic and sauté, stirring frequently, until shallots are softened but not browned. Stir in the ginger and saffron.

Add the wine, tomato juice, and clams. Cover the skillet and increase the heat to high. Simmer until the clams are open about halfway. Add the mussels and cover the skillet again, and simmer until the mussels have opened.

Remove the skillet from the heat and, using a slotted spoon, remove the clams and mussels from the skillet (discarding any shellfish that haven't opened), set aside, and keep warm.

Add the olive oil and salt and pepper to taste to the sauce remaining in the skillet and return to a simmer. Stir in the tarragon and chives and return the clams and mussels to the skillet.

TO SERVE, divide the clams and mussels with their vegetables and broth among 6 warm soup bowls. Place 3 flounder pinwheels on each serving of ragout.

*Game meats are a significant part of
my repertoire during the colder months.
This recipe was inspired by the spice
rub my sous-chef Ross Midgley uses
to coat a nice Sunday roast of beef. By*

Fennel Seed and Juniper Crusted Venison Loin
with Winter Squash Purée and Pinot Noir Sauce

*applying it to the venison and serv-
ing it with a rich squash purée and an
intense red wine sauce, we've created
the quintessential winter dish: warming, filling, and satisfying.*

SERVES 6

WINTER SQUASH PURÉE

1 large butternut squash

¼ cup (60 mL) unsalted butter,
    softened

kosher salt and white pepper to taste

2 Tbsp (30 mL) maple syrup

grated zest of 1 orange

pinch cinnamon

PREHEAT THE OVEN to 350°F (180°C).

Using a large chef's knife, carefully cut the squash in half lengthwise.
Using a large spoon, scrape out and discard the seeds and strings. Rub the
cut sides and the hollows of the squash halves with 2 Tbsp (30 mL) of the
butter, then season with salt and pepper to taste.

Place squash halves cut sides down in a shallow roasting pan and add
¼ cup (60 mL) water to the pan. Bake for 30 to 40 minutes or until the
squash is fork tender.

Using a large spoon, scoop out the flesh from the squash halves and
transfer to a food processor or blender. Add the remaining butter, the
maple syrup, and the orange zest. Purée until smooth. With the motor
running, season with a pinch of cinnamon, and more salt and pepper to
taste. Set aside and keep warm until ready to serve.

PINOT NOIR SAUCE

⅓ cup (80 mL) cold unsalted
   butter, cubed
1 onion, finely chopped
¼ cup (60 mL) diced carrots
¼ cup (60 mL) chopped mushrooms
2 cloves garlic, finely chopped
6 black peppercorns
1 bay leaf

kosher salt and black pepper to taste
2 tsp (10 mL) tomato paste
1 cup (250 mL) veal, chicken,
   or vegetable stock (pages 254–55)
1 bottle (750 mL) Pinot Noir
3 sprigs thyme, leaves picked off
   from stems and finely chopped
pinch granulated sugar

HEAT A HEAVY SAUCEPAN over medium heat and add 2 Tbsp (30 mL) of the butter. When the butter foams, add the onion, carrots, mushrooms, and garlic and cook for 10 minutes, stirring frequently, until the vegetables have softened and are golden brown. Add the peppercorns and bay leaf and season with salt and pepper to taste.

Reduce the heat to medium-low and add the tomato paste. Cook for 5 minutes, stirring frequently to prevent scorching. Stir in the stock and simmer until almost completely reduced. Increase the heat to medium and stir in the Pinot Noir. Simmer until the wine has reduced by half.

Remove the saucepan from the heat and carefully pour the sauce through a fine-mesh sieve into a clean saucepan, discarding the solids in the sieve. Bring the sauce to a simmer over medium heat and stir in the thyme and sugar. Reduce the heat to low and whisk in the remaining butter a little at a time, allowing each addition to melt before you add the next, then whisk until the sauce has a nice creamy consistency. Keep the sauce warm until ready to serve, whisking the sauce well before serving.

FENNEL SEED AND JUNIPER CRUSTED VENISON LOIN

2 Tbsp (30 mL) toasted whole
   fennel seeds

1 Tbsp (15 mL) toasted juniper berries

¼ cup (60 mL) fresh, soft
   breadcrumbs

¼ cup (60 mL) olive oil, divided

1 Tbsp (15 mL) Dijon mustard

1 Tbsp (15 mL) honey

2¼ lb (1.1 kg) venison loin, trimmed
   and cut into six 6 oz (175 g)
   medallions

kosher salt and black pepper to taste

PREHEAT THE OVEN to 400°F (200°C).

Combine the fennel seeds and juniper berries in a spice mill and grind to a coarse consistency. On a plate, stir together fennel mixture and breadcrumbs and set aside.

In a small saucepan over low heat, stir together 2 Tbsp (30 mL) of the oil, the mustard, and the honey until well combined. Remove the saucepan from the heat.

Pat the venison dry and season with salt and pepper to taste. Using a pastry brush, coat the entire surface of the venison with the honey mustard, then press the top side of each piece in the breadcrumb mixture.

In a large ovenproof skillet, heat the remaining oil over medium-high heat. Carefully place the venison pieces in the skillet, crumb side up. Immediately transfer the skillet to the oven and cook for about 15 minutes or until an instant-read thermometer inserted into a piece of venison registers 130°F (54°C) for medium-rare (cook a little longer for well-cooked meat, a little less for rare). Remove the venison to a board and let stand, loosely covered, for 5 minutes.

TO SERVE, spoon the winter squash purée down the centre of a large warm serving platter. Slice the venison loins thinly and arrange on either side of the squash purée. Spoon the Pinot Noir sauce over and around the meat.

Bourbon Rice Pudding with Caramelized Pears and Brandy Snaps

SERVES 6

BRANDY SNAPS

non-stick baking spray	5 Tbsp (75 mL) unsalted butter
½ cup (125 mL) all-purpose flour	½ cup (125 mL) granulated sugar
½ tsp (2 mL) ground ginger	¼ cup (60 mL) corn syrup

PREHEAT THE OVEN to 350°F (180°C). Line a large baking sheet with parchment paper and spray the paper with non-stick baking spray.

In a medium bowl, whisk together the flour and ginger.

In a small saucepan over medium heat, melt the butter. Stir in the sugar and syrup and cook, stirring often, until the sugar has melted.

Remove the saucepan from the heat and gradually stir the melted butter mixture into the flour mixture until well combined.

Drop about twenty 1 Tbsp (15 mL) portions of the batter about 3 inches (8 cm) apart onto the prepared baking sheet. Bake for about 8 minutes or until flattened and golden brown. Remove the baking sheet from the oven and let the cookies cool slightly. Using a spatula and your fingertips, carefully lift each cookie off the baking sheet and place on a wire rack. Let cool completely until brittle. Store in an airtight container in cool, dry place until ready to serve.

BOURBON RICE PUDDING

1 cup (250 mL) arborio rice

4 cups (1 L) milk

1 cup (250 mL) granulated sugar

½ cup (125 mL) bourbon (my favourite
   brand is Woodford Reserve)

½ vanilla bean, split in half lengthwise

BRING A LARGE SAUCEPAN of water to a boil over high heat. Add the rice and blanch for 3 minutes. Strain the rice through a sieve then refresh under cold running water for several minutes.

Meanwhile, in a large heavy saucepan, stir together the milk, sugar, bourbon, and vanilla bean. Bring to a gentle simmer over medium heat. Stir in the rice and cook for about 18 minutes, stirring constantly, until the rice is just tender but still al dente and the pudding is creamy. Keep warm until ready to serve.

CARAMELIZED PEARS

3 ripe pears, peeled and cored

2 Tbsp (30 mL) granulated sugar

¼ cup (60 mL) unsalted butter

CUT THE PEARS in half lengthwise. Using a small sharp paring knife, thinly slice each pear half, cutting almost but not quite through the blossom end of each so that the slices fan out but don't separate. (Or simply quarter the pears if you wish.)

In a large skillet, stir together the sugar and butter over low heat until melted and smooth. Continue cooking, stirring frequently, until the mixture is golden brown and bubbly.

Add the pears to the skillet core side down, fanning out the slices slightly (you may have to cook the pears in batches), then cook until the pears are caramelized. Using a spatula, carefully turn the pears over and cook until caramelized on the other side.

TO SERVE, divide the rice pudding among 6 warm dessert bowls. Carefully place a caramelized pear half (or 2 quarters) on top of each portion, and serve with brandy snaps on the side.

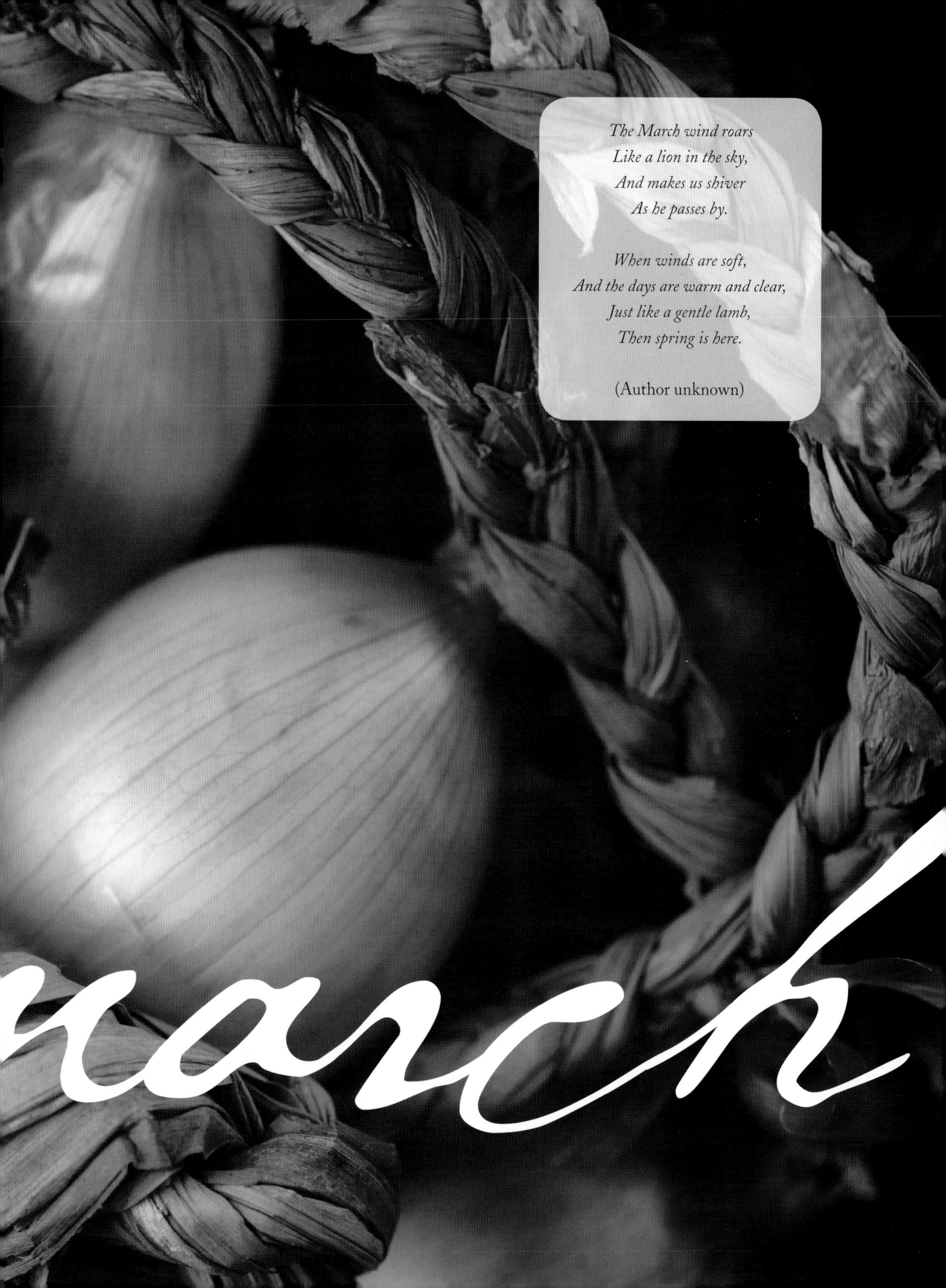

The March wind roars
Like a lion in the sky,
And makes us shiver
As he passes by.

When winds are soft,
And the days are warm and clear,
Just like a gentle lamb,
Then spring is here.

(Author unknown)

march

March I can't really hate March. As the days become longer and the weather turns milder, the month is a harbinger of warm weather to come. March comes in like a lion and goes out like a lamb, they say. Nestled between lakes Erie and Ontario, the Niagara region is fortunate to miss the worst of the typical Canadian winter weather, the area's unique microclimate making our winters tolerable.

In March, I keep an eye out for those days when Mother Nature sends us a hint of what's to come. You know the days I'm speaking of—brisk and sunny with the steady drip of melting snow. As we lose that extra hour of sleep and the evenings become lighter, I love to start planning our garden and organizing more outdoor activities.

In the kitchen, the way we cook is influenced by the coming season. We might taste the season's first fresh herbs and edible flowers, while different seedlings and sprouts make their way onto the menu. The blending of winter and spring defines the cuisine. We may have had our fill of root vegetables and hearty, comforting food, but new crops are on their way, such as young leeks for a bacon and potato chowder—perhaps with my favourite beer, Guinness—or cabbage leaves to stuff and serve with roast Cornish hens, and with them a brand new season of tempting, awe-inspiring food.

Leek, Bacon, and Potato Chowder with Guinness

Nothing cheers a chef more than being able to eat his beer as well as drink it! This hearty soup combines two of my favourite ingredients: Guinness and potatoes.

SERVES 6

¼ cup (60 mL) olive oil
1 cup (250 mL) finely chopped bacon
3 cups (750 mL) chopped leeks
   (white parts only)
1 onion, chopped
2 stalks celery, chopped
2 potatoes, peeled and chopped
2 sprigs thyme

4 cups (1 L) chicken or vegetable
   stock (page 255)
1 cup (250 mL) 35% cream
1 cup (250 mL) Guinness or other
   dark beer
kosher salt and black pepper to taste
2 Tbsp (30 mL) finely chopped chives
paprika for garnish

HEAT A LARGE SAUCEPAN over medium heat and add the olive oil. When the oil is hot, add the bacon and sauté, stirring frequently, until it is lightly browned and crisp. With a slotted spoon, remove half of the bacon to a plate lined with paper towels, and reserve for garnishing the soup.

Add the leeks and onion to the bacon remaining in the saucepan and sauté, stirring frequently, for about 12 minutes or until vegetables are very soft but not brown.

Stir in the celery, potatoes, and thyme. Add the stock and bring to a boil. Simmer for 10 minutes or until the potatoes and celery are tender. Stir in the cream and bring to a simmer again. Discard the thyme.

In a blender (not a food processor), blend the soup until smooth. Return to the rinsed-out saucepan. Add the Guinness and bring to a simmer. Season with salt and pepper to taste.

Ladle the soup into 6 warm soup bowls. Garnish with the reserved bacon and the chives. Sprinkle each portion with a little paprika.

I adore Indian food. Regrettably, there are not many really good Indian restaurants in the Niagara area, but thanks to the memories I have of the great Indian meals I enjoyed when I

Curried Onion Rings with Tamarind Dipping Sauce

lived in England, this recipe is a way for me to pay my respects. March is a somewhat arbitrary choice for this recipe, since onions are in season in Ontario from December to May. (Pictured on page 105.)

SERVES 6

TAMARIND DIPPING SAUCE

1 Tbsp (15 mL) vegetable oil	1 Tbsp (15 mL) ketchup
1 clove garlic, crushed	1 Tbsp (15 mL) tamarind paste
½-inch (1 cm) piece fresh ginger, chopped	2 tsp (10 mL) granulated sugar
	1½ tsp (7.5 mL) soy sauce
1 cup (250 mL) chicken stock (page 255)	½ tsp (2 mL) chili paste
1 Tbsp (15 mL) aged sherry vinegar	1 tsp (5 mL) cornstarch

IN A MEDIUM SAUCEPAN, heat the oil over medium heat. Add the garlic and ginger and sauté, stirring frequently, until the garlic is translucent but not browned. Stir in the chicken stock, vinegar, ketchup, tamarind paste, sugar, soy, and chili paste. Bring to a boil then reduce the heat to low and simmer for 10 minutes.

In a small bowl, whisk together the cornstarch and 1 Tbsp (15 mL) cold water until smooth. Add the cornstarch mixture to the simmering sauce and cook, stirring frequently, until just thickened. Strain the sauce through a fine-mesh sieve into a serving bowl. Set aside until ready to serve.

CURRIED ONION RINGS

1¾ cups (435 mL) all-purpose flour
3 Tbsp (45 mL) curry powder
2 tsp (10 mL) baking powder
pinch table salt
1½ cups (375 mL) milk
2 eggs

½ tsp (2 mL) cider vinegar
   or white wine vinegar
2 large sweet onions (I like to use
   local Vidalias), cut crosswise into
   ¼-inch-thick (6 mm) rings
vegetable oil for deep-frying
kosher salt to taste

IN A MEDIUM BOWL, whisk together the flour, curry powder, baking powder, and salt. In a separate medium bowl, whisk together the milk, eggs, and vinegar until well combined.

Gradually add the flour mixture to the milk mixture, whisking to create a smooth batter. Add the onion rings to the batter and let stand for 30 minutes.

Heat the oil in a deep pot until a candy thermometer registers 375°F (190°C), or use a deep fat fryer and follow the manufacturer's instructions. Remove the onion rings a few at a time from the batter, shaking off the excess. Fry for 2 to 3 minutes or until golden brown and crisp. Remove the onion rings from the pot with a slotted spoon and let drain on a plate lined with paper towels.

TO SERVE, pile the onion rings on a platter and sprinkle with salt. Serve the tamarind dipping sauce alongside.

When I first introduced sardines to the menu at the Old Winery Restaurant, it took a while for my staff and guests to appreciate what a marvellous, tasty fish they are, and how happily they

Grilled Sardines on Frisée Salad with Gribiche Sauce

can be matched to both red and white wines. In this recipe, a simple, classic gribiche sauce—a type of vinaigrette containing cornichons, capers, herbs, and eggs—highlights the meatiness and full-bodied flavour of the sardines. Any leftover sauce can be spread on roasted salmon, or on slices of toasted baguette to serve with salad.

SERVES 6

GRIBICHE SAUCE

3 hard-cooked eggs

1½ tsp (7.5 mL) Dijon mustard

1 Tbsp (15 mL) lemon juice

¾ cup (185 mL) vegetable oil

3 Tbsp (45 mL) chopped drained
    cornichons

1½ Tbsp (22.5 mL) drained
    capers, chopped

2 tsp (10 mL) white wine vinegar

1 tsp (5 mL) finely chopped
    Italian parsley

1 tsp (5 mL) finely chopped tarragon

1 tsp (5 mL) finely chopped chervil

kosher salt and black pepper
    to taste

SHELL THE EGGS and cut in half lengthwise. Separate the yolks from the whites. Rub the yolks and whites separately through a fine sieve. Set whites aside.

In a medium bowl, whisk together the egg yolks, mustard, and lemon juice. Gradually whisk in the oil until well combined. Stir in the cornichons, capers, vinegar, parsley, tarragon, and chervil and season with salt and pepper to taste. Cover and refrigerate until ready to serve.

GRILLED SARDINES

12 large sardines, cleaned and rinsed
    under cold water
½ cup (125 mL) finely chopped
    Italian parsley

¼ cup (60 mL) olive oil
juice of 1 lemon
kosher salt and black pepper
    to taste

PREHEAT THE BARBECUE to medium-high.

In a large bowl, toss the sardines with the remaining ingredients until evenly coated. Place the sardines on the grill and cook for 5 minutes without moving them. Using a spatula, carefully turn over each sardine and cook for another 5 minutes or until nicely charred and crisp. Keep warm until ready to serve.

FRISÉE SALAD

¼ cup (60 mL) olive oil
2 Tbsp (30 mL) finely chopped chives
1 Tbsp (15 mL) grated lemon zest
juice of 2 lemons

kosher salt and black pepper
    to taste
3 cups (750 mL) frisée, washed,
    dried, and torn

IN A MEDIUM BOWL, whisk together the oil, chives, lemon zest, lemon juice, and salt and pepper to taste. Add the frisée and toss well.

TO SERVE, divide the salad among 6 salad plates. Top each salad with 2 sardines arranged in an X. Spoon the gribiche sauce randomly around each plate and garnish with reserved sieved egg whites.

*This is wine country comfort food.
Choose a good-quality cheddar for the
scalloped potatoes that's at least three
years old. The stuffed cabbage leaves
are an adaptation of a vegetable*

Roast Cornish Hens with Stuffed Cabbage Leaves and Aged Cheddar Cheese Scalloped Potatoes

*garnish that I first saw prepared by chef
Jean-Louis Palladin in Washing-
ton, D.C.*

    *Ask your butcher to bone the Cor-
nish hens for you.*

SERVES 6

CORNISH HEN STUFFING

5 cups (1.25 L) cubed crustless white
    bread (2-inch/5 cm cubes)

1 cup (250 mL) milk

2 oz (60 g) finely chopped prosciutto

½ onion, finely chopped

2 shallots, finely chopped

3 large cloves garlic, crushed

¼ cup (60 mL) lightly packed Italian
    parsley (leaves only)

2 sprigs thyme, leaves picked off
    from stems

6 oz (175 g) chicken livers,
    cleaned of all sinew

1 egg

1 Tbsp (15 mL) all-purpose flour

2 tsp (10 mL) granulated sugar

2 tsp (10 mL) kosher salt

black pepper to taste

IN A LARGE BOWL, soak the bread in the milk for about 5 minutes. Using
your hands, squeeze out the milk from the bread. Set the bread aside,
discarding the milk.

    In a food processor, combine the prosciutto, onion, shallots, garlic, pars-
ley, and thyme leaves. Process until finely chopped. Add the chicken livers
and process until quite smooth.

    Scrape the chicken liver mixture into a large bowl and add the egg,
flour, sugar, salt, reserved bread, and pepper to taste. Mix with your hands
until the ingredients are well combined. Cover and refrigerate for at least
3 hours or overnight.

STUFFED CABBAGE LEAVES

1 medium to large head green or
    Savoy cabbage

½ cup (125 mL) very finely
    chopped carrots

½ cup (125 mL) very finely
    chopped turnip or rutabaga

½ cup (125 mL) very finely
    chopped celery root

½ cup (125 mL) very finely chopped
    leek (white part only)

3 Tbsp (45 mL) unsalted butter

2 shallots, finely chopped

½ cup (125 mL) tomato
    concassé (page 257)

⅓ cup (80 mL) toasted pine nuts

¼ cup (60 mL) chicken or vegetable
    stock (page 255) or water

kosher salt and black pepper
    to taste

BRING A LARGE POT of salted water to a rapid boil and have ready a large bowl of ice water. Remove 6 of the largest, darkest green, and most perfect leaves from the cabbage, reserving the remainder of the cabbage. Add the 6 cabbage leaves to the pot of boiling water, and blanch for 2 minutes. Using a strainer, transfer the leaves to the bowl of ice water, being careful not to rip them while lifting them out. Carefully remove the leaves from the ice water and drain on paper towels. Using a small sharp knife, cut away any thick stems from the cabbage leaves to make the leaves easier to fold. Set aside.

Add the carrots, turnip, celery root, and leek to the pot of boiling water and blanch, chill, and drain the same way as the cabbage. Set aside.

Cut enough of the remaining cabbage into very fine julienne strips to yield about 5 cups (1.25 L), discarding the core. Set aside.

In a large skillet, melt the butter over medium heat. Add the shallots and sauté, stirring frequently, for 2 minutes or until shallots are softened but not browned. Add the julienned cabbage, blanched chopped vegetables, tomato concassé, pine nuts, and stock and stir to combine well. Cook until the liquid has evaporated. Season with salt and pepper to taste and set aside.

Cut 6 large square pieces of strong plastic wrap and lay them on a work surface. Place 1 blanched cabbage leaf in the centre of each piece of plastic wrap with the outer side of the leaf down. Divide the vegetable mixture evenly among the leaves. Fold in the sides of each leaf and, using the plastic wrap, roll each into a tight log. Refrigerate for 3 hours or until thoroughly chilled.

When ready to cook, steam the cabbage leaves (still in their plastic wrap) in a covered steamer over boiling water for 20 minutes. Turn the heat off under the steamer and, when the steam subsides, use a pair of tongs to remove the cabbage leaves. Keep warm until ready to serve.

AGED CHEDDAR CHEESE SCALLOPED POTATOES

2 lb (1 kg) potatoes, peeled and cut
   into ⅛-inch (3 mm) slices
1 Tbsp (15 mL) finely chopped
   rosemary
1 clove garlic, minced
cayenne, freshly grated nutmeg,
   kosher salt, and black pepper
   to taste

2 cups (500 mL) milk (approx.)
6 Tbsp (90 mL) 35% cream
1 cup (250 mL) shredded aged cheddar
   cheese (at least 3 years old)
2 Tbsp (30 mL) unsalted butter

PREHEAT THE OVEN to 300°F (150°C).

In a large bowl, toss the potatoes with the rosemary, garlic, and cayenne, nutmeg, and salt and pepper to taste. Tip the mixture into a large saucepan and pour in enough of the milk to barely cover the potatoes.

Bring the potato mixture to a simmer over medium-low heat and cook, uncovered, for 10 minutes. Add the cream and bring to a boil. Remove the saucepan from the heat and tip the potato mixture into a shallow baking dish, spreading it out evenly. Sprinkle the cheese evenly over the top and dot with the butter. Bake, uncovered, for 1 hour or until the potatoes feel tender when pierced with a slim knife. If the top starts to brown too much, cover the dish with foil. Keep warm until ready to serve.

ROAST CORNISH HENS

6 medium Cornish hens, boned
kosher salt and black pepper to taste

Cornish hen stuffing
olive oil for rubbing

PREHEAT THE OVEN to 350°F (180°C).

Season the hens on both sides with salt and pepper to taste. Lay the hens skin side down on a work surface and divide the stuffing evenly among them. Fold in the sides of the hens to enclose the stuffing and secure with kitchen twine or toothpicks. Rub all over with olive oil and place seam side down in a shallow roasting pan.

Roast for 45 minutes or until an instant-read thermometer inserted in the thickest part of one of the hens registers 160°F (71°C). Remove the hens from the oven and let rest for 10 minutes before serving.

TO SERVE, remove the twine or toothpicks from the hens and place each on a warm dinner plate. Carefully cut away the plastic wrap from the stuffed cabbage leaves and cut each one in half. Arrange stuffed cabbage leaves next to the hens, along with a spoonful of scalloped potatoes.

Saupiquet is a culinary term from antiquity that referred to a sauce thickened with bread to form a sort of sloppy mass that accompanied dried and roasted meats. I have adapted the

Roasted Rabbit Tenderloins with Saupiquet, Fava Beans, and Thyme Sauce

term and refined the recipe to create a sauce-like purée thickened with rabbit livers. You'll need an aged balsamic vinegar for the saupiquet, and the older the vinegar the better the saupiquet will be.

When ordering the rabbit, ask your butcher not to remove the stomach flaps as these will hold the thyme inside the cavities during roasting.

SERVES 4

THYME SAUCE

12 sprigs thyme

2 Tbsp (30 mL) grapeseed oil

1 stalk celery, cut into ½-inch (1 cm) dice

1 leek (white part only), cut into ½-inch (1 cm) dice

1 small turnip, cut into ½-inch (1 cm) dice

1 small carrot, cut into ½-inch (1 cm) dice

½ red onion, cut into ½-inch (1 cm) dice

1 shallot, finely chopped

1 cup (250 mL) chicken stock (page 255)

½ cup (125 mL) veal jus (page 254)

1 tsp (5 mL) aged sherry vinegar

kosher salt and black pepper to taste

PICK the leaves off 6 of the thyme sprigs and chop them, setting the remaining sprigs aside. Heat a large saucepan over medium-high heat and add the oil. When the oil is hot, add the celery, leek, turnip, carrot, onion, shallot, and chopped thyme. Reduce the heat to medium and cook for 5 minutes, stirring frequently, until the vegetables are softened but not browned.

Add the stock and simmer for about 30 minutes or until the stock is reduced to ½ cup (125 mL). Add the veal jus and simmer, stirring frequently, for about 10 minutes or until the liquid has reduced slightly and is thick enough to coat the back of a spoon.

Strain through a fine-mesh sieve into a smaller saucepan, discarding the solids in the sieve. Return the sauce to medium heat. Once it starts to steam (do not let sauce boil), remove the saucepan from the heat and add the reserved thyme sprigs. Set aside to steep for 5 minutes.

Discard the thyme sprigs. Stir in the vinegar and season with salt and pepper to taste. Keep warm until ready to serve.

SAUPIQUET

2 tsp (10 mL) grapeseed oil

2 green onions, trimmed
    and finely chopped

1 shallot, finely chopped

2 sprigs thyme, leaves picked off
    from stems and finely chopped

½ cup (125 mL) rabbit livers (from
    2 rabbits), cleaned of any sinew

kosher salt and black pepper
    to taste

1 Tbsp (15 mL) aged balsamic vinegar

IN A MEDIUM SKILLET, heat the grapeseed oil over medium heat. Add the green onions, shallot, and thyme, then sauté for 1 minute, stirring frequently.

Add the livers and season with salt and pepper to taste. Reduce the heat to medium-low and sauté, stirring frequently, for about 7 minutes or until the centres of the livers are only slightly pink. Add the vinegar, stir for 30 seconds, then remove the skillet from the heat.

Let cool for 2 minutes, then transfer to a food processor or blender and purée until smooth. Scrape the saupiquet into a small saucepan and keep warm until ready to serve.

ROASTED RABBIT TENDERLOINS

4 saddles of rabbit with tenderloins
    attached (each 1 lb/500 g)

kosher salt and black pepper to taste

12 sprigs thyme

3 Tbsp (45 mL) vegetable oil

PREHEAT THE OVEN to 400°F (200°C).

Season each saddle inside and out with salt and pepper to taste. Lay the saddles on a work surface breast side up and spread open the stomach flaps. Place 3 sprigs thyme in the cavity of each saddle, then fold the stomach flaps back over to enclose the herbs.

In a large ovenproof skillet, heat the oil over moderate heat. Add the rabbit saddles stomach side down and cook for 8 to 10 minutes or until golden brown. Using tongs, carefully turn over the saddles and continue to cook for a further 5 minutes or until golden brown.

Transfer the skillet to the oven and cook for about 15 minutes or until the rabbit saddles are tender and an instant-read thermometer inserted into the rabbit saddles but not touching any bones registers 150°F (65°C).

Remove the saddles to a cutting board and let rest for 5 minutes. Using a very sharp thin knife, cut away each tenderloin in 1 piece (these are the slim fillets on either side of the saddles). Cover the tenderloins and keep warm until ready to serve (reserve the carcasses for making stock).

FAVA BEANS

3 lb (1.5 kg) fresh unshelled fava beans   kosher salt and black pepper
¼ cup (60 mL) unsalted butter   to taste

BRING A LARGE POT of salted water to a rapid boil and have ready a large bowl of ice water. Shell the fava beans, add the shelled beans to the pot of boiling water, and blanch for 4 minutes. Using a strainer or a slotted spoon, transfer the fava beans to the bowl of ice water. Drain the beans through a colander.

Using a small knife or your fingernail, make an incision in the membrane of each bean then squeeze out the bean with your thumb and forefinger.

Just before serving, melt the butter in a medium skillet over medium heat. When the butter foams, add the fava beans and season to taste with salt and pepper.

TO SERVE, spoon the saupiquet down the centre of each of 4 warm dinner plates. Cut the rabbit tenderloins crosswise into thin slices and arrange over the saupiquet. Spoon the fava beans decoratively on top of the rabbit and drizzle each plate with thyme sauce.

Floating Islands with Vanilla Sauce and Caramel

SERVES 6

VANILLA SAUCE

2 cups (500 mL) whole milk

pinch table salt

4 egg yolks

¼ cup (60 mL) granulated sugar

1 tsp (5 mL) vanilla

IN A MEDIUM SAUCEPAN, bring the milk to a simmer over medium heat. Add the salt.

Meanwhile, in a small bowl and using an electric mixer, beat together the egg yolks and sugar for 5 minutes or until pale in colour and smooth.

Whisk the hot milk into the egg mixture. Strain the milk mixture through a fine-mesh sieve into a clean saucepan. Cook over medium heat (do not boil), stirring constantly, until the sauce thickens enough to coat the back of a spoon and an instant-read thermometer placed in the sauce registers 170°F (77°C).

Strain the sauce once again through a fine-mesh sieve into a clean bowl. Stir in the vanilla. Let cool to room temperature.

CARAMEL

¼ cup (60 mL) granulated sugar

IN A SMALL SAUCEPAN, combine the sugar with ¼ cup (60 mL) water and bring to a boil over medium-high heat, stirring often. Continue to boil, without stirring, for 5 to 10 minutes or until it is a light golden colour.

Immediately remove the saucepan from the heat and let the caramel cool until it is the consistency of maple syrup. Keep warm until ready to serve.

FLOATING ISLANDS

2 cups (500 mL) milk

4 egg whites

pinch table salt

¼ cup (60 mL) granulated sugar

6 sprigs mint

LINE A LARGE BAKING SHEET with paper towels. In a large shallow saucepan, bring the milk and 2 cups (500 mL) water to a simmer over medium heat.

Meanwhile, in a medium bowl, beat the egg whites and salt until soft peaks form. Gradually beat in the sugar and continue beating until stiff peaks form, about 15 minutes.

Use 2 large serving spoons to form the meringue into oval-shaped quenelles. Drop them gently, a few at a time, into the simmering milk mixture. Poach for 8 minutes or until firm. Using a slotted spoon, carefully remove the quenelles from the hot milk and place them on the prepared baking sheet. Repeat with the remaining egg white mixture.

(Instead of poaching the egg whites in milk, try this shortcut: Spoon the whipped egg whites into six ½-cup/125 mL ramekins, and microwave on low for 45 to 60 seconds, or until they firm up. Wait until cool enough to handle before inverting the ramekins onto the dessert bowls.)

TO SERVE, whisk the vanilla sauce and divide it among 6 dessert bowls. Top each portion of sauce with floating islands and drizzle with caramel. (If the caramel has become too thick to drizzle, warm it slightly over low heat.) Garnish with the mint.

april

April is the time to get busy. The month starts off with all the nasty April Fool's shenanigans, but as the days go by it settles down nicely, revealing the new season in all its optimism. It should come as no surprise that some people believe the word "April" comes from the Latin verb *aperire*, which means "to open."

Personally, I love April. It truly is a month of transition. You can feel it in the bright blue skies and the temperate air that suck people outdoors again. As the last of the winter gives way to the gentler, warmer days, this is the month we start our gardening in earnest and are rewarded with the first green shoots. Even the air seems cleaner, sweeter, and fresher. It's a generous month that gives us back the feeling of being more alive. Is it any wonder that one of April's birth flowers is the pretty, fragrant sweet pea?

Since Easter often falls in April, I have fond memories of the celebrations we had when I was a kid. On Easter Sunday, after attending church—and if I had behaved during Mass—my parents would allow me to break open one of the many chocolate Easter eggs I'd been given. I used to love discovering the surprise hidden in the centre of each egg.

Easter Sunday always meant a big beautiful meal with dear relatives, usually mid-afternoon, and my mother would spend hours the week before preparing the specialties of our Italian heritage. But the meal on Good Friday was my favourite. My mom would prepare a magnificent fish feast that became legendary in our extended family. As I grew older and more comfortable around the stove, I'd help her prepare it.

From antipasti of shrimps, cuttlefish, and smoked salmon, to pastas with clams, mussels, and scallops, and more shrimp, to platters of king crab legs, salt cod baked in tomato sauce, stuffed clams, mussels, and lobster tails, it was an endless stream of oceanic delights. My wife, a seafood lover, craves this feast and I'm quite sure it was one of the reasons she agreed to marry me. In fact, I've never seen anyone eat as much lobster as my wife is capable of consuming, good Maritimer that she is!

The meal on Easter Sunday was also a marvel. We would always have numerous antipasti, pastas, and, always, a nice braised leg of lamb. Often my mom would prepare her lasagna with the tiny little meatballs between each delicate layer of pasta. Or perhaps, hand-rolled fusilli baked in a rich tomato sauce. Whatever was on our plates, we were always grateful to have such abundance and especially appreciated the blessing of sharing it with each other.

From a culinary point of view, this is the first month we start to move away from the more substantial foods of winter to spring's lighter, fresher cuisine. April is also the time when we break out the barbecue in earnest and start wearing funny aprons! By the end of the month, we may be enjoying spring's first harvest of delicate herbs, such as chives and tarragon, baby lettuces, and cress.

This rich savoury cheesecake can be served as an appetizer course for an elegant dinner, as a brunch or lunch entrée, or even as part of a buffet. The cheesecake recipe makes a 9-inch (23 cm)

Savoury Blue Cheese Cheesecake with Onion Confit and Baby Greens in Verjus Dressing

cake (enough for 8 to 12 portions), so refrigerate the remainder for up to three days to serve at another meal.

SERVES 6

SAVOURY BLUE CHEESE CHEESECAKE

2 Tbsp (30 mL) unsalted butter

1 cup (250 mL) fresh, soft
   breadcrumbs

⅔ cup (160 mL) ground
   toasted walnuts

1¾ lb (875 g) cream cheese, softened

12 oz (375 g) blue cheese (such as
   roquefort), crumbled

4 eggs

3 shallots, finely chopped,
   sautéed, and cooled

¼ cup (60 mL) 35% cream

2 Tbsp (30 mL) all-purpose flour

2 Tbsp (30 mL) finely chopped dill

white pepper to taste

½ cup (125 mL) chopped toasted
   walnuts (to serve)

PREHEAT THE OVEN to 300°F (150°C). Place a 10-inch (3 L) springform pan on 2 pieces of aluminum foil and fold the foil up the outside of the pan.

Melt the butter in a small skillet over medium heat. Add the breadcrumbs and cook, stirring frequently, until the breadcrumbs are golden brown. Stir in the ground walnuts. Press the breadcrumb mixture evenly into the prepared pan and let cool to room temperature.

In a food processor, combine the cream cheese and blue cheese. Process until smooth. Add the eggs, shallots, cream, flour, dill, and pepper to taste. Process until well combined.

Pour the cheese mixture into the prepared pan over the base, smoothing the top level. Place the springform pan in a shallow roasting pan. Pour boiling water into the roasting pan to come halfway up the sides of the springform pan. Bake for 1 hour or until the cheesecake is set around the edges but still jiggles slightly in the centre.

Remove the cheesecake from the roasting pan and let cool to room temperature. Cover the springform pan with plastic wrap and refrigerate overnight. Bring the cheesecake to room temperature before serving. Release the sides of the pan and remove the cheesecake.

ONION CONFIT

¼ cup (60 mL) olive oil

2 Tbsp (30 mL) unsalted butter

2 onions (white or red), cut crosswise
   into ¾-inch-thick (2 cm) rings

2 Tbsp (30 mL) maple syrup

1 sprig rosemary

1 sprig thyme

1 bay leaf

½ cup (125 mL) red wine vinegar

kosher salt and black pepper to taste

HEAT A LARGE SKILLET over medium heat and add the olive oil and butter. When the butter foams, add the onions and sauté, stirring frequently, until the onions are softened but not browned. Stir in the maple syrup, rosemary, thyme, and bay leaf and cook for an additional 5 minutes, stirring frequently, to prevent burning.

Reduce the heat to low and add the vinegar and 2 Tbsp (30 mL) water. Simmer for 20 to 30 minutes or until the liquid has completely evaporated. Season with salt and pepper. Remove from the heat and let cool to room temperature. Discard the rosemary, thyme, and bay leaf before serving.

BABY GREENS IN VERJUS DRESSING

1 cup (250 mL) verjus

1 cup (250 mL) port

2 Tbsp (30 mL) finely chopped shallots

1 cup (250 mL) grapeseed oil

kosher salt and black pepper
   to taste

3 cups (750 mL) lightly packed baby
   greens, washed and dried

COMBINE THE VERJUS, port, and shallots in a small saucepan over medium heat and bring to a boil. Reduce the heat to low and simmer until the liquid is reduced by half. Pour through a fine-mesh sieve into a clean bowl and let cool to room temperature.

Pour the reduced verjus mixture into a food processor or blender. With the motor on low speed, slowly add the grapeseed oil in a slow steady stream. Blend until the dressing is creamy. Season with salt and pepper to taste. Cover and refrigerate. One hour before serving, remove the dressing from the fridge. Just before serving, whisk the dressing and toss the baby greens in enough dressing to coat the leaves.

TO SERVE, dip a long sharp carving knife into hot water then dry it. While the knife is still warm, cut 6 wedges from the cheesecake. Top each slice with chopped walnuts. Place each wedge on a dinner plate, along with some of the baby greens. Spoon some of the remaining verjus dressing over each piece of cheesecake, and serve with a small mound of onion confit.

The inspiration for this recipe is two-fold. First, Pierre Chevillard, the chef I worked for at the Chewton Glen hotel in England, was a devoted sausage master, and a version of his seafood

Seafood Sausages with Carrot-Top Sauce and Tarragon and Roasted Garlic Timbales

sausage was always on the menu. Also while in England, I was introduced to the cuisine of chef Anton Mosimann. Years later, when he was in Toronto as a guest chef at the Mövenpick restaurant in Yorkville, chef Mosimann served a carrot-top sauce that blew me away. I'd been throwing them out for years, never realizing the delicate, fresh green flavour that could be coaxed out of them.

If you cannot find sausage casings (they are available from any good butcher), form the seafood mixture into individual sausages and wrap each tightly in strong plastic wrap, twisting the wrap to seal the ends.

SERVES 6

FROMAGE BLANC

⅔ cup (160 mL) non-fat cottage cheese

⅓ cup (80 mL) plain yogurt

IN A FOOD PROCESSOR, combine the cottage cheese and yogurt and purée until smooth. Cover and refrigerate until needed.

SEAFOOD SAUSAGES

5 oz (150 g) skinless, boneless salmon fillet, cut into ½-inch (1 cm) dice (dark parts discarded)

5 oz (150 g) skinless, boneless monkfish, cut into ½-inch (1 cm) dice (dark parts discarded)

6 black tiger shrimp, peeled, deveined, and cut into ½-inch (1 cm) dice

4 fresh large sea scallops, cut into ½-inch (1 cm) dice

kosher salt and white pepper to taste

½ lb (250 g) skinless, boneless whitefish fillet, cut into ½-inch (1 cm) dice (dark parts discarded)

2 egg whites

½ cup (125 mL) Fromage Blanc

2 Tbsp (30 mL) finely chopped dill

20-inch (50 cm) piece sausage casing, soaked in cold water

IN A STAINLESS STEEL BOWL, combine the salmon, monkfish, shrimp, scallops, and salt and pepper to taste. Refrigerate until needed.

In a food processor, combine the whitefish, egg whites, and more salt and pepper to taste. Pulse until a fine purée forms. Using a rubber spatula, scrape the whitefish purée into a stainless steel bowl set over a larger bowl one-third-full of ice cubes. Stir in the fromage blanc and dill until well combined. Add the reserved seafood and stir until well combined. Refrigerate for 1 hour.

Spoon the chilled seafood mixture into a piping bag fitted with a large round tip. Tie 1 end of the sausage skin securely with kitchen twine. Gather the other end of the sausage skin on the tip of the piping bag. Squeeze the piping bag gently to fill the sausage skin.

When all the seafood mixture has been piped into the sausage skin, use kitchen twine to tie off the sausage skin at 3-inch (8 cm) intervals to make sausages. Refrigerate for 1 hour.

Bring 8 cups (2 L) water to a simmer in a large pot over medium-low heat. Have ready a large bowl of ice water. Add the sausages to the simmering water and place a plate slightly smaller than the circumference of the pot on top of the sausages to keep them submerged. Cook for 10 minutes or until sausages are firm. Do not let the water boil.

Remove the sausages from the pot and plunge immediately into the ice water. Remove from the ice water and dry on paper towels. Refrigerate for 1 hour.

Just before serving, preheat the barbecue to medium-high. Use the tip of a small, sharp knife to peel away the sausage skins from the sausages. Grill the sausages for about 5 minutes, turning often, until evenly browned and hot all the way through. Keep warm until ready to serve.

CARROT-TOP SAUCE

4 cups (1 L) lightly packed carrot tops, washed and dried

1 cup (250 mL) fish or vegetable stock (page 255)

½ cup (125 mL) 35% cream

juice of ½ lemon

kosher salt and black pepper to taste

BRING A LARGE POT of salted water to a rapid boil over high heat and have ready a large bowl of ice water. Add the carrot tops to the pot of boiling water, and blanch for 10 seconds. Using a strainer or a slotted spoon, transfer the carrots tops to the bowl of ice water, reserving the blanching liquid. Drain the carrot tops through a colander and drain on paper towels.

Recipe continued . . .

Place the blanched carrot tops in a blender with ½ cup (125 mL) of the reserved blanching liquid. Purée until smooth, then rub through a fine-mesh sieve into a bowl.

In a small saucepan, simmer the fish stock over medium heat until it has reduced by half. Add the cream and continue to simmer until the sauce is slightly thickened. Stir in the carrot-top purée, lemon juice, salt, and pepper. Keep warm until ready to serve, but do not boil.

TARRAGON AND ROASTED GARLIC TIMBALES

non-stick baking spray

3 eggs

3 Tbsp (45 mL) lightly packed tarragon
    leaves, blanched

1½ Tbsp (22.5 mL) roasted garlic
    (page 257)

1 tsp (5 mL) kosher salt

½ tsp (2 mL) black pepper

¾ cup (185 mL) milk

¾ cup (185 mL) vegetable
    or chicken stock (page 255)

PREHEAT THE OVEN to 350°F (180°C). Spray six ½-cup (125 mL) ramekins with non-stick baking spray.

In a blender or a food processor, combine the eggs, tarragon, garlic, salt, and pepper. Pulse until smooth then add the milk and stock and pulse briefly until well combined.

Pour the custard into the prepared ramekins, dividing evenly. Place ramekins in a shallow roasting pan. Pour enough boiling water into the roasting pan to come halfway up the sides of the ramekins. Bake for 35 minutes or until the centres of the timbales are just set and lightly browned. Remove the roasting pan from the oven and let the timbales cool slightly in the roasting pan.

TO SERVE, divide the carrot-top sauce among 6 warm dinner plates, spooning it into the centre of each plate. Place 1 or 2 sausages on each portion of sauce. Run a thin sharp knife or a small spatula around the edges of the timbales to release them. Invert each ramekin next to the sausages on each plate to turn out the timbales. Remove the ramekins.

This lovely Mediterranean-inspired dish uses halibut, one of my absolute favourite fish. We always use wild, line-caught Pacific halibut in season and find it to be amazingly fresh and

Chardonnay-Steamed Halibut with Israeli Couscous Salad, Pickled Lemon Rind, and Black Olive Tapenade

sweet tasting. In this recipe, I've paired the fish with Israeli couscous (which is a nice light way to introduce some starch), pickled lemon for the acidity needed to accentuate the sweetness of the fish, and a sharp olive tapenade for depth of flavour. The technique of wrapping the halibut in leek leaves isn't new, but it's an effective way to keep the fish moist while adding a subtle onion flavour.

SERVES 6

PICKLED LEMON RIND

3 lemons	2 bay leaves
2 Tbsp (30 mL) kosher salt	1 cinnamon stick
1 Tbsp (15 mL) grated fresh turmeric	1 tsp (5 mL) red chili flakes
4 allspice berries	1 tsp (5 mL) coriander seeds

CUT RIND FROM EACH LEMON in long wide strips. Wrap salt, turmeric, allspice, bay leaves, cinnamon stick, chili flakes, and coriander seeds in a double layer of cheesecloth to make a spice bag.

In a medium saucepan, bring 2 cups (500 mL) water to a boil over medium-high heat. Add spice bag and bring back to a boil. Reduce the heat and simmer for 10 minutes. Add the lemon rind and simmer for 15 minutes or until the lemon rind has softened.

Remove the saucepan from the heat and let the lemon rind mixture cool to room temperature. Discard the spice bag. Pour the lemon rind and liquid into a clean Mason jar, cover, and refrigerate for at least 1 month before using.

BLACK OLIVE TAPENADE

1¼ cups (310 mL) pitted black olives

⅓ cup (80 mL) coarsely chopped
    anchovy fillets

¼ cup (60 mL) drained capers

2 Tbsp (30 mL) coarsely
    chopped garlic

black pepper to taste

½ cup (125 mL) olive oil

juice of ½ lemon

1 Tbsp (15 mL) finely chopped basil

1 Tbsp (15 mL) finely chopped oregano

IN A FOOD PROCESSOR, combine the olives, anchovies, capers, garlic, and pepper. With the motor running, gradually add the olive oil and lemon juice and process until chunky and spreadable.

Scrape into a non-reactive bowl and stir in the basil and oregano. Cover and refrigerate until ready to serve.

ISRAELI COUSCOUS SALAD

2 Tbsp (30 mL) olive oil

2 shallots, finely chopped

¼ cup (60 mL) finely diced sweet
    red pepper

¼ cup (60 mL) finely diced sweet
    yellow pepper

1 Tbsp (15 mL) chopped Pickled
    Lemon Rind (optional)

1½ cups (375 mL) Israeli couscous

1 tsp (5 mL) curry powder

1 sprig fresh thyme

1 bay leaf

2 cups (500 mL) chicken, fish,
    or vegetable stock (page 255)
    or water

½ cup (125 mL) golden raisins
    or currants

¼ cup (60 mL) finely chopped
    green onions

1 Tbsp (15 mL) finely chopped mint

HEAT A MEDIUM SAUCEPAN over medium heat and add the olive oil, shallots, sweet red and yellow peppers, and pickled lemon rind (if using). Sauté, stirring frequently, until shallots are softened but not browned.

Add the couscous and cook, stirring frequently, to allow the couscous to toast slightly. Stir in the curry powder, thyme, and bay leaf, then add the stock and bring to a simmer. Simmer, covered, for 10 minutes.

Stir in the raisins, green onions, and mint. Remove the saucepan from the heat and let stand, covered, for 5 minutes or until the couscous is tender and the liquid has been absorbed. Discard thyme and bay leaf. Keep warm until ready to serve.

CHARDONNAY-STEAMED HALIBUT

3 leeks (white parts only), cut in half
    lengthwise and washed well
2¼ lb (1.1 kg) halibut fillets, cut into
    6 even-size pieces
2 Tbsp (30 mL) olive oil
kosher salt and white pepper to taste
3 sprigs Italian parsley

2 cups (500 mL) Chardonnay
2 cups (500 mL) fish stock
    (page 255)
1 lemon, thinly sliced
3 sprigs thyme
6 white peppercorns
1 bay leaf

BRING A LARGE POT of salted water to a rapid boil over high heat and have ready a large bowl of ice water. Add the leeks to the pot of boiling water, and blanch for 3 minutes. Using a strainer or a slotted spoon, transfer the leeks to the bowl of ice water. Set aside.

Rub the halibut all over with the olive oil then season with salt and pepper to taste. Pick the parsley leaves off the sprigs, discarding the stems. Stick the parsley leaves generously over both sides of each piece of fish.

Drain the leeks, separate into individual leaves, and pat dry on paper towels. Divide the leek leaves into 6 portions. On a work surface, arrange each portion of leaves in a single layer and slightly overlapping. Place a piece of halibut on one-half of each portion of leaves. Slide a spatula or a long knife under 1 portion of leeks and fold the leeks over the halibut to enclose the fish completely. Trim away any excess leeks. Repeat with the remaining portions. Refrigerate until ready to steam.

In the base of a steamer, combine the Chardonnay, stock, lemon, thyme, peppercorns, and bay leaf. Bring to a simmer over medium heat and simmer for 5 minutes. Put the halibut in a steamer over the Chardonnay mixture and steam, covered, for 12 minutes or until the fish feels firm. Turn off the heat and let stand for 2 minutes. Carefully remove halibut from the steamer with a spatula, leaving it wrapped in leek leaves.

TO SERVE, divide the Israeli couscous salad among 6 warm dinner plates. Place 1 piece of halibut on each portion of salad. Spoon a generous amount of tapenade on top of each piece of fish.

My version of beef carpaccio is actually more of a cross between classic carpaccio and bresaola. In truth, these dishes are very different. Carpaccio is usually made from raw beef tenderloin, while

Cured Beef Tenderloin and Arugula Salad with Truffle Vinaigrette and Ricotta Flan

bresaola is generally a piece of inside or outside round that's cured in salt and spices then air-dried for months. My take treats beef tenderloin to a 24-hour "cure" to create an updated version of carpaccio that's similar to bresaola.

SERVES 6

CURED BEEF TENDERLOIN

2 cups (500 mL) granulated sugar	10 sprigs mint
2 cups (500 mL) kosher salt	1 tsp (5 mL) crushed dried chili
1 cup (250 mL) orange juice	8 black peppercorns, cracked
½ cup (125 mL) citrus-flavoured vodka	1 star anise
½ cup (125 mL) olive oil	2 lb (1 kg) beef tenderloin, trimmed
1 Tbsp (15 mL) grated fresh ginger	of all fat and sinew and cut
1 Tbsp (15 mL) soy sauce	crosswise in half

IN A NON-REACTIVE BOWL large enough to hold the beef, stir together the sugar, salt, orange juice, vodka, oil, ginger, soy sauce, mint, chili, peppercorns, and star anise. Add the beef and turn several times. Lay a piece of plastic wrap on the surface and weigh it down with a can of fruit or soup to ensure the beef is completely submerged. Refrigerate for 24 hours.

Remove the beef from the bowl, discarding the liquid, and pat dry with paper towel. Wrap each piece of beef in several layers of plastic wrap and freeze for 1 hour or until chilled enough to slice thinly.

Using a large, very sharp knife or a meat slicer, cut each piece of beef into very thin slices. Refrigerate, tightly wrapped in plastic wrap, until ready to serve.

RICOTTA FLAN

non-stick baking spray

½ lb (250 g) fresh ricotta cheese

½ cup (125 mL) 35% cream

2 egg yolks plus 1 egg

¼ cup (60 mL) freshly grated
   Parmesan cheese

pinch freshly grated nutmeg

kosher salt and white pepper to taste

PREHEAT THE OVEN to 325°F (160°C). Spray six ½-cup (125 mL) ramekins with non-stick baking spray.

Combine the remaining ingredients in a food processor or blender and process on medium-low speed for 3 minutes or until smooth. Pour the ricotta mixture into the prepared ramekins and tap each on the counter to remove any air bubbles.

Place the ramekins in a shallow roasting pan. Pour enough boiling water into the pan to come halfway up the sides of the ramekins. Bake for 35 minutes or until the tops of the flans are golden brown and a toothpick inserted in the centre comes out clean. Remove the roasting pan from the oven and let the flans cool slightly in the water bath. Remove the flans from the water bath and keep warm until ready to serve.

ARUGULA SALAD WITH TRUFFLE VINAIGRETTE

¾ cup (185 mL) red wine vinegar

¾ cup (185 mL) olive oil

¼ cup (60 mL) aged balsamic vinegar

3 Tbsp (45 mL) truffle oil

1 tsp (5 mL) Dijon mustard

1 shallot, finely chopped

1 tsp (5 mL) granulated sugar

1 tsp (5 mL) kosher salt

¼ tsp (1 mL) black pepper

½ black truffle, chopped

3 cups (750 mL) lightly packed
   arugula, tough stems discarded,
   leaves washed and dried

IN A NON-REACTIVE BOWL, whisk together the red wine vinegar, olive oil, balsamic vinegar, truffle oil, mustard, and 2 Tbsp (30 mL) water. Whisk in the shallot, sugar, salt, and pepper until the sugar has dissolved. Fold in the truffle. Cover and refrigerate.

One hour before serving, remove the dressing from the fridge. Just before serving, whisk the vinaigrette and toss the arugula in enough vinaigrette to coat the leaves, reserving the remaining vinaigrette.

TO SERVE, divide the arugula salad between 6 large, chilled dinner plates. Arrange slices of beef, slightly overlapping, to cover the salad (wrap any remaining slices tightly in plastic wrap and refrigerate for up to 1 week). Run a thin sharp knife or a small spatula around the edges of the flans to release them from the ramekins onto a plate. Using your hands, crumble the ricotta flan (1 flan per serving) overtop the beef slices. Spoon any remaining truffle vinaigrette around each plate.

I find pork and mustard are a great flavour combo. In this recipe, a grainy mustard crust makes ordinary grilled pork chops way more interesting. And, serving them with a caramelized onion

Mustard-Crusted Pork Chops with Caramelized Onion Sauce

and beer sauce creates a meal fit for a grill master!

In my kitchens, we try to use Kozlik's Canadian Mustard whenever possible. Since 1948, Anton Kozlik has been making some of the world's best mustards right here in Canada. If you're surprised by that, you may be even more stunned to learn that Canada grows more than 90 percent of the world's mustard seed and is home to one of the biggest and oldest mustard mills on the planet.

For the juiciest pork, choose the thickest bone-in chops you can find.

SERVES 6

CARAMELIZED ONION SAUCE

3 Tbsp (45 mL) unsalted butter

2 cups (500 mL) finely chopped onions

2 cloves garlic, crushed

2 Tbsp (30 mL) maple syrup

2 Tbsp (30 mL) all-purpose flour

1 bottle (330 mL) dark beer or ale

1 cup (250 mL) veal or chicken stock (page 254–55)

kosher salt and black pepper to taste

HEAT A LARGE SAUCEPAN over medium heat and add the butter. When the butter foams, add the onions and sauté, stirring frequently, for 15 minutes or until onions are golden brown. Add the garlic and cook, stirring, for 2 minutes. Stir in the maple syrup, then the flour, stirring until well combined.

Add the beer and bring to a simmer, stirring constantly. Simmer, stirring occasionally, until the liquid has reduced by three-quarters. Add the stock and continue to simmer until the sauce has reduced a little more and is thick enough to coat the back of a spoon.

Remove the saucepan from the heat. Transfer the sauce to a blender and blend until smooth. Strain through a fine-mesh sieve into a clean saucepan. Return the sauce to a simmer, and season with salt and pepper to taste. Set aside and reheat gently when ready to serve.

MUSTARD-CRUSTED PORK CHOPS

2 Tbsp (30 mL) unsalted butter

¼ cup (60 mL) olive oil, divided

1 shallot, finely chopped

2 cloves garlic, minced

2 cups (500 mL) fresh, soft
   breadcrumbs

¼ cup (60 mL) apple cider

2 Tbsp (30 mL) Kozlik's mustard
   (or any grainy mustard)

2 sprigs rosemary, leaves picked off
   from stems and finely chopped

1 egg, lightly beaten

kosher salt and black pepper to taste

6 bone-in rib pork chops, 1½ inches
   (4 cm) thick

HEAT A MEDIUM SKILLET over medium heat and add the butter and 2 Tbsp (30 mL) of the oil. When the butter foams, add the shallot and garlic and sauté, stirring frequently, for 2 minutes. Add the breadcrumbs and cook, stirring frequently, until the oil and butter are completely absorbed by the breadcrumbs and the crumbs begin to toast slightly.

Stir in the apple cider, mustard, and rosemary and cook, stirring frequently, for 2 minutes or until mixture is slightly moist. Remove the skillet from the heat and let stand for 5 minutes. Stir in the egg and season with salt and pepper to taste. Set aside.

Preheat the barbecue to high. Brush the pork chops on both sides with the remaining olive oil and grill on 1 side for 5 minutes, rotating them through 90 degrees after 2 or 3 minutes to make a lovely crosshatch pattern.

Turn the chops over and spoon the breadcrumb mixture on top of the chops, dividing evenly. Close the lid, reduce the heat to medium, and cook the chops, without disturbing them, for 4 to 5 minutes or until an instant-read thermometer inserted into thickest part of chops and not touching any bones registers 150°F (65°C). Remove the chops from the grill and let rest, loosely covered, for 10 minutes.

TO SERVE, place 1 pork chop on each of 6 warm dinner plates. Spoon caramelized onion sauce alongside each chop. Serve with more mustard alongside in ramekins if you wish.

We always have a leg of lamb at Easter. Often we grill it on the barbecue (weather permitting, of course), but sometimes we braise it. When I was a kid, I got a kick out of stuffing the

Braised Leg of Lamb "Nonna de Luca" with Salsa Verde

garlic into the meat. The real treat, of course, is to get served a slice with the garlic still in it. Truly delicious.

The cooking liquid in this dish is reduced slightly; then, with the addition of some olive oil and parsley, it's transformed into a flavourful gravy.

SERVES 6

SALSA VERDE

1 cup (250 mL) finely chopped
    Italian parsley
½ cup (125 mL) finely chopped mint
¼ cup (60 mL) finely chopped
    drained gherkins
4 anchovy fillets, finely chopped
2 cloves garlic, minced

1 Tbsp (15 mL) drained capers,
    squeezed dry and finely chopped
3 Tbsp (45 mL) red wine vinegar
1 Tbsp (15 mL) Dijon mustard
¾ cup (185 mL) olive oil
black pepper to taste

COMBINE the parsley, mint, gherkins, anchovies, garlic, and capers in a medium bowl and toss to combine. Whisk in the vinegar and mustard. Slowly add the olive oil in a steady stream, whisking constantly to combine the ingredients. Whisk in black pepper to taste then refrigerate until ready to serve.

BRAISED LEG OF LAMB

8 cloves garlic

1 boneless leg of lamb (6 lb/2.7 kg),
   trimmed of excess fat, rolled, and
   tied with butcher's twine

kosher salt and black pepper to taste

⅓ cup (80 mL) olive oil, divided

2 onions, chopped

2 carrots, chopped

3 stalks celery, chopped

2 fennel bulbs, trimmed
   and chopped

6 tomatoes, peeled, seeded,
   and chopped

6 cups (1.5 L) chicken stock (page 255)

¼ cup (60 mL) finely chopped
   Italian parsley

PREHEAT THE OVEN to 375°F (190°C).

Cut 3 cloves of the garlic lengthwise into 6 slices each. Using the tip of a small, sharp knife, poke 18 deep holes all over the leg of lamb. Stuff 1 slice of garlic into each hole. Season the lamb liberally with salt and pepper. Crush the remaining garlic and set aside.

Pour ¼ cup (60 mL) of the olive oil into a large flameproof roasting pan and heat over medium-high heat. Add the seasoned lamb to the roasting pan and sear the meat on all sides for 15 to 20 minutes or until golden brown and very aromatic. Remove the lamb to a large plate.

Add the crushed garlic, onions, carrots, celery, and fennel to the roasting pan. Sauté, stirring frequently, for 10 minutes or until vegetables start to brown. Season the vegetables with more salt and pepper to taste. Stir in the tomatoes and return the lamb to the roasting pan. Cover the pan with aluminum foil. Transfer the roasting pan to the oven and cook for 1 hour, stirring the vegetables occasionally.

NONNA DE LUCA CARVING THE EASTER LEG OF LAMB

Bring the stock to the boil in a medium saucepan. Add the stock to the roasting pan and reduce the temperature to 300°F (150°C). Recover the pan with foil and continue to cook for another 2½ hours or until the lamb is very tender.

Remove the roasting pan from the oven and carefully transfer the lamb to a warm serving platter. Using a slotted spoon, remove the vegetables from the roasting pan and spoon them around the lamb. Cover the platter loosely and keep warm until ready to serve.

There should be about 2 cups (500 mL) cooking liquid left in the roasting pan (if there's less, add chicken stock or water to make 2 cups/ 500 mL). Put the roasting pan over medium-high heat and simmer the liquid until it is reduced to 1½ cups (375 mL). Remove the roasting pan from the heat and stir in the parsley and remaining olive oil. Pour the sauce into a small saucepan and keep warm until ready to serve.

Carve the lamb at the table and serve with the vegetables, reduced cooking liquid, and salsa verde.

In honour of my time spent cooking in Germany, I've decided to include a classic Austrian dessert! Actually, I lived in a town called Passau near the Austrian border, and during my

Classic Linzer Torte with Toasted Hazelnut Ice Cream

break on Sunday afternoons, I'd slip over the border for a slice of linzer torte and a cup of tea. How civilized I was back then.

SERVES 6

TOASTED HAZELNUT ICE CREAM

1½ cups (375 mL) whole milk

1½ cups (375 mL) 35% cream

1 Tbsp (15 mL) maple syrup

1 vanilla bean, spit in half lengthwise

4 egg yolks

¾ cup (185 mL) granulated sugar

1 Tbsp (15 mL) Frangelico hazelnut liqueur (optional)

1 cup (250 mL) toasted hazelnuts (page 18), coarsely chopped

IN A MEDIUM SAUCEPAN, combine the milk, cream, maple syrup, and vanilla bean and bring to a simmer over medium heat. Remove the saucepan from the heat, cover, and set aside to steep for 15 minutes.

Meanwhile, in a small bowl and using an electric mixer, beat together the egg yolks and sugar for 5 minutes or until pale in colour and smooth.

Temper the eggs by whisking a small amount of the hot cream mixture into the egg mixture. Pour this back into the hot cream and return the saucepan to medium heat. Cook, stirring frequently with a wooden spoon, for about 15 minutes or until the mixture thickens slightly (do not boil).

Immediately pour the custard through a fine-mesh sieve into a clean bowl and stir in the hazelnut liqueur (if using). Stir in the hazelnuts. Cover and refrigerate until chilled.

Freeze in an ice-cream maker following the manufacturer's instructions. (Or, pour the mixture into a shallow container, cover, and freeze for 2 to 3 hours or until a 1-inch/2.5 cm frozen border has formed around the edge. Scrape the ice cream into a bowl and beat until smooth. Scrape the ice cream back into the container. Repeat freezing and beating process once more, then cover and freeze until firm.)

LINZER TORTE DOUGH

1 cup (250 mL) toasted slivered
  almonds
½ cup (125 mL) toasted hazelnuts
  (page 18)
1½ cups (375 mL) all-purpose flour
⅔ cup (160 mL) granulated sugar
grated zest of 1 orange
1 tsp (5 mL) cinnamon

½ tsp (2 mL) baking powder
¼ tsp (1 mL) table salt
⅛ tsp (0.5 mL) ground cloves
½ cup plus 6 Tbsp (215 mL)
  cold unsalted butter, cubed
2 egg yolks
1 tsp (5 mL) vanilla
softened unsalted butter for greasing

IN A FOOD PROCESSOR, combine the almonds, hazelnuts, and half of the flour. Pulse until the nuts are finely ground. Add the rest of the flour, along with the sugar, orange zest, cinnamon, baking powder, salt, and cloves. Process until well combined. Add the butter and pulse until the mixture resembles fine crumbs. Add the egg yolks and vanilla and process until the dough comes together into a ball.

Divide the dough into 2 pieces, one slightly larger than the other. Press the larger piece into the bottom and up the sides of a buttered 10-inch (25 cm) tart pan with a removable base. Wrap the smaller piece of dough in plastic wrap. Let the lined tart pan and the ball of dough rest in the refrigerator for 1 hour while you make the filling.

LINZER TORTE FILLING

2 cups (500 mL) fresh or frozen
    raspberries

¼ cup (60 mL) granulated sugar

juice of 1 lemon

2 Tbsp (30 mL) raspberry jam

icing sugar for dusting

PREHEAT THE OVEN to 350°F (180°C).

In a small saucepan over medium heat, combine the raspberries and sugar and bring to a boil. Reduce the heat to medium-low and simmer, stirring occasionally, for 15 minutes or until all the liquid has evaporated.

Remove the saucepan from the heat and stir in the lemon juice and jam. Let cool to room temperature.

Pour the raspberry filling into the chilled tart shell. Unwrap the reserved ball of dough and roll it out between 2 sheets of parchment paper to form a 10- × 6-inch (25 × 15 cm) rectangle. With a sharp knife, cut dough lengthwise into 10 strips (about ½-inch/15 mm wide).

Using an offset spatula or an egg lifter, gently place 5 evenly spaced strips on top of the torte. Lay the remaining strips across the torte at right angles to the first strips to form a lattice. Trim any excess dough from the edges of the torte.

Bake the torte for 30 minutes or until the pastry is golden brown. Let the torte cool slightly before removing it from the pan. Let cool to room temperature before slicing.

TO SERVE, cut the torte into 6 wedges and place each wedge on a dessert plate. Dust each wedge of the torte with icing sugar. Scoop toasted hazelnut ice cream onto each plate.

TONY, TODD CLARMO,
AND CHEF NIGEL DIDCOCK
AT LANGDON HALL, 1989

FIDDLEDEE

by Maria Giuliani

A young fern
Bow and fiddle
Softly strummed
By the fingers of the warming sun.

Both unite
In light
Exuberance
And relief
At the changing season.

Fiddledee

A young fern
Waking from a cocooned slumber
Ready to unfurl

Tender tendrils
Rejuvenated

Fiddlehead
Plucked
At just the right height
For happiness.

may

May If April showers bring forth May flowers, then in May a young man's fancy turns to . . . why, food of course. Especially if that young man (or woman) is a chef. If I had been responsible for laying out the months of the year, I'd have made May the first month. To any chef with an interest in seasonal food, May is the start of the gastronomic year. Now is when spring's slow transformation from winter darkness is complete. May is light, May is colour, May is exuberance, rejuvenation, and optimism. In May we realize that winter has finally gone away for another year, and we can breathe a collective sigh of relief.

Professionally and personally, May is a busy time filled with much hustle and bustle, and it's a month that's always held special food memories for me. May is also a time for family. On Mother's Day we typically honour our moms with the ubiquitous Sunday brunch. It's also a month for confirmations, communions, and spring weddings, and Victoria Day and Memorial Day both fall in May. As a restaurateur, it can be heartwarming to see entire families, often several generations grouped together, enjoying the fruits of our kitchen labours.

With the chill of the spring mostly behind us, May grabs hold of April's teasing and reveals its culinary promise in the bountiful produce of the season. In May we say hello again to much-anticipated fiddleheads, to wild leeks, and to prized morel mushrooms. We complement our repertoire with delicate edible flowers, sweet peppers, and fava bean sprouts, cresses of every description, baby spinach, sweet Nantes carrots, Ratte and Roseval potatoes, red icicle radishes, rainbow chard, and cherry tomatoes. And, of course, asparagus: glorious green and white asparagus, baby asparagettes, and even wild asparagus when we're in luck.

Two wonderful spring ingredients combine in this dish. I love soft-shell crabs because they're delicious and only available for about four weeks in the spring. The crabs are not indigenous

Soft-Shell Crabs with Spicy Pistachio Crust and New-Asparagus Salsa

to the Niagara region—this recipe is my way of saying thank you to the many guests who travel to see us from the eastern United States, where we source the crabs from. As for asparagus, when the first stalks of the vegetable come to the back door, it fills the entire kitchen with that unmistakable aroma—what can only be described as "greenness." Asparagus is the quintessential spring vegetable. Eaten raw or cooked, it brings smiles to all who love it (including me!).

SERVES 6

SPICY PISTACHIO CRUST

¾ cup (185 mL) unsalted shelled
  pistachios, finely chopped
½ cup (125 mL) all-purpose flour
½ cup (125 mL) freshly grated
  Parmesan cheese
¼ cup (60 mL) finely chopped
  Italian parsley
2 tsp (10 mL) cayenne
2 tsp (10 mL) paprika
grated zest and juice of 2 lemons
kosher salt and black pepper to taste

IN A LARGE BOWL, toss together all the ingredients until thoroughly combined and set aside.

NEW-ASPARAGUS SALSA

1 lb (500 g) asparagus, peeled,
  blanched, and cut into 1-inch
  (2.5 cm) pieces
1 cup (250 mL) tomato concassé
  (page 257)
½ cup (125 mL) olive oil
2 shallots, finely chopped
2 Tbsp (30 mL) finely chopped cilantro
juice of 2 lemons
2 Tbsp (30 mL) aged sherry vinegar
1 clove garlic, minced
pinch granulated sugar
kosher salt and black pepper
  to taste

COMBINE all the ingredients in a non-reactive bowl and set aside until ready to serve.

SOFT-SHELL CRABS

1 cup (250 mL) vegetable oil

1 cup (250 mL) milk

3 eggs

kosher salt and black pepper to taste

all-purpose flour for dredging

6 soft-shell crabs, thoroughly cleaned
   (no more than ¼ lb/125 g each)

spicy pistachio crust

baby salad greens for garnish

lemon wedges for garnish

POUR THE VEGETABLE OIL into a large skillet and heat over medium heat until a candy thermometer registers 360°F (182°C).

Meanwhile, whisk together the milk and eggs in a shallow bowl and season with salt and pepper to taste. In a large bowl, put enough all-purpose flour to dredge the crabs.

Working with 3 crabs at a time, toss them one at a time in the flour. Dip them one at a time into the milk mixture then immediately into the spicy pistachio crust, making sure each crab is completely and generously coated in the pistachio mixture.

Immediately plunge the crabs carefully into the hot oil and fry for 3 to 5 minutes on each side until golden brown. If the crabs brown too rapidly, reduce the heat to low. Using tongs, remove the crabs from the hot oil and drain on paper towels. Reheat the oil to 360°F (182°C) and repeat with the remaining crabs.

TO SERVE, line a large platter with salad greens. Top the greens with the soft-shell crabs and garnish with lemon wedges. Spoon the asparagus salsa into a serving bowl and serve alongside the crabs.

When fish is so fresh and healthy look-
ing and so sparkling with vitality, I
love eating it raw. Here, I've given
raw tuna a Mediterranean twist—the
nearest I get to "fusion" cuisine—by

Tuna and Fennel Tarts with Vegetable Vinaigrette

laying thin slices over just-warmed
fennel tarts. The ratatouille-style vin-
aigrette adds a spectacular visual touch
to this tasty dish.

SERVES 6

VEGETABLE VINAIGRETTE

½ cup (125 mL) olive oil

¼ cup (60 mL) aged sherry vinegar

2 Tbsp (30 mL) soy sauce

kosher salt and black pepper to taste

2 Tbsp (30 mL) finely chopped shallots

2 Tbsp (30 mL) finely chopped
    zucchini, blanched

2 Tbsp (30 mL) finely chopped
    beets, blanched

2 Tbsp (30 mL) finely chopped
    fennel, blanched

2 Tbsp (30 mL) tomato concassé
    (page 257)

2 Tbsp (30 mL) blanched lemon
    zest (see sidebar)

1 Tbsp (15 mL) finely
    chopped chives

IN A MEDIUM BOWL, whisk together the olive oil, vinegar, soy sauce, 2 Tbsp (30 mL) hot water, and salt and pepper to taste. Whisk in the shallots, zucchini, beets, fennel, tomato concassé, lemon zest, and chives. Cover and refrigerate. Let come to room temperature and whisk well before using.

TO BLANCH
LEMON ZEST

Zest the lemon using a Microplane, making sure that no pith is attached. Submerge the lemon zest in boiling water for 15 seconds. Strain zest with a fine-mesh strainer and submerge in ice water. Drain and use as directed. (If you don't have a Microplane, remove zest with a vegetable peeler and mince finely after blanching.)

TUNA AND FENNEL TARTS

¾ lb (375 g) puff pastry

2 Tbsp (30 mL) unsalted butter

1½ cups (375 mL) thinly sliced fennel

⅓ cup (80 mL) chicken stock
  (page 255)

2 tsp (10 mL) whole fennel seeds

kosher salt and white pepper to taste

10 oz (300 g) sushi-grade tuna,
  in 1 piece

coarse salt for garnish

PREHEAT THE OVEN to 400°F (200°C).

Roll out the pastry thinly on a lightly floured surface. Using a saucer or a small plate as a guide, cut out six 3-inch (8 cm) discs from the pastry. Place on an ungreased baking sheet and prick the pastry discs all over with a fork. Bake for 8 to 10 minutes or until golden brown. Set aside on baking sheet.

In a small skillet, melt the butter over medium heat. Add the fennel slices and stir to coat with the butter. Stir in the stock, fennel seeds, and salt and pepper to taste and simmer, stirring frequently, until the fennel is very soft and very little liquid remains.

Transfer the fennel mixture to a food processor or blender and purée until smooth. Spread fennel purée on each puff pastry disc, dividing evenly. Return the baking sheet to the oven for a few minutes to warm the tarts.

TO SERVE, place 1 tart on each of 6 dinner plates. Slice the tuna thinly and arrange attractively on top of the tarts, dividing evenly. Drizzle each tart with vegetable vinaigrette and sprinkle with coarse salt.

One of the benefits of marrying into a Maritime family is that each spring I receive regular shipments of fiddleheads from Nova Scotia. Fiddleheads are one of Mother Nature's gifts. These

Creamy Fiddlehead and New Potato Chowder

edible shoots of the wild ostrich fern are actually young fern fronds that have not yet opened up. Their taste is often compared to asparagus.

SERVES 6

2 Tbsp (30 mL) olive oil
2 Tbsp (30 mL) unsalted butter
1 cup (250 mL) chopped onions
1 cup (250 mL) peeled and diced
    new potatoes
¼ cup (60 mL) chopped carrot
¼ cup (60 mL) chopped celery
2 cloves garlic, crushed

4 cups (1 L) chicken or vegetable
    stock (page 255) or water
3 cups (750 mL) fresh or frozen
    fiddleheads
1 cup (250 mL) 35% cream
pinch cayenne
kosher salt and black pepper
    to taste

HEAT A LARGE SAUCEPAN over medium heat and add the olive oil and butter. When the butter foams, add the onions, potatoes, carrot, celery, and garlic. Sauté, stirring frequently, until the vegetables are softened but not browned.

Add the stock and bring to a boil. Reduce heat to low and simmer for 15 minutes or until the vegetables are tender. Add the fiddleheads and simmer for another 5 minutes or until the fiddleheads are cooked through but still a vibrant green.

Transfer the soup to a blender (not a food processor) and process until smooth. Strain the soup through a fine-mesh sieve, discarding the solids, and return it to the rinsed-out saucepan.

To serve, add the cream to the soup and bring back to a boil. Reduce the heat to a simmer, add the cayenne, and season with salt and pepper to taste. Ladle the soup into 6 warm soup bowls.

Have you figured out yet that I love asparagus? This is a quick and easy yet very attractive soup that is sure to impress your dinner guests. It is another example of how foods that

Asparagus Soup with Morel Mushrooms and Quail Eggs

share the same season have an affinity to each other and often are harmonious in flavour.

SERVES 4

ASPARAGUS SOUP

24 medium asparagus spears

12 thin asparagus spears

⅓ cup (80 mL) unsalted butter

½ cup (125 mL) cooked, peeled, and diced potatoes

1 cup (250 mL) 35% cream

kosher salt and white pepper to taste

cayenne to taste

BRING A LARGE POT of salted water to a rapid boil over high heat and have ready a large bowl of ice water.

Meanwhile, snap off and discard the tough ends from all the asparagus. Cut about 2 inches (5 cm) off the tips of the thin asparagus.

Add all of the asparagus (including the tips) to the pot of boiling water, and blanch for 30 seconds. Using a strainer or a slotted spoon, transfer the asparagus to the bowl of ice water, reserving the blanching water. Remove the asparagus from the ice water and set the tips aside.

Heat a large pot over medium heat and add half of the butter. When the butter foams, add the asparagus (excluding the tips), potatoes, and 2 cups (500 mL) of the reserved blanching water. Simmer for 12 to 15 minutes or until the asparagus is tender. Stir in the cream and salt and pepper to taste. Simmer for an additional 5 minutes.

Remove the saucepan from the heat and let cool for 5 minutes. Transfer the soup and the remaining butter to a blender (not a food processor) and blend on medium speed until smooth.

Strain the soup through a fine-mesh sieve back into the rinsed-out pot and season with cayenne. Keep warm until ready to serve.

MOREL MUSHROOMS AND QUAIL EGGS

¼ lb (125 g) fresh morel mushrooms (or 1 oz/30 g dried)	2 shallots, finely chopped
	kosher salt and black pepper to taste
3 Tbsp (45 mL) grapeseed oil	2 quail eggs

IF USING FRESH MUSHROOMS, wash them in cold water and drain on paper towels. If using dried mushrooms, soak them in hot water for 20 minutes, then rinse and drain them well and dry on paper towels.

In a medium skillet, heat the grapeseed oil over high heat. Add the mushrooms and sauté, stirring frequently, for 2 to 3 minutes. Reduce the heat to medium-low and add the shallots and salt and pepper to taste. Sauté, stirring frequently for 6 to 8 minutes or until the mushrooms are tender and golden and the shallots are softened but not browned.

Meanwhile, in a small saucepan of simmering water, cook the quail eggs for 3 minutes. Drain well and immediately cool under cold running water. Remove the shells and cut the eggs in half lengthwise. Set aside until ready to serve.

TO SERVE, bring the soup back to a simmer. Ladle the soup into 4 warm soup bowls. Spoon the mushrooms in a pile in the centre of each bowl, dividing evenly, and garnish each with the reserved asparagus tips and half a quail egg.

In this dish, two great spring ingredients—one from the land, one from the sea—combine to create a French-inspired dish of wonderful nuance and delicate flavour. The simple recipe

Fresh Asparagus with Oyster Cream Sauce

involves what is called a "liaison" sauce where fresh egg yolks, mixed with a bit of cream, are folded back into the oyster reduction.

For several years, I have been buying oysters from my good friend Michel Longuet whom I first met when I worked at the Four Seasons Hotel in Yorkville. Michel represents Canada's foremost oyster supplier, the legendary Rodney Clark, and I've always been proud to serve these magnificent molluscs.

SERVES 6

36 asparagus spears
12 large oysters
¼ cup (60 mL) dry white wine
4 egg yolks
2 Tbsp (30 mL) 35% cream
pinch cayenne

kosher salt and white pepper to taste
3 Tbsp (45 mL) cold unsalted
    butter, cubed
2 Tbsp (30 mL) tomato concassé
    (page 257)
chervil for garnish

TRIM OFF AND DISCARD the tough ends of the asparagus to make 4-inch (10 cm) spears. Peel the stalk ends of the spears, discarding the peelings. Cook the asparagus spears in boiling salted water for about 10 minutes or until tender. Remove from the heat and set aside in the hot water to keep warm.

Meanwhile, open the oysters and save their juices. Cut the oysters into ⅛-inch-thick (3 mm) strips and set aside.

Pour the oyster juices through a fine-mesh sieve into a small heavy saucepan. Add the wine and simmer over medium-high heat until reduced by two-thirds. Remove the saucepan from the heat.

In a small bowl, beat together the egg yolks, cream, and ½ cup (125 mL) of the asparagus cooking water. Add this mixture to the oyster juice reduction. Whisk over very low heat until the mixture is very foamy and slightly thickened. Do not let it boil. Add cayenne and season with salt and pepper to taste. Gradually whisk in the butter until blended. Stir in the oyster strips.

Drain the asparagus. Cut one ¼-inch (6 mm) slice from the stem end of each asparagus spear. Stir these slices into the oyster cream sauce, along with the tomato concassé.

To serve, arrange 6 asparagus spears in a fan shape on each of 6 warm plates and spoon the oyster cream sauce over each portion. Garnish with chervil.

This is the first of two burger recipes in this chapter. This rich vegetarian version is a great favourite of my wife's. This recipe makes 12 burgers, so freeze the ones you don't need before you cook

The Ultimate Wine Country Veggie Burger

them. Wrap each separately in plastic wrap, then freeze for up to one month. Cook them straight from the freezer for 12 to 15 minutes.

SERVES 6

¼ cup (60 mL) olive oil

1 cup (250 mL) minced onions

1 Tbsp (15 mL) minced garlic

1 cup (250 mL) minced carrots

1 jalapeño pepper, seeded and minced

1 tsp (5 mL) ground cumin

½ tsp (2 mL) ground ginger

1 cup (250 mL) chopped roasted
    eggplant (unpeeled)

1 cup (250 mL) chopped cooked
    potatoes (unpeeled)

1 cup (250 mL) grated green zucchini,
    wrapped in paper towel and
    squeezed very dry

3 Tbsp (45 mL) finely chopped
    cilantro (optional)

1 cup (250 mL) panko-style
    breadcrumbs

1 egg, lightly beaten

2 Tbsp (30 mL) whole wheat flour

kosher salt and black pepper to taste

2 Tbsp (30 mL) unsalted butter

6 toasted burger buns

HEAT A LARGE SKILLET over medium heat and add the olive oil. When the oil is hot, add the onions and garlic and sauté, stirring frequently, until onions are golden brown. Reduce the heat to medium-low and add the carrots, jalapeño, cumin, and ginger and continue to cook, stirring frequently, until the carrots begin to soften.

Stir in the eggplant, potatoes, zucchini, and cilantro (if using). Cook for another 5 minutes, stirring to combine the ingredients thoroughly. Remove the skillet from the heat and let cool to room temperature.

Transfer the mixture to the bowl of a food mixer fitted with a paddle attachment. With the motor running at low speed, add the breadcrumbs, egg, flour, and salt and pepper to taste.

Form the mixture into 12 even-size patties. Wrap and freeze 6 of the patties as described above. In a large skillet, heat half of the butter over medium heat. When the butter foams, add 3 patties and cook for 8 to 10 minutes, turning carefully once, until golden brown on both sides. Remove from the skillet and keep warm. Repeat with the remaining butter and patties.

Serve the burgers in the toasted buns, along with your favourite garnishes and condiments.

You may think it premature to feature burger recipes in May, but this is the time of year when many of us look forward to bringing out the barbecue and firing it up again. My wife simply

Salmon and Seafood Burgers on Herb Buns

adores this burger recipe, which I created in honour of her Maritime roots. Feel free to use store-bought hamburger buns if you don't have time to make them from scratch.

SERVES 6

HERB BURGER BUNS

2 cups (500 mL) milk

¼ cup (60 mL) unsalted butter

2 Tbsp (30 mL) granulated sugar

2 tsp (10 mL) quick-rising yeast

1 Tbsp (15 mL) table salt

6 cups (1.5 L) bread (hard) flour

2 Tbsp (30 mL) olive oil

1 Tbsp (15 mL) finely chopped herbs
	(a mix of rosemary, thyme, and/or
	Italian parsley)

WARM THE MILK in a small saucepan over medium heat until it is warm to the touch. Remove the saucepan from the heat and stir in the butter, sugar, yeast, and ¼ cup (60 mL) water. Let stand for 10 minutes. Stir in the salt until it dissolves.

Put the flour in the bowl of a stand mixer fitted with a dough hook attachment. With the motor on low speed, slowly pour in the milk mixture. Mix until the dough has come together into a smooth mass. If it seems sticky, add a little more flour until the dough comes away easily from the sides of the bowl. Using the mixer, knead for 5 minutes.

Transfer the dough to a well-floured work surface, divide into 6 pieces, and form into round buns. Place the buns on a baking sheet lined with parchment paper and cover loosely with plastic wrap. Let proof for 30 minutes in the warmest part of the kitchen until the buns have doubled in size.

Preheat the oven to 325°F (160°C). Brush the buns with the olive oil and sprinkle with the herbs. Bake for 35 minutes or until golden brown. Let cool on a wire rack.

Pictured with Curried Onion Rings (page 51)

SALMON AND SEAFOOD BURGERS

1½ lb (750 g) skinless, boneless salmon
    fillet, minced
1 lb (500 g) black tiger shrimp, peeled,
    deveined, and minced
¾ cup (185 mL) dry breadcrumbs
    (plus a little extra if necessary)
3 egg whites
grated zest and juice of 2 lemons
¼ cup (60 mL) finely chopped
    Italian parsley

¼ cup (60 mL) sour cream
    or mayonnaise
2 Tbsp (30 mL) drained capers, minced
2 Tbsp (30 mL) dry white wine
    with nice acidity, such as a
    cold-climate Riesling
3 cloves garlic, minced
2 tsp (10 mL) minced anchovy fillets
kosher salt and white pepper
    to taste

IN A LARGE BOWL, combine all the ingredients and mix gently with your hands until well combined. Form the mixture into 6 even-size patties, adding more breadcrumbs if the mixture is too moist to hold together.

Preheat the barbecue to high. Grill the burgers for 8 to 10 minutes, turning carefully once, until golden brown. Split the herb buns and toast them lightly on the barbecue. Serve the burgers in the buns, along with your favourite garnishes and condiments.

Sometimes a recipe enjoys a strong supporting cast. Here, the delicate, neutrally flavoured pots de crème have the support of much-anticipated co-stars. The season's first strawberries always

Vanilla Pots de Crème with Strawberry-Rhubarb Compote

receive an enthusiastic welcome, and rhubarb, our first truly local crop of the year here in Niagara, goes perfectly with both.

SERVES 6

STRAWBERRY-RHUBARB COMPOTE

1 lb (500 g) strawberries

1 lb (500 g) rhubarb, trimmed

¾ cup (185 mL) granulated sugar

grated zest of 1 lemon

1 Tbsp (15 mL) lemon juice

CUT THE STRAWBERRIES in half and any larger ones into quarters. Peel any strings from the rhubarb and cut each stalk into 1-inch (2.5 cm) pieces.

In a large non-reactive saucepan, combine the strawberries, rhubarb, sugar, lemon zest, and lemon juice. Simmer over low heat, stirring occasionally, until the rhubarb is tender but not broken up. Remove the saucepan from the heat and let cool to room temperature. Refrigerate, covered, until ready to serve.

VANILLA POTS DE CRÈME

2½ cups (625 mL) 35% cream

⅔ cup (160 mL) milk

½ cup + 1 Tbsp (140 mL) granulated
   sugar, divided

1 vanilla bean, split in half
   lengthwise

6 egg yolks

COMBINE the cream, milk, and 5 Tbsp (75 mL) of the sugar in a saucepan. Scrape the seeds from the vanilla bean and add both the seeds and the bean to the saucepan. Simmer over medium heat, stirring to dissolve the sugar. Remove the saucepan from the heat and let steep for 20 minutes.

Meanwhile, whisk the egg yolks with the remaining sugar in a medium bowl until well combined. Reheat the milk mixture until warm then slowly whisk the warm liquid into the egg yolks to temper them. Strain the mixture through a fine-mesh sieve into a pitcher and refrigerate, covered, for 24 hours.

When ready to bake, preheat the oven to 300°F (150°C). Pour the chilled custard into six ¾-cup (185 mL) ramekins (or coffee cups, like in the photograph), dividing evenly. Cover each ramekin with plastic wrap. Place ramekins in a shallow roasting pan. Pour enough boiling water into the roasting pan to come halfway up the sides of the ramekins. Bake for 45 to 50 minutes or until the centres of the custards are just set. Remove the roasting pan from the oven and let the custards cool slightly in the roasting pan. Remove the plastic wrap from each ramekin. Remove the custards from the roasting pan and let them cool to room temperature before serving.

TO SERVE, run a thin sharp knife or a small spatula around the edges of the pots de crème to release them. Invert each ramekin on a chilled dessert plate to turn out the pots de crème. Remove the ramekins. Spoon the strawberry-rhubarb compote around each pot de crème, and garnish with fresh strawberries if you like. If instead of ramekins you used elegant coffee cups, just serve as is, with the compote on top.

*What is one to say about June, the time of perfect young summer,
the fulfillment of the promise of the earlier months, and with as yet no sign
to remind one that its fresh young beauty will ever fade.*

(Gertrude Jekyll, English garden designer and writer, 1843–1932)

june

June I have always had a soft spot for June. It's my birth month, and, speaking as a former kid, it was the last month of the school year. It elicited a huge sigh of relief and at the same time was a month filled with anticipation of exciting summer adventures ahead. Nothing changes. Our children are still beside themselves, revelling in the thought that the end of the month brings the cry of , "School's out!"

Parents and youngsters alike adopt a more relaxed state of mind. The ever-lengthening days and warm evenings mean it's a time for T-shirts, shorts, and sunglasses and long strolls through our neighbourhood enjoying the last rays of the late-evening sun. June seems to me to be the month when we see and feel summer settling in. And, whether on our patio at the restaurant or the deck at home, this is the month when barbecuing starts in earnest.

June is also the time we embark on another of my favourite types of dining. My wife and I love to picnic, and we believe we have perfected the art. Since I was a small child, picnicking has always meant time with the family, and today our picnics are always a fun, relaxing way to spend a Sunday with our kids, far from the hectic nature of our jobs. We'll head to a park along the Niagara river with a bottle of good local wine and a basket of our favourite summer foods.

June is a busy time in Niagara. The orchards are in bloom, and the vines, after the May bud break, are starting to fill in. June is also the month when the farmers' markets hit their full stride, and vendors from all over the region flock in to sell their wares. Our menus reflect this bounty and change frequently, sometimes daily. It's this subtle rhythm of the season that sets my creative juices flowing. At this time of the year, our menus, and indeed the recipes, almost write themselves. The region's local harvest is a source of endless creativity with a momentum that takes us through the entire summer and well into the fall.

During the early weeks of June, we're still heavily into asparagus season, and will have welcomed the beautiful white asparagus that floods our markets at this time. We enjoy cooking with a variety of greens and vegetables such as baby fennel, rainbow heirloom tomatoes, purple snow peas, and squash blossoms. Sometimes we find wild dandelions or fiddleheads and, if it is a particularly good year, maybe even wild cattail hearts.

This is also the month for salads. I was once referred to by a restaurant reviewer as "Niagara's salad king," and in June, it's easy to see why. Perhaps because of the more relaxed nature of our surroundings, the longer days, and the warmer weather, I crave more greens and vegetables, and lighter fare in general.

Credit for this recipe must go to my good friend and fellow chef Jason Parsons of Peller Estates Winery Restaurant. My friendship with Jason goes back to our early days at

Smoked Salmon, Crab, and Lobster Terrine

Langdon Hall. When he worked with me at Hillebrand, this delectable terrine was one of his creations.

SERVES 12

2 tsp (10 mL) vegetable oil

1 lb (500 g) thinly sliced smoked salmon

2 cups (500 mL) sour cream

8 sheets gelatin or 2 Tbsp (30 mL) unflavoured powdered gelatin

cooked meat from 1 lobster (page 36), diced

1 lb (500 g) cooked crabmeat, well drained

2 Tbsp (30 mL) mixed finely chopped tarragon, chives, chervil, and dill

grated zest and juice of 1 lemon

1 cup (250 mL) seeded and finely diced mixed red and yellow sweet pepper

kosher salt and white pepper to taste

sliced toasted baguette to serve

LINE THE BASE and sides of a 10- × 3-inch (1.5 L) terrine pan with plastic wrap. Pour in the vegetable oil and, using a pastry brush, coat the bottom and sides of the pan. Carefully line the base and sides of the pan with the smoked salmon being careful to overlap the slices slightly so that the entire base and sides are covered, and leaving an overhang of smoked salmon slices around the top. Refrigerate until needed.

In a stainless steel bowl set over a saucepan of simmering water, whisk the sour cream until it becomes quite runny.

Meanwhile, soak the gelatin sheets in ½ cup (125 mL) cold water for about 5 minutes or until softened. Drain well. Transfer the gelatin sheets to a small saucepan and melt over low heat. (If you are using powdered gelatin, sprinkle the gelatin over 2 Tbsp/30 mL cold water in a small bowl and let stand for 5 minutes or until puffy. Set the bowl in a small saucepan of simmering water and stir gently until melted.)

Recipe continued . . .

In a large bowl, stir together the warm sour cream, melted gelatin, lobster, crab, herbs, lemon zest and juice, sweet pepper, and salt and pepper to taste until well combined. Pour the mixture into the prepared pan. Carefully fold the overhanging smoked salmon over the top of the mixture to cover it. Cover the pan with plastic wrap and gently tap the filled pan on the counter to expel any trapped air. Refrigerate overnight.

To serve, remove the plastic wrap from the top of the terrine and invert the terrine on a cutting board. Remove the pan from the terrine, shaking the pan and the cutting board together gently if necessary.

TO SERVE, hold a long, sharp knife under hot running water until it is warm. Wipe the knife dry and, while it is still warm, cut the terrine crosswise into ½-inch (1 cm) slices. Arrange the slices, slightly overlapping, on a large platter. Serve with toasted baguette and a selection of chutneys and pickles.

Green Pea Soup with Minted Crème Fraîche and Cheddar Cheese Scones

SERVES 6

CHEDDAR CHEESE SCONES

4 slices bacon, chopped (optional)

3 cups (750 mL) all-purpose flour

1 Tbsp (15 mL) baking powder

1 Tbsp (15 mL) granulated sugar

1½ tsp (7.5 mL) table salt

½ cup (125 mL) cold unsalted
   butter, cubed

1½ cups (375 mL) shredded sharp
   cheddar cheese (about 6 oz/175 g)

½ cup (125 mL) thinly sliced
   green onions

½ tsp (2 mL) black pepper

1 cup plus 2 Tbsp (280 mL) 35% cream

PREHEAT THE OVEN to 400°F (200°C).

In a medium skillet over medium heat, cook the bacon (if using) for about 5 minutes, stirring frequently, until crisp. Remove the bacon with a slotted spoon and drain well on paper towels.

In a large bowl, whisk together the flour, baking powder, sugar, and salt. Cut in the butter with a pastry blender or 2 knives until the mixture resembles coarse crumbs. Stir in the cooked bacon, cheese, green onions, and pepper.

Using a fork, stir in 1 cup (250 mL) of the cream until a sticky dough forms. Turn out the dough onto a lightly floured surface and form it into a disc. Dust the dough lightly with flour then roll to ¾-inch (2 cm) thickness. Using a cookie cutter, cut out loonie-size rounds (about 1 inch/2.5 cm across) from the dough.

Place scones ½ inch (1 cm) apart on a large baking sheet. Brush the tops with the remaining cream. Bake 20 to 25 minutes or until golden brown. Remove the baking sheet from the oven and let the scones cool slightly before serving.

MINTED CRÈME FRAÎCHE

2 Tbsp (30 mL) crème fraîche
  or sour cream

1 tsp (5 mL) finely chopped mint

IN A SMALL BOWL, stir together the crème fraîche and mint. Set aside.

GREEN PEA SOUP

2 Tbsp (30 mL) olive oil
2 Tbsp (30 mL) unsalted butter
4 green onions, finely chopped
¼ cup (60 mL) finely diced
  cooked ham, prosciutto,
  or cooked pancetta
1 shallot, finely chopped
1 clove garlic, minced

4 cups (1 L) chicken or vegetable
  stock (page 255)
1 cup (250 mL) diced peeled potatoes
3 cups (750 mL) shelled fresh
  green peas
¼ cup (60 mL) 35% cream
kosher salt, white pepper,
  and cayenne to taste

HEAT a large saucepan over medium heat and add the olive oil and butter. When the butter foams, add the green onions, ham, shallot, and garlic. Sauté, stirring frequently to prevent browning, then add the stock and potatoes. Simmer for 10 minutes then add the peas, cream, and salt, pepper, and cayenne to taste. Simmer for 5 minutes or until the potatoes and peas are tender.

Remove the saucepan from the heat. Transfer the soup to a blender (not a food processor) and blend until smooth. Return the soup to the rinsed-out saucepan and bring to a simmer.

TO SERVE, ladle the soup into 6 warm soup bowls and top each serving with 1 tsp (5 mL) minted crème fraîche. Serve with cheddar cheese scones.

Fresh Tuna Salad "Niagar-oise" with Canadian Mustard

This is my version of the famous French salade niçoise. I figured that with all of Niagara's bounty so close at hand, this would be the quintessential summer salad and a way of expressing my love of the French original.

SERVES 6

ANCHOVY-CAPER DRESSING

5 hard-cooked eggs, cut in half
　lengthwise
24 black olives, pitted and
　coarsely chopped
¼ cup (60 mL) drained capers
4 anchovy fillets, coarsely chopped

juice of 1 lemon
1 Tbsp (15 mL) Kozlik's mustard
　(or any grainy mustard)
½ cup (125 mL) olive oil
kosher salt and black pepper to taste
3 sprigs Italian parsley, finely chopped

REMOVE the yolks from the hard-cooked eggs, reserving the whites for use in another recipe. In a food processor, combine the yolks, olives, capers, anchovy fillets, lemon juice, and mustard and process to a smooth paste.

With the motor running, add the olive oil and season with salt and pepper to taste. Process until smooth and creamy. Add the chopped parsley and process just until combined. Scrape into a small bowl, cover, and refrigerate. Let come to room temperature and whisk well before using.

MARINATED VEGETABLES

juice of 1 lemon
1 Tbsp (15 mL) aged sherry vinegar
1 shallot, finely chopped
1 clove garlic, minced
¼ cup (60 mL) olive oil
1 Tbsp (15 mL) Kozlik's mustard
　(or any grainy mustard)

2 cups (500 mL) sliced or diced
　blanched vegetables, such
　as green beans, peas, asparagus,
　sweet peppers, and/or cherry
　tomatoes
kosher salt and black pepper
　to taste

IN A MEDIUM BOWL, whisk together the lemon juice, vinegar, shallot, and garlic. Whisk in the olive oil and mustard until smooth. Add the vegetables and toss well. Season with salt and pepper to taste. Set aside until ready to serve.

OVEN-DRIED TOMATOES

½ cup (125 mL) olive oil

12 thin slices yellow tomato

12 thin slices red tomato

1 tsp (5 mL) finely chopped
   fresh tarragon

1 tsp (5 mL) finely chopped
   fresh chervil

1 tsp (5 mL) finely chopped chives

kosher salt and black pepper
   to taste

PREHEAT THE OVEN to 350°F (180°C).

Combine the olive oil and tomato slices in a large bowl. Add the herbs, season with salt and pepper to taste, and toss gently.

Place the tomato slices in a single layer on a large baking sheet and bake, without turning, for 10 minutes or until the slices have warmed through and wrinkled up but aren't browned.

Remove the baking sheet from the oven and let cool slightly before serving.

SEARED TUNA

1 Tbsp (15 mL) olive oil

12 oz (375 g) fresh tuna loin, sliced
   into 12 even-size pieces

kosher salt and black pepper
   to taste

JUST BEFORE SERVING, heat a medium skillet over high and add the olive oil. When the oil is hot, sear the tuna slices on one side for 1 minute then using kitchen tongs, carefully turn each piece over and sear for another 1 minute. Season with salt and pepper to taste. Drain on paper towels.

TO SERVE, place 2 red oven-dried tomato slices and 2 yellow oven-dried tomato slices in the centre of each of 6 salad plates. Drizzle anchovy-caper dressing over each portion of tomatoes. Divide the marinated vegetables among the plates and top each portion with 2 pieces of warm seared tuna.

King oyster mushrooms are very fat, very meaty cultivated mushrooms that are also called king eryngii. *I love them because they are flavour chameleons and can take on the taste of any*

King Oyster Mushroom and White Asparagus Salad

ingredient they're cooked with. The mushrooms don't have a high moisture content so can be a bit chewy if over-cooked. They also don't lose much volume so a few go a long way. I have used them in braised dishes (adding them during the last 45 minutes), and in stir-fries and salads, such as this one.

White asparagus is a premium ingredient. Often available in the spring and summer, the spears are kept white by piling earth over them as they grow, keeping them away from sunlight. It's important to peel white asparagus and serve only the tender top third of each spear as the stem ends are often stringy and bitter.

SERVES 4

16 white asparagus spears
8 king oyster mushrooms (or
    substitute about ½ lb/250 g other
    seasonal mushrooms), each cut
    into 4 even-size slices
½ cup (125 mL) all-purpose flour
½ cup (125 mL) olive oil
2 Tbsp (30 mL) unsalted butter

kosher salt and black pepper
    to taste
¼ cup (60 mL) hazelnut oil
2 Tbsp (30 mL) aged balsamic vinegar
2 cups (500 mL) lightly packed baby
    mâche, washed and dried
3 Tbsp (45 mL) toasted hazelnuts
    (page 18), chopped

TRIM OFF and discard the tough ends of the asparagus to make 4-inch (10 cm) spears. Peel the stalk ends of the spears, discarding the peelings. Using a mandoline slicer, carefully slice the white asparagus spears diagonally into wafer-thin slices. Set aside.

Dust the mushroom slices with the flour. Heat a large skillet over high heat and add the olive oil and butter. When the butter foams, carefully add the mushrooms, 1 slice at a time so they don't touch each other, and sauté for 45 seconds to 1 minute or until golden brown on both sides (you may have to do this in batches). Remove the mushrooms from the skillet and drain on paper towels. Season with salt and pepper to taste and set aside.

In a medium bowl, whisk together the hazelnut oil and vinegar. Add the baby mâche, and more salt and pepper to taste. Toss well until the leaves are coated with dressing. Add the reserved asparagus and toss gently to combine.

To serve, divide the mushroom slices among 4 salad plates. Pile the asparagus salad in the centre of each plate, dividing evenly. Garnish with hazelnuts.

Halibut Fillets Crusted in Peanuts, Capers, and Sultanas with Warm Spicy Romaine Salad

refreshing, the dish is satisfying yet not heavy at all.

SERVES 4

HALIBUT FILLETS WITH PEANUT-CAPER-SULTANA CRUST

2 Tbsp (30 mL) unsalted butter	kosher salt and black pepper to taste
¼ shallot, chopped	1½ lb (750 g) skinless, boneless halibut
¼ clove garlic, minced	fillets, cut into 4 even-size pieces
¼ cup (60 mL) sultana raisins	½ cup (125 mL) finely chopped
1½ tsp (7.5 mL) drained capers	roasted, unsalted peanuts
juice of ½ lemon	2 Tbsp (30 mL) finely chopped
1½ Tbsp (22.5 mL) grapeseed oil	Italian parsley

PREHEAT THE OVEN to 400°F (200°C).

Heat the butter in a small skillet over low heat. Add the shallot and garlic and sauté, stirring frequently, for about 2 minutes until softened but not browned. Stir in the sultana raisins and capers and remove the skillet from the heat.

Transfer the mixture to a food processor. With the motor running, slowly add the lemon juice and grapeseed oil until well combined. Season with salt and pepper to taste.

Place the halibut fillets on a non-stick baking sheet. Top each fillet with about 1 Tbsp (15 mL) caper-sultana mixture, spreading to cover top of the fillets completely. Sprinkle the peanuts evenly over each fillet, then sprinkle evenly with the parsley. Bake the fillets for 12 minutes or until they flake easily with a fork. Keep warm until ready to serve.

WARM SPICY ROMAINE SALAD

2 Tbsp (30 mL) unsalted butter

1 Tbsp (15 mL) grapeseed oil

12 cherry tomatoes, cut in half

1 cup (250 mL) honey mushrooms

½ shallot, finely chopped

½ clove garlic, finely chopped

½ cup (125 mL) dry white wine

3 cups (750 mL) fish stock (page 255)

12 cloves garlic confit (page 257)

juice of 1 lemon

kosher salt and white pepper to taste

2 Tbsp (30 mL) finely chopped chives

4 cups (1 L) lightly packed chopped
    romaine lettuce

HEAT A MEDIUM SAUCEPAN over medium heat and add 1 Tbsp (15 mL) of the butter and the grapeseed oil. When the butter foams, add the cherry tomatoes, honey mushrooms, shallot, and garlic. Sauté, stirring frequently, for 5 minutes or until softened but not browned. Add the wine and bring to a simmer. Add the fish stock and the garlic confit and bring to a simmer.

Remove the saucepan from the heat, stir in the lemon juice, and season with salt and pepper to taste. Whisk in the remaining butter and the chives, whisking until the butter has melted. Add the chopped romaine and stir gently until the romaine is just slightly wilted, yet still crunchy.

TO SERVE, divide the warm spicy romaine salad among 4 dinner plates. Top each portion with garlic confit, and then with a halibut fillet.

Rosemary-Skewered Lamb Brochettes with Spring Vegetable Stew

In this new take on lamb kebabs, each piece of meat is wrapped in a leek leaf before being threaded onto rosemary "skewers" with sweet cipollini onions.

SERVES 8

ROSEMARY-SKEWERED LAMB BROCHETTES

3 leeks (pale green parts only)

8 large sprigs rosemary

3 lb (1.5 kg) boneless lamb loins, cut into 24 pieces

¼ cup (60 mL) olive oil

kosher salt and black pepper to taste

24 cipollini onions, blanched and peeled

BRING A LARGE POT of salted water to a rapid boil over high heat and have ready a large bowl of ice water.

Split each leek halfway through lengthwise and wash well. Cut each leek into 4-inch (10 cm) lengths and separate into individual leaves. Take 24 of the best-looking leaves, add them to the pot of boiling water, and blanch for 2 minutes. Using a strainer or a slotted spoon, transfer the leek leaves to the bowl of ice water, reserving the blanching liquid. Drain the leek leaves through a colander and drain on paper towels.

Remove all the leaves from the rosemary sprigs, except a few at the tip of each (reserve the rosemary leaves for use in another recipe).

Combine the lamb pieces in a bowl with the olive oil and salt and pepper to taste and toss with your hands until well coated. Roll each piece of lamb in a blanched leek leaf.

On each rosemary skewer, thread the lamb alternately with the onions, using 3 pieces of lamb and 3 onions for each skewer. Refrigerate until ready to cook.

SPRING VEGETABLE STEW

2 Tbsp (30 mL) olive oil

2 Tbsp (30 mL) unsalted butter

¼ cup (60 mL) finely diced prosciutto

2 cloves garlic, finely chopped

8 cups (2 L) chicken or vegetable
   stock (page 255)

3 sprigs thyme

2 bay leaves

½ cup (125 mL) white navy beans,
   picked over, rinsed, and soaked
   in water overnight

2 cups (500 mL) julienned
   green cabbage

2 carrots, diced

2 leeks (white parts only), cut into
   ½-inch (1 cm) slices

½ cup (125 mL) diced peeled potatoes

½ cup (125 mL) pearl onions, peeled

1 cup (250 mL) shelled sweet peas
   (or substitute snow peas cut into
   ½-inch/1 cm pieces)

kosher salt and black pepper to taste

PREHEAT THE OVEN to 400°F (200°C).

Heat a large pot over medium heat and add the olive oil and butter. When the butter foams, add the prosciutto and garlic and stir to combine. Add the chicken stock, thyme, and bay leaves and bring to a simmer. Add the beans and simmer for about 40 minutes or until the beans are cooked through and soft.

Add the cabbage, carrots, leeks, potatoes, and onions and simmer until the vegetables are tender. Add the peas and cook for another few minutes until the peas are just cooked. Discard the thyme sprigs and bay leaves and season with salt and pepper to taste.

Meanwhile, place the lamb brochettes on a non-stick baking sheet and cook in the oven for about 10 minutes for medium-rare lamb.

TO SERVE, divide the vegetable stew among 8 warm soup bowls and top each portion with a lamb brochette.

New Carrot Risotto with Carrot Broth, Braised Mushrooms, and Basil Pesto

In this visually appealing recipe, the risotto is cooked in a carrot broth/sauce, which gives the rice a bright orange colour. When dotted with the pesto and served with the mushrooms, the risotto makes a spectacular meal.

SERVES 4

BASIL PESTO

4 stalks fresh basil, leaves only

1 Tbsp (15 mL) toasted pine nuts

1 Tbsp (15 mL) freshly grated
   Parmesan cheese

½ cup (125 mL) olive oil

kosher salt and black pepper
   to taste

COMBINE all the ingredients in a food processor and process until smooth. Scrape into a small bowl and set aside at room temperature.

CARROT BROTH

1 Tbsp (15 mL) olive oil

1 stalk celery, chopped

2 shallots, chopped

1 clove garlic, minced

2 carrots, shredded

1 cup (250 mL) dry white wine

2 cups (500 mL) chicken or vegetable
   stock (page 255)

kosher salt and white pepper
   to taste

HEAT A SAUCEPAN over medium heat and add the olive oil. When the oil is hot, add the celery, shallots, and garlic and sauté, stirring frequently, until softened but not browned. Add the carrots and wine and simmer until the wine has all but evaporated. Add the chicken stock and simmer until the carrots are soft.

Transfer to a blender and blend until smooth. Strain the carrot mixture through a fine-mesh sieve into a clean saucepan. Season with salt and pepper to taste, set aside, and keep warm until ready to serve.

NEW CARROT RISOTTO

6 cups (1.5 L) chicken stock (page 255)

2 shallots, finely chopped

¼ cup (60 mL) finely diced carrot

2 Tbsp (30 mL) olive oil

1 clove garlic, finely chopped

2 cups (500 mL) arborio, Vialone Nano, or Carnaroli rice

¾ cup (185 mL) dry white wine

2 Tbsp (30 mL) carrot broth

BRING the chicken stock to a simmer in a medium saucepan and keep warm over low heat.

In a medium heavy saucepan, stir together the shallots, carrots, olive oil, and garlic for a few minutes. Stir in the arborio rice, then add the wine and carrot broth. Simmer, stirring frequently, until the rice has turned slightly orange and the liquid has evaporated.

Using a small ladle, gradually add the warm chicken stock to the rice, stirring constantly and allowing the stock to be fully absorbed by the rice before adding the next ladleful of hot stock. Keep adding the stock in small batches and stirring, continuing for 15 to 18 minutes or until the rice is al dente and has a creamy consistency. You may or may not need more stock. Remove the saucepan from the heat and keep warm until ready to serve.

BRAISED MUSHROOMS

2 Tbsp (30 mL) unsalted butter

4 large seasonal wild mushrooms, such as king oysters, morels, or chanterelles, brushed clean and stems removed

2 green onions, finely chopped

kosher salt and black pepper to taste

freshly grated Parmesan cheese for garnish (optional)

MELT THE BUTTER in a small non-stick skillet and add the mushrooms. (You may wish to slice the larger mushrooms before cooking.) Cover with a lid and cook until the mushrooms have started to wilt. Add 2 Tbsp (30 mL) water and simmer, uncovered, until all the liquid has evaporated. Stir in the green onions, remove the skillet from the heat, and season with salt and pepper to taste.

TO SERVE, divide the risotto among 4 large warm dinner plates and pour the carrot broth around the risotto (like a moat around a castle). Top each serving with a mushroom. Dot the carrot broth with pesto and garnish with Parmesan (if using).

White Chocolate and Raspberry Crème Brûlée

This is a nice light yet intensely satis-fying version of a classic crème brûlée. I like to hide fresh berries under the custard ready to be discovered.

SERVES 6

48 raspberries

5 egg yolks

⅓ cup (80 mL) granulated sugar

pinch table salt

1 cup (250 mL) 35% cream

1 cup (250 mL) milk

3½ oz (105 g) good-quality white
  chocolate, finely chopped

3 Tbsp (45 mL) packed brown sugar

biscotti to serve

PREHEAT THE OVEN to 300°F (150°C). Place 7 raspberries in the bottom of each of six ½-cup (125 mL) ramekins and set aside.

Whisk together the egg yolks, sugar, and salt in a medium bowl until well combined.

Pour the cream and milk into a medium saucepan. Bring to a gentle simmer over medium heat. Remove the saucepan from the heat and stir in the white chocolate until it is melted and smooth.

Gradually whisk the warm cream mixture into the egg yolk mixture. Strain the custard through a fine-mesh sieve into a pitcher.

Pour the custard into the ramekins, dividing evenly. Place the ramekins in a shallow roasting pan. Pour enough boiling water into the roasting pan to come halfway up the sides of the ramekins. Bake for about 1 hour or until the centres of the custards are just set. Shake one of the ramekins in the centre of the roasting pan and if the custard does not shake or appear liquid it is set. Remove the roasting pan from the oven. Remove the rame-kins from the roasting pan and cool to room temperature on a wire rack. Cover and refrigerate for at least 3 hours.

Just before serving, sprinkle the brown sugar evenly over tops of cus-tards to cover them completely. Ignite a blowtorch and caramelize the sugar, moving the torch constantly so the sugar doesn't burn. Place each ramekin on a round plate with a vine leaf under the ramekin so it does not shift on the plate. Garnish each crème brûlée with one of the remaining raspberries, and serve with biscotti.

No bought potpourri is so pleasant as that made from one's own garden, for the petals of the flowers one has gathered at home hold the sunshine and memories of summer, and of past summers only the sunny days should be remembered.

(Eleanour Sinclair Rohde, English gardener and writer, 1881–1950)

july

July is unadulterated summer. Everything that is good about being a chef is highlighted and celebrated during this glorious, sunny time of the year. Have you ever noticed how happy people are during July? That's because we are all, in our own special ways, reaping the rewards of enduring the long, cold winter. July is Mother Nature's way of saying thank you.

I have many fond memories of July. When I was about 10 years old, my dad bought a one-acre parcel of land in the small rural town of Oak Ridges just north of Toronto. Well, it was rural back in 1975, not so much these days. It was a good piece of land dominated at the centre by a huge oak tree. With its deep black soil, the land was perfectly suited for farming. Every spring weekend, my parents would load up our yellow Fiat 124 and go to the "farm." While my brother and I spent hours climbing the tree, my parents would work the land, planting a mind-blowing array of produce.

In July, my brother and I would often be conscripted into the harvest as various fruits and vegetables became ready for picking. It was during these times I learned the joy of feeling the cool, dark earth between my fingers. And although I didn't know it at the time, I wasn't just cultivating crops but a sincere love of produce. The smell and feel of ripe, just-harvested fruits and vegetables still bring me joy today.

As a chef, July is the start of a very busy and often overwhelming time of year for me. Not only are the restaurants humming with activity, but the farmers are delivering products at an alarming rate. Often several of them gather in the back doorway, enjoying each other's company and swapping stories (and equally complaining about the weather, if you can believe that!). Our market menu changes frequently in July. Food delivered to the back door and waiting to be put away and processed is often the inspiration for an innovative flavour combination or a new dish.

At this time of year, too, the grill takes on a more prevalent role in my repertoire, and I often rely on marinades, like the one my mother has used for years, to bring out the true flavour of a good piece of meat. These are inspiring times!

Dungeness Crab Salad with Apricots and Sparkling Wine Sabayon

The combination of sweet crabmeat and luscious ripe apricots creates a quint-essential summer taste experience you won't soon forget.

SERVES 6

DUNGENESS CRAB SALAD

2 cups (500 mL) cooked Dungeness
    crabmeat

8 large ripe apricots, pitted and diced

2 Tbsp (30 mL) mayonnaise

2 Tbsp (30 mL) finely chopped
    green onion

2 Tbsp (30 mL) finely chopped chives

1 tsp (5 mL) blanched lemon
    zest (page 94)

1 tsp (5 mL) Dijon mustard

IN A LARGE BOWL, gently combine the crabmeat, apricots, mayonnaise, green onion, chives, lemon zest, and mustard. Cover and refrigerate for 1 hour.

SPARKING WINE SABAYON

½ cup (125 mL) chilled sparkling wine

2 eggs yolks

½ cup (125 mL) unsalted butter

2 Tbsp (30 mL) 35% cream

kosher salt and white pepper
   to taste

IN A STAINLESS STEEL BOWL set over a saucepan of simmering water, cook the wine and egg yolks over medium heat, whisking constantly, for about 15 minutes or until the mixture is light and fluffy and an instant-read thermometer placed in the mixture registers 140°F (60°C).

Meanwhile, melt the butter in the microwave on medium power (50%) for 45 seconds or until completely melted. In a small saucepan, bring the cream to a boil then remove the saucepan from the heat.

Gradually whisk the melted butter into the fluffy egg mixture until completely incorporated, then do the same with the cream. Season with salt and pepper to taste.

TO SERVE

1 cup (250 mL) lightly packed frisée, washed, dried, and torn (some set aside for garnish)

2 Tbsp (30 mL) olive oil

kosher salt and black pepper to taste

2 large ripe apricots, pitted and each cut into 8 wedges

¼ cup (60 mL) tomato concassé (page 257)

TOSS THE FRISÉE in a large bowl with the olive oil, and salt and pepper to taste. Place a small "nest" of frisée on the centre of each of 6 chilled salad plates. Divide the crab salad among the plates, placing it on top of the frisée. Scatter the apricot wedges evenly around each crab salad and the tomato concassé over each salad. Drizzle each portion with the sparkling wine sabayon. Garnish with undressed frisée.

This is a very popular appetizer that I've included in my menus on and off for the past ten years. People love the juxtaposition of textures of the cured, mildly salty salmon and the rich, fatty

Duo of Tuna Confit and Fennel-Cured Salmon with Lemon-Garlic Cream and Fried Capers

tuna cooked slowly in olive oil. It's important when making any confit that the oil or fat not ever boil or simmer; it's at the proper temperature when just small bubbles appear.

SERVES 6

FENNEL-CURED SALMON

1 cup (250 mL) packed light
  brown sugar

⅔ cup (160 mL) granulated sugar

⅔ cup (160 mL) kosher salt

1 side salmon, boneless but with skin

¼ cup (60 mL) Pernod

1 fennel bulb, trimmed and very
  thinly sliced

½ cup (125 mL) toasted fennel seeds

2 Tbsp (30 mL) cracked white
  peppercorns

IN A MEDIUM BOWL, stir together the light brown sugar, granulated sugar, and salt. Spread half of the mixture over the bottom of a shallow glass dish large enough to hold the salmon. Place the salmon on the sugar mixture, skin side down, and sprinkle evenly with the Pernod.

Cover the salmon with the remaining sugar mixture. Top with the shaved fennel, fennel seeds, and peppercorns. Lay a piece of plastic wrap directly on the surface of the fennel-topped fish. Place a board or large plate that fits inside the perimeter of the dish on top of the plastic wrap and weigh it down lightly (with 2 cans of fruit or soup, for instance). Refrigerate for 48 hours.

Remove the salmon from the dish, discarding the curing ingredients. Carefully rinse off any sugar mixture that remains on the salmon. Refrigerate the salmon, uncovered, for 1 hour to dry. Before serving, thinly slice the salmon on the diagonal, removing each slice from the skin.

LEMON-GARLIC CREAM

¾ cup (185 mL) olive oil

juice of 2 lemons

1 hard-cooked egg, shelled and
    coarsely chopped

1 Tbsp (15 mL) 35% cream

1 clove garlic, coarsely chopped

kosher salt and white pepper
    to taste

IN A BLENDER or a food processor, combine all the ingredients and blend until smooth and creamy. Cover and refrigerate until ready to serve.

FRIED CAPERS

1 cup (250 mL) vegetable oil

¼ cup (60 mL) drained capers,
    patted very dry

HEAT THE OIL in a small saucepan over medium heat until a candy thermometer registers 350°F (180°C). Add the capers and fry for 3 minutes or until golden brown and crisp. Remove from the oil with a slotted spoon and drain on paper towels. Set aside until ready to serve.

TUNA CONFIT

1 cup plus 2 Tbsp (280 mL) olive oil

⅔ cup (160 mL) aged sherry vinegar

2 shallots, finely sliced

2 cloves garlic, crushed

1 Tbsp (15 mL) Pernod

4 sprigs Italian parsley

2 bay leaves

1 sprig thyme

5 white peppercorns

pinch saffron

½ lb (250 g) tuna loin, in 1 piece

thyme sprigs for garnish

IN A LARGE SAUCEPAN over medium heat, combine 1 cup (250 mL) of the olive oil, the vinegar, shallots, garlic, Pernod, parsley, bay leaves, thyme, peppercorns, and saffron. Simmer over medium heat for 20 minutes for the flavours to infuse. Keep warm over very low heat. Heat the remaining olive oil in a small skillet over high heat. Add the tuna and sear it for 1 minute on each side. Remove from the skillet and submerge in the flavoured olive oil. Keep warm over very low heat for up to 30 minutes.

TO SERVE, remove the tuna confit from the oil and cut crosswise into 6 slices. Arrange 4 or 5 slices of fennel-cured salmon in a "fan" pattern on each of 6 chilled dinner plates. Spoon the lemon-garlic cream in a neat line across the salmon and top each portion with a piece of tuna confit. Sprinkle with the fried capers and garnish with thyme.

As I've mentioned elsewhere in this book, I love taking old ideas and making them fresh and relevant again. This is especially true when I find I can add a local Niagara twist, as I've

Niagara Bouillabaisse

done here by using Lake Erie whitefish in a traditional fish soup.

SERVES 6

SEAFOOD BROTH

2 Tbsp (30 mL) olive oil

2 Tbsp (30 mL) unsalted butter

½ onion, finely chopped

3 cloves garlic, finely chopped

1 bottle (750 mL) dry white wine, such as Chardonnay

24 tightly closed fresh littleneck clams, scrubbed

2 sprigs thyme

24 tightly closed fresh mussels, scrubbed

HEAT A LARGE POT over medium-high heat and add the olive oil and butter. When the butter foams, add the onion and garlic and sauté, stirring frequently, for 5 minutes or until softened but not browned. Add the wine, clams, and thyme. Put a lid on the pot and increase the heat to high.

Cook for 10 minutes or until the clams have opened slightly. Add the mussels, put the lid back on, and continue cooking for about 5 minutes or until the mussels have opened (discard any shellfish that don't open). Remove the pot from the heat and set aside to cool a little.

When the clams and mussels are cool enough to handle, remove the meat from the shells. Discard the shells and refrigerate the meat. Strain the cooking liquid through a colander, discarding the solids. There should be about 3 cups (750 mL) seafood broth. If not, top up the broth with water. Refrigerate the broth until needed.

BOUILLABAISSE

¼ cup (60 mL) diced pancetta

2 Tbsp (30 mL) olive oil

½ cup (125 mL) chopped onion

½ cup (125 mL) diced celery

¼ fennel bulb, trimmed and diced

2 cloves garlic, finely chopped

1 cup (250 mL) chopped tomatoes
   (peeled and seeded)

1 tsp (5 mL) tomato paste

3 cups (750 mL) seafood broth

3 sprigs thyme, leaves picked off from
   stems and finely chopped

pinch cayenne, or to taste (optional)

2 cups (500 mL) diced scrubbed
   potatoes

1 lb (500 g) skinless, boneless Lake
   Erie whitefish fillets (or substitute
   pickerel or halibut fillets), cut into
   1-inch (2.5 cm) pieces

clam and mussel meat reserved from
   seafood broth

kosher salt and black pepper to taste

sprigs of chervil, dill, and chives
   for garnish

HEAT A LARGE POT over medium heat and add the pancetta and olive oil. Sauté, stirring frequently, until the pancetta has crisped up. Add the onion, celery, and fennel and sauté, stirring frequently, for 10 minutes or until the vegetables are softened but not browned. Add the garlic and cook for a few minutes longer.

Stir in the tomatoes and tomato paste. Add the seafood broth, thyme, and cayenne (if using) and bring to a simmer. Add the potatoes and reduce heat to medium-low. Cook for about 5 minutes or until the potatoes are almost tender but still a bit firm. Add the whitefish and the clam and mussel meat. Cook, covered, for 5 minutes, then remove the pot from the heat and let stand for 5 minutes or until the whitefish is opaque and firm.

TO SERVE, using a slotted spoon, divide the whitefish, shellfish, and vegetables among 6 warm soup bowls. Return the pot to the heat and bring the soup to a rapid boil. Season with salt and pepper to taste. Ladle the soup into the bowls, dividing evenly. Garnish with chervil, dill, and chives.

Adding sparkling wine to this chilled soup just before serving gives it a lovely effervescence. The flavour of any soup generally improves after some time sitting in the fridge so, if you can,

Sparkling Wine and Yellow Tomato Gazpacho with Zucchini Bread

make the soup two or three days before serving. The recipe for zucchini bread makes two loaves, but the bread freezes beautifully if wrapped well in plastic wrap and foil.

SERVES 8

ZUCCHINI BREAD

non-stick baking spray	2 cups (500 mL) granulated sugar
3 cups (750 mL) all-purpose flour	1 cup (250 mL) vegetable oil
1 Tbsp (15 mL) cinnamon	3 eggs
1 tsp (5 mL) baking powder	¼ cup (60 mL) honey
1 tsp (5 mL) baking soda	2 cups (500 mL) shredded zucchini
1 tsp (5 mL) table salt	1 cup (250 mL) chopped walnuts
pinch freshly grated nutmeg	(optional)

PREHEAT THE OVEN to 350°F (180°C). Spray two 8- × 4-inch (1.5 L) loaf pans with baking spray.

In a large bowl, whisk together the flour, cinnamon, baking powder, baking soda, salt, and nutmeg.

In the bowl of a stand mixer fitted with the paddle attachment, mix the granulated sugar, oil, eggs, and honey until well blended. Gradually add the flour mixture to the oil mixture and mix until well blended. Stir in the zucchini and walnuts (if using) until well combined.

Scrape the batter into the prepared pans, dividing evenly. Bake for 50 minutes or until a toothpick inserted in the centre of the loaves comes out clean. Remove the pans from the oven and allow the loaves to cool in the pans on a wire rack for 5 minutes. Remove the loaves from the pans and let cool completely on the wire rack.

SPARKLING WINE AND YELLOW TOMATO GAZPACHO

3 large, ripe yellow tomatoes,
   chopped

1 sweet yellow pepper, seeded
   and chopped

½ English cucumber, peeled
   and seeded

¼ cup (60 mL) chopped red onion

¼ cup (60 mL) red wine vinegar

1 shallot, finely chopped

2 Tbsp (30 mL) olive oil

1 Tbsp (15 mL) kosher salt

1 clove garlic, coarsely chopped

juice of 1 lemon

1 cup (250 mL) sparkling wine

black pepper to taste

Tabasco sauce to taste

8 basil leaves, cut into julienne
   strips, for garnish

IN A FOOD PROCESSOR, combine the tomatoes, sweet pepper, cucumber, red onion, vinegar, shallot, olive oil, salt, garlic, and lemon juice. Process until fairly smooth.

Strain the soup through a fine-mesh sieve into a large serving bowl. Refrigerate for at least 1 hour or overnight.

Just before serving, add the sparkling wine to the soup. Season with more salt, and black pepper and Tabasco to taste.

TO SERVE, ladle the soup into 8 chilled soup bowls and garnish with basil. Cut zucchini bread into 1-inch (2.5 cm) slices and serve with soup.

Chilled Spicy Maritime Mussel Salad with Saffron Mayonnaise, Black Olives, and Roasted Peppers

This is an attractive summer salad that's full of flavour and provides an unexpected way to eat mussels—chilled and out of their shells. If you wish, keep a few shells for garnishing each plate.

SERVES 4

SAFFRON MAYONNAISE

1 egg yolk

1 clove garlic, coarsely chopped

1½ tsp (7.5 mL) Kozlik's mustard
   (or any grainy mustard)

2 pinches saffron threads

½ cup (125 mL) olive oil

kosher salt and white pepper
   to taste

IN A FOOD PROCESSOR or blender, combine the egg yolk, garlic, mustard, and saffron. Process until smooth. With the motor running, gradually add the olive oil in a slow, steady stream. Process until thickened and creamy. Scrape the mayonnaise into a small bowl and season with salt and pepper to taste. Cover and refrigerate until ready to serve.

CHILLED SPICY MARITIME MUSSEL SALAD

¼ cup (60 mL) grapeseed oil

¼ cup (60 mL) chopped onion

2 cloves garlic, finely chopped

1 bay leaf

48 tightly closed large fresh
   mussels, scrubbed

½ cup (125 mL) dry white wine

½ cup (125 mL) fish stock (page 255)

2 sprigs thyme

1 cup (250 mL) lightly packed baby
   arugula leaves, washed and dried

juice of 1 lemon

3 Tbsp (45 mL) olive oil

½ cup (125 mL) pitted,
   dry-cured black olives

4 roasted sweet red peppers,
   seeded, peeled, and cut
   lengthwise into strips

4 chives, minced

Recipe continued . . .

HEAT A LARGE POT over high heat and add the grapeseed oil and onion. Sauté, stirring frequently, until the onions are softened but not browned. Stir in the garlic and bay leaf.

Add the mussels, wine, fish stock, and thyme. Cover the pot and bring to a simmer. Cook for 8 to 10 minutes or until all the mussels have opened (discard any that don't open). Remove the pot from the heat and let cool slightly.

When the mussels are cool enough to handle, remove the meat from the shells. Discard the shells (saving a few for garnish, if you wish) and refrigerate the meat. Strain the cooking liquid through a colander, discarding the solids.

In a small saucepan over low heat, simmer the cooking liquid until it has reduced to about 1 Tbsp (15 mL). Remove the saucepan from the heat and strain the reduced cooking liquid through a fine-mesh sieve. Refrigerate until ready to serve.

TO SERVE, spoon the saffron mayonnaise onto the centres of 4 chilled salad plates, dividing evenly and using the back of the spoon to spread the mayonnaise into a thin puddle on each plate. Arrange 12 mussels around the perimeter of the mayonnaise on each plate.

In a small bowl, toss the arugula with the lemon juice and olive oil and pile on top of the saffron mayonnaise in the centre of each plate. Scatter the black olives around each plate, dividing evenly. Arrange strips of red pepper like spokes of a wheel between the mussels on each plate. Scatter each salad with chives and drizzle with the reserved reduced mussel liquid.

This is the basting recipe my mom uses on any meat she throws on the barbecue, and it's perfect for the summer grilling season. I find it tastes best slathered on the thick sirloins or rib-eyes she grills

My Mother's Steak-Basting Recipe

up. The unique part is that, instead of a basting brush, she uses leaves cut from the middle of a bunch of celery. The number of celery stalks you'll need depends on how long you grill your steaks. The recipe makes enough basting sauce for 10 or 12 steaks so refrigerate any unused sauce to use another time (it will keep for up to one week).

MAKES ABOUT 1½ CUPS
(375 ML)

1 cup (250 mL) olive oil
¼ cup (60 mL) red wine vinegar
6 cloves garlic, thinly sliced
1 Tbsp (15 mL) packed brown sugar
1 Tbsp (15 mL) dried oregano

1 Tbsp (15 mL) finely chopped
   Italian parsley
6 to 10 leafy stalks celery cut from
   the centre of a bunch of celery
sirloin or rib-eye steaks
kosher salt and black pepper to taste

COMBINE THE OIL, vinegar, garlic, sugar, oregano, and parsley in a sealable jar. Put on the lid and shake well to combine. Take the lid off the jar and put the celery stalks, leafy ends down, in the jar.

Preheat the barbecue to high. Season the steaks with salt and pepper to taste. Put the steaks on the grill. Remove 1 celery stalk from the jar and brush the basting sauce clinging to its leaves over the steaks (do not put the celery stalk back in the jar after it's touched the steaks). Discard the celery stalk. Continue grilling the steaks, turning once, until they are done to your taste, basting them often and using a new celery stalk each time.

Cornish hen is a wonderful alternative to chicken, its breast meat delicate, the legs full of flavour. Frozen Cornish hens are available in most larger supermarkets, but I prefer fresh birds.

Cornish Hens and Egg Spaetzle with Pinot Noir Sauce and Glazed Baby Carrots

I cherish the relationships I have with all my food purveyors, but I nurture most the one I have with my butcher. So, when I order Cornish hens, he sends them to me boned out and ready to cook, but includes the bones so I can use them to make stock.

In this recipe, the hens are cooked skin side down on a hot baking sheet. This caramelizes the skin beautifully and ups the visual and taste quotient. Spaetzle is a very easy-to-make dumpling and a nice change to sides of potato, rice, or pasta.

SERVES 4

EGG SPAETZLE

4 eggs	2 Tbsp (30 mL) finely chopped herbs,
½ cup (125 mL) milk	such as thyme, sage, and rosemary
pinch freshly grated nutmeg	1½ cups (375 mL) all-purpose flour
pinch table salt	1 Tbsp (15 mL) olive oil
	1 Tbsp (15 mL) unsalted butter

COMBINE THE EGGS, milk, nutmeg, and salt in a bowl and whisk to combine. Gradually add the flour a little at a time, mixing until a smooth, elastic dough forms. Blend in the chopped herbs. Let stand for 10 minutes.

Meanwhile, bring a large pot of salted water to a rapid boil. Set a colander over the pot, ensuring the water does not touch the colander. Have ready a large bowl of ice water. Place the spaetzle dough, a little at a time, into the colander and using a pastry scraper, push the dough through the holes in the colander to form spaghetti-like strings.

Simmer the spaetzle dumplings until they float to the surface. Using a slotted spoon, carefully remove the dumplings from the pot and immediately plunge them into the ice water. Drain well then refrigerate until ready to use.

Just before serving heat the olive oil and butter in a large non-stick skillet. When the butter foams, add the spaetzle dumplings and sauté them until golden brown.

PINOT NOIR SAUCE

¾ cup (185 mL) Pinot Noir

2 shallots, finely chopped

2 sprigs thyme

3 black peppercorns

¾ cup (185 mL) veal jus (page 254)

1 Tbsp (15 mL) cold unsalted butter

1 tsp (5 mL) red wine vinegar

IN A SMALL SAUCEPAN over medium heat, combine the Pinot Noir, shallots, thyme, and peppercorns and simmer until reduced by three-quarters. Add the veal jus and bring back to a simmer. Strain the sauce through a fine-mesh sieve into a clean saucepan and set aside.

Just before serving, warm the sauce gently over low heat and whisk in the butter until melted. Stir in the vinegar.

CORNISH HENS

4 Cornish hens, boned

kosher salt and black pepper to taste

3 Tbsp (45 mL) olive oil

12 baby carrots

2 Tbsp (30 mL) unsalted butter

1 Tbsp (15 mL) maple syrup

1 sprig thyme

2 Tbsp (30 mL) slivered almonds, lightly toasted (optional)

PREHEAT THE OVEN to 375°F (190°C). Place a large rimmed baking sheet in the oven for about 10 minutes to get hot.

Meanwhile, lay the hens skin side down on a work surface. Season them generously with salt and pepper to taste and drizzle with the olive oil. Remove the hot baking sheet from the oven and carefully lay the Cornish hens skin side down on the baking sheet. Return the baking sheet to the oven and roast for 25 minutes or until the skins have browned and an instant-read thermometer inserted in the thickest part of one of the hens registers 160°F (71°C). Remove the hens from the oven and let rest for 10 minutes before serving.

Meanwhile combine the carrots, butter, maple syrup, and thyme in a small saucepan and simmer for 25 minutes or until the carrots are tender and glazed, and the liquid has evaporated. Season with more salt and pepper to taste and keep warm until ready to serve.

TO SERVE, divide the carrots among 4 warm dinner plates. Spoon the spaetzle beside the carrots on each plate. Lay a Cornish hen skin side up on top of the carrots and spaetzle. Spoon the Pinot Noir sauce around the edge of the plate. Garnish with almonds, if desired.

The beauty of this dish is its simplicity. Panna cotta literally translates to "cooked cream," and that's really all there is to it. I particularly love pairing the panna cotta with the warm blue-

Sour Cream Panna Cotta with Blueberry Beignets

berry beignets, as the contrast in temperatures and textures is delicious.

SERVES 8

SOUR-CREAM PANNA COTTA

1 cup (250 mL) sour cream

1 cup (250 mL) 35% cream

1 cup (250 mL) half-and-half cream (10%)

1 cup (250 mL) granulated sugar

½ cup (125 mL) lemon juice

10 sheets gelatin or 2½ Tbsp (37.5 mL) unflavoured powdered gelatin

IN A MEDIUM SAUCEPAN, combine the sour cream, 35% cream, and half-and-half and bring to a simmer. Add the sugar and lemon juice, stirring until the sugar has dissolved. Remove the saucepan from the heat.

Meanwhile, in a large bowl, soak the gelatin sheets in enough cold water just to cover them, for about 5 minutes or until softened. Remove the gelatin from the bowl, squeezing the sheets to remove the excess water. (If you are using powdered gelatin, sprinkle the gelatin over 3 Tbsp/45 mL cold water in a small bowl and let stand for 5 minutes or until puffy. Set the bowl in a small saucepan of simmering water and stir gently until melted.)

Add the gelatin to the hot cream mixture and stir well. Pour into eight ½-cup (125 mL) espresso cups or ramekins. Refrigerate until set.

BLUEBERRY BEIGNETS

¼ cup (60 mL) granulated sugar, divided

1½ tsp (7.5 mL) active dry yeast

½ cup (125 mL) evaporated milk

1 egg, lightly beaten

2 Tbsp (30 mL) shortening

½ tsp (2 mL) table salt

3½ cups (875 mL) all-purpose flour

1 cup (250 mL) fresh blueberries

non-stick baking spray

vegetable oil for deep-frying

icing sugar for dusting

IN SMALL BOWL, dissolve 2 tsp (10 mL) of the granulated sugar in ¾ cup (185 mL) warm water. Sprinkle in the yeast and let stand for 10 minutes or until the yeast is bubbly.

In the bowl of a stand mixer fitted with the paddle attachment, mix together the remaining sugar, the evaporated milk, egg, shortening, and salt. Add the yeast mixture and beat until smooth. Beat in the flour, ½ cup (125 mL) at a time, until a soft, sticky dough forms. Stir in the blueberries just until combined.

Spray a clean bowl with baking spray and transfer the dough to the bowl. Cover with plastic wrap and refrigerate for at least 6 hours or overnight.

On a lightly floured surface, roll out the dough to form a rectangle about 20 × 16 inches (50 × 40 cm) and ¼ inch (6 mm) thick. Using a sharp chef's knife, cut the dough into squares about 2½ inches (6 cm).

Heat the oil in a deep pot until a candy thermometer registers 360°F (182°C), or use a deep fat fryer and follow the manufacturer's instructions. Fry the beignets, a few at a time to avoid overcrowding, for about 2 minutes, turning frequently, until golden brown. Using a slotted spoon, transfer the beignets to a rack lined with paper towels and set over a baking sheet to cool.

TO SERVE, place each espresso cup of sour cream panna cotta on its saucer or a dessert plate. Or if you used ramekins, run a thin sharp knife or a small spatula around the edges of the panna cotta to release them. Invert each ramekin onto a dessert plate. Dust the blueberry beignets generously with icing sugar and serve alongside the panna cottas.

AUGUST: THE KING OF PLENTY
by Maria Giuliani

August is a nobleman
Robust with cheeks and belly
Offering up all he owns
Known as the King of Plenty.

August, like a mother bird
Providing warmth and shaded nests
And bearing fruits of graceful work,
Serves us as we lay in rest.

August is a farmer man
A quiet soul with gentle hands
In pink hours, with hat on hair
He tends the land with extra care.

His fields are freshly ripening
Delightfully auspicious
The mounds of maize are quite august,
Bursting and delicious,

It finds its way from farm to feast.
We all sit down to eat
Our mouths are full from all the good
Our hearts have skipped a beat.

August is our humble host
Our diligent gardener
With gusto grows all season long
That which will soon be reaped.

August Like June, August is a marvellous bookend to July. In August, we start to realize that all good things must pass, and we feel a gentle reminder that hectic September is just around the corner. Luckily, the long slow days of summer are still upon us, and we lounge around enjoying the warmth, savouring every moment.

Typically, I like to get away with my family in August. Some of my fondest memories of this month are of vacations we've spent in Nova Scotia, where my wife, Kaleen, is from. Nova Scotia is still my favourite holiday destination. The pace of life, the people, and the beautiful scenery are all truly amazing there. We particularly enjoy visiting Kaleen's uncle Sandy, who owns 300 acres in the centre of the province. With several lakes and streams on the property, it is my perfect getaway.

My sons and I will spend hours lingering at the lakes, trying our hands at fishing, and on the rare occasions when we do catch some nice large lake trout, it's a real ceremony to bring them in and have them for dinner. Kaleen and I will spend hours hiking the land, recharging our batteries, and making plans for the coming year.

The seafood of this Maritime paradise is truly legendary. Nothing stimulates the culinary juices like walking along the docks in Digby and watching the scallop boats come in, or stopping at a roadside diner and having the best clam chowder imaginable.

Back in the kitchen, this is the time of year when we can truly say that we're not hindered by seasonal limitations. We can flex our creative muscles, and Mother Nature responds to our every whim, whether we crave peaches, corn, tomatoes, watermelon, or any other summer treat. In August we realize how truly blessed we are to be living in such a wonderfully bountiful land. Now is when we revel in its generosity and that helps ease us into the realization that autumn is just around the corner.

August is the perfect time to enjoy corn. It's best served straight from the pot slathered with butter, but another great way to enjoy corn is in a soup, such as this satisfying chowder. If you

August Corn Chowder

are an ambitious cook, make a stock from the ears that you've removed the kernels from and use the stock for this soup (instead of chicken or vegetable stock). Simply simmer the ears in enough water to cover them for about one hour. Any leftover corn stock can be frozen for future use.

SERVES 6

2 Tbsp (30 mL) unsalted butter
4 slices double-smoked bacon, finely chopped
2 stalks celery, finely chopped
½ cup (125 mL) chopped onion
½ cup (125 mL) finely chopped carrot
1 clove garlic, minced
2 cups (500 mL) fresh corn kernels (about 4 medium ears)

1½ cups (375 mL) diced peeled potatoes (about ¼-inch/6 mm dice)
4 cups (1 L) chicken or vegetable stock (page 255)
1 cup (250 mL) 35% cream
kosher salt and black pepper to taste
1 Tbsp (15 mL) finely chopped parsley or chives
smoked paprika for garnish (optional)

HEAT A LARGE HEAVY POT over medium heat and add the butter. When the butter foams, add the bacon, reduce the heat to low, and cook the bacon until it is brown and crispy. Add the celery, onion, carrot, and garlic and sauté, stirring frequently, for 15 minutes or until softened but not browned. Add the corn and potatoes and stir to combine.

Add the stock and bring to a simmer over medium heat. Cover and simmer until the vegetables are just tender. Add the cream and season with salt and pepper to taste. Bring the soup to a simmer again, then remove the saucepan from the heat and let cool slightly.

Transfer half of the soup to a blender (not a food processor) and blend until smooth. Return the blended soup to the saucepan and stir to combine. Bring to a simmer once more.

To serve, ladle the soup into 6 warm soup bowls and sprinkle each portion with parsley or chives, and smoked paprika if desired.

I had never considered eating watermelon as an appetizer until I was invited to the wedding of my friends Steven Klc and Colleen Apte in Washington, D.C. The reception was at

Watermelon and Watercress Salad

Jaleo Tapas Bar, and the chef there made a watermelon and tomato tapa that opened my eyes to the versatility of this wonderful fruit.

You can use cubes of melon or stamp out shapes from slices of melon with a fluted cookie cutter. While using both red and yellow watermelons adds a "wow" factor to this dish, choosing only the ripest fruit is more important as this will dictate whether the salad is remarkable or has diners wondering, "What was Tony thinking?"

SERVES 6

⅓ cup (80 mL) olive oil
⅓ cup (80 mL) aged sherry vinegar
2 Tbsp (30 mL) honey
1 shallot, finely chopped
2 red onions, cut crosswise into
   thin rings
2 bunches watercress, washed, dried,
   and stems removed

kosher salt and black pepper to taste
8 cups (2 L) cubed watermelon
   (1-inch/2.5 cm cubes) (you may also
   use a decorative cookie cutter)
additional olive oil for garnish
fleur de sel for garnish
2 Tbsp (30 mL) finely chopped
   basil (optional)

IN A MEDIUM BOWL, whisk together the olive oil, vinegar, honey, and shallot. Add the red onions and watercress, season with salt and pepper to taste, and toss well.

To serve, arrange the watermelon and salad on 6 dinner plates. Drizzle each plate with olive oil and sprinkle with fleur de sel. Garnish with chopped basil if desired.

Foie Gras with Grilled Peaches and Juniper Jus

Grilled peaches are amazing. The flames caramelize them beautifully, exposing the hidden flavour deep within the warmed peach and rendering them wonderfully juicy. This dish is a typical example of one of my summertime tasting menu starters.

SERVES 6

JUNIPER JUS

1 Tbsp (15 mL) grapeseed oil
1 shallot, finely chopped
1 clove garlic, finely chopped
4 button mushrooms, cleaned
   and chopped
1 sprig thyme, leaves picked off from
   stems and finely chopped

⅓ cup (80 mL) gin
2 tsp (10 mL) crushed juniper berries
⅓ cup (80 mL) dry red wine
⅓ cup (80 mL) veal jus (page 254)
¼ cup (60 mL) fresh blueberries
1 Tbsp (15 mL) cold unsalted butter

HEAT A SMALL SAUCEPAN over medium heat and add the grapeseed oil. When the oil is hot, add the shallot and garlic and sauté, stirring frequently, for 3 minutes. Add the mushrooms and thyme and cook until the mushrooms are wilted and their liquid has evaporated.

Add the gin and juniper berries and simmer until the liquid has reduced by half. Add the wine and simmer until the liquid has reduced by half. Add the veal jus and simmer for about 5 minutes or until just slightly reduced. Add the fresh blueberries and simmer for 5 minutes or until the blueberries have softened.

Transfer the sauce to a blender (not a food processor) and blend until smooth. Strain through a fine-mesh sieve into a clean saucepan. Return the sauce to a simmer and whisk in the butter until it melts. Remove the saucepan from the heat and set aside. Just before serving, reheat the sauce gently over low heat.

FOIE GRAS WITH GRILLED PEACHES

1½ lb (750 g) foie gras, large veins removed and cut into 6 even-size pieces

kosher salt and black pepper to taste

6 ripe peaches, preferably freestone

2 cups (500 mL) lightly packed frisée, washed, dried, and torn

1 cup (250 mL) lightly packed baby arugula, washed and dried

2 Tbsp (30 mL) finely chopped chives

juice of 1 lemon

2 Tbsp (30 mL) hazelnut oil

SEASON THE FOIE GRAS with salt and pepper to taste. Cover and refrigerate until needed.

Preheat the barbecue to high.

Bring a large pot of water to a rapid boil over high heat and have ready a large bowl of ice water. Add the peaches to the pot of boiling water, and blanch for 10 seconds. Using a strainer or a slotted spoon, transfer the peaches to the bowl of ice water. Remove the peaches from the ice water and, using a small, sharp knife, peel off their skins and cut the peaches in half and remove the pits.

In a medium bowl, combine the frisée, arugula, chives, lemon juice, and more salt and pepper to taste. Set aside.

In a large bowl, gently toss the peach halves with the hazelnut oil, and more salt and pepper to taste. Grill the peach halves, cut sides down, for 1 minute. Rotate the peaches through 90 degrees and grill for 1 minute longer to make a crosshatch pattern. Remove the peaches from the grill and place, cut sides up, in the centre of 6 salad plates. Leave the barbecue on.

Remove the seasoned foie gras from the refrigerator and place on the grill. Cook for 1 minute. Carefully turn the foie gras over and grill for 1 minute longer or until it is caramelized on the outside but the centre is still soft.

TO SERVE, place 2 peach halves on each of 6 plates. Spoon a small pile of salad on each of the grilled peach halves. Top each with a piece of foie gras. Spoon juniper jus around each plate.

Roasting the onions first in grapeseed oil gives this soup a luxurious texture and great depth of flavour. We call these slow-cooked onions "onion confit" in the kitchens, and because it's such a

Roasted Tomato Bisque with Onion Confit and Tomato Jam

flavourful ingredient, we tend to keep it as a staple, using it in many recipes where onions are required. The onion oil is also great for dressings and marinades, and even for searing fish and meat. It will keep in the fridge for up to one week.

SERVES 6

ONION CONFIT

1 cup (250 mL) chopped onions
1 cup (250 mL) grapeseed oil

3 sprigs thyme
1 bay leaf

PREHEAT THE OVEN to 300°F (150°C).

Combine all the ingredients in a baking dish. Cover and bake for 1 hour or until very soft and mushy.

Remove the dish from the oven and let cool to room temperature. Strain the onion mixture through a fine-mesh sieve, discarding the thyme and bay leaf but reserving the onion confit and the oil separately.

TOMATO JAM

2 cups (500 mL) tomato concassé
  (page 257) made with plum
  tomatoes
1 cup (250 mL) carrot juice
2 Tbsp (30 mL) packed brown sugar
2 Tbsp (30 mL) tomato paste

juice of ½ lemon
1 Tbsp (15 mL) ground fennel seed
  (optional)
1 Tbsp (15 mL) grated lemon zest
1 large clove garlic, finely chopped
1 tsp (5 mL) kosher salt

COMBINE all the ingredients in a food processor (not a blender) and process until well combined.

Transfer the mixture to a saucepan and simmer over medium-low heat, stirring occasionally, until the mixture has reduced by one-third and is thickened. Remove the saucepan from the heat and let cool to room temperature. Set aside at room temperature until ready to serve.

ROASTED TOMATO BISQUE

4 cups (1 L) chopped ripe tomatoes
2 Tbsp (30 mL) onion oil (from
  onion confit)
1 cup (250 mL) onion confit
¼ cup (60 mL) chopped carrot
¼ cup (60 mL) chopped leek (white
  part only)

¼ cup (60 mL) chopped fennel
2 cloves garlic, minced
2 cups (500 mL) chicken or vegetable
  stock (page 255)
1 cup (250 mL) tomato juice
kosher salt and black pepper to taste
additional onion oil to taste

PREHEAT THE OVEN to 400°F (200°C).

Spread the chopped tomatoes out on a baking sheet and roast, stirring frequently, for 35 minutes or until the liquid has evaporated and the tomatoes are browned.

Meanwhile, in a large pot, heat the onion oil over medium heat. Add the onion confit, carrot, leek, fennel, and garlic and sauté, stirring frequently, for 15 minutes or until softened but not browned.

Stir in the roast tomatoes and cook for 15 minutes longer. Add the stock and tomato juice and bring to a simmer, stirring frequently.

Transfer the bisque to a blender (not a food processor) and blend until smooth. Strain the bisque through a fine-mesh sieve into a clean pot. Return the bisque to a simmer and continue to simmer until it has thickened slightly. Season with salt and pepper to taste.

TO SERVE, ladle the bisque into 6 warm soup bowls. Drizzle each portion with additional onion oil and top with a dollop of tomato jam.

Lobster Salad with Tomato Confit and Pink Mayonnaise

This is just a nice little salad that I created for my wife, Kaleen, to satisfy her love of lobster. I was too tired to come up with one of my usual convoluted recipes, so I put this together and found it totally delicious and beautiful in its simplicity.

SERVES 4

LOBSTER SALAD

cooked meat from 3 lobsters
  (page 36), roughly diced
grated zest and juice of 1 lemon

1 Tbsp (15 mL) olive oil
1½ tsp (7.5 mL) finely chopped chives
kosher salt and white pepper to taste

IN A SALAD BOWL, combine all the ingredients. Cover and refrigerate until ready to serve.

TOMATO CONFIT

12 vine-ripened cherry tomatoes

½ cup (125 mL) olive oil

1 clove garlic, thinly sliced

2 sprigs thyme, leaves picked off
   from stems and finely chopped

1 tsp (5 mL) granulated sugar

kosher salt and black pepper to taste

PREHEAT OVEN to 300°F (150°C).

Bring a large pot of water to a rapid boil over high heat and have ready a large bowl of ice water. With a small, sharp knife, make an X in the skin of the bottom of each tomato. Add the tomatoes to the pot of boiling water and blanch for 5 seconds. Using a strainer or a slotted spoon, transfer the tomatoes to the bowl of ice water.

Drain the tomatoes. Using a small, sharp knife, peel away the skin from where the incision was made. Cut each tomato in half and discard the seeds.

In an ovenproof dish, toss the tomato quarters with the remaining ingredients. Bake for 10 minutes or until the tomatoes are soft but do not fall apart. Remove the dish from the oven and set aside at room temperature until ready to serve.

PINK MAYONNAISE

⅓ cup (80 mL) olive oil

juice of 1 lemon

1 egg yolk

1 Tbsp (15 mL) finely chopped
   tarragon

2 tsp (10 mL) tomato paste

1 tsp (5 mL) honey

1 tsp (5 mL) Armagnac or brandy

½ tsp (2 mL) Dijon mustard

kosher salt and white pepper
   to taste

2 Tbsp (30 mL) finely chopped chives

COMBINE all the ingredients in a food processor or blender and process until smooth. Cover and refrigerate until ready to serve.

TO SERVE, spoon the pink mayonnaise onto 4 chilled salad plates. Spoon the lobster salad on top of each portion of mayonnaise. Garnish each plate with tomato confit and sprinkle with chives.

Since this time of the year is also the height of picnic season, it would be remiss of me if I didn't include a nice chicken pasta salad recipe that's perfect for alfresco eating. If you can't find

Smoked Chicken and Orecchiette Salad with Fresh Corn and Pine Nuts

orecchiette (a small ear-shaped pasta), then substitute any other short pasta. Unsmoked, cooked chicken would also be delicious in this.

SERVES 6

½ cup (125 mL) olive oil
½ cup (125 mL) rice wine vinegar
juice of 3 limes
2 Tbsp (30 mL) honey
2 sprigs thyme, leaves picked off
    from stems and finely chopped
1 tsp (5 mL) minced canned chipotle
    chilis in adobo sauce
3 cups (750 mL) cooked orecchiette
    pasta

¾ lb (375 g) smoked chicken,
    cut into bite-size pieces
2 cups (500 mL) fresh corn kernels
    (from 4 medium ears), blanched
½ sweet red pepper, seeded and cut
    into julienne strips
3 green onions, finely chopped
6 basil leaves, finely chopped
kosher salt and black pepper to taste
½ cup (125 mL) toasted pine nuts
    (optional)

IN THE BOWL of a food processor, combine the olive oil, vinegar, lime juice, honey, thyme, and chipotle chilis and process until the ingredients are well combined and emulsified. Set aside.

In a large salad bowl, toss together the pasta, smoked chicken, fresh corn, and sweet pepper. Pour the chipotle dressing over the pasta mixture and toss to combine. Stir in the green onions, basil, and salt and pepper to taste. Garnish with the toasted pine nuts if desired.

*Along with the sweet goodness of hali-
but, the other seafood I adore is the scallop. I find scallops so versatile as they
marry well with many different flavours and wines. I love putting them*

Oven-Dried Tomato and Olive Crusted Sea Scallops with a Light Caponata

*in different situations as in this recipe
where they're topped with an olive-
tomato "cap" and served on an Italian
version of ratatouille.*

SERVES 6

LIGHT CAPONATA

2 cups (500 mL) diced peeled eggplant
  (½-inch/1 cm dice)

2 Tbsp (30 mL) kosher salt

½ cup (125 mL) plus 2 Tbsp (30 mL)
  olive oil

2 stalks celery, cut into ½-inch
  (1 cm) dice

½ small onion, cut into ½-inch
  (1 cm) dice

2 cloves garlic, minced

2 large ripe tomatoes, cut into
  ½-inch (1 cm) dice

½ cup (125 mL) pitted green olives

2 Tbsp (30 mL) drained capers,
  chopped

1 Tbsp (15 mL) red wine vinegar

2 tsp (10 mL) granulated sugar

6 mint leaves, finely chopped

black pepper to taste

IN A LARGE BOWL, toss the eggplant with the salt. Transfer to a colander
and let the eggplant "sweat" for 20 minutes.

Meanwhile, in a large pot, heat 2 Tbsp (30 mL) of the olive oil over
medium heat and add the celery, onion, and garlic. Sauté, stirring frequently, for about 15 minutes or until the vegetables are softened but not
browned. Add the tomatoes and cook, stirring frequently, until the liquid
from the tomatoes has completely evaporated. Stir in the olives, capers,
vinegar, and sugar. Remove the saucepan from the heat.

Rinse the excess salt from the eggplant by standing the colander under
cold running water for a few minutes. Transfer eggplant to a clean kitchen
towel and squeeze dry.

Heat the remaining olive oil in a large skillet over high heat. Add the
prepared eggplant and sauté, stirring frequently, for about 5 minutes or
until golden brown. Remove the skillet from the heat and pour contents
into a colander set over a bowl to drain off the excess oil, reserving the oil
in the refrigerator to use as a garnish.

Stir the sautéed eggplant and mint into the tomato mixture. Season
with pepper and more salt to taste. Set aside at room temperature until
ready to serve.

OVEN-DRIED TOMATO AND OLIVE CRUSTED SEA SCALLOPS

3 large ripe tomatoes or 1 cup
   (250 mL) ripe cherry tomatoes

1 clove garlic, thinly sliced

2 sprigs thyme, leaves picked off from
   stems and finely chopped

julienned rind of ½ lemon, pith
   removed

pinch granulated sugar

3 slices crustless white bread,
   torn into pieces

¼ cup (60 mL) pitted black olives

2 Tbsp (30 mL) unsalted butter,
   softened

2 anchovy fillets, coarsely chopped

2 sprigs Italian parsley, stems
   discarded and leaves coarsely
   chopped

18 large fresh sea scallops

¼ cup (60 mL) olive oil

kosher salt and white pepper to taste

PREHEAT THE OVEN to 400°F (200°C).

Bring a large pot of water to a rapid boil over high heat and have ready a large bowl of ice water. With a small, sharp knife, make an X in the skin of the smooth end of each tomato. Add the tomatoes to the pot of boiling water and blanch for 5 seconds. Using a strainer or a slotted spoon, transfer the tomatoes to the bowl of ice water.

Drain the tomatoes. Using a small, sharp knife, peel away the skin from where the incision was made. Cut large tomatoes in quarters or cherry tomatoes in half, discarding the seeds and tough stem ends.

On a large non-stick baking sheet, toss the tomatoes with the garlic, thyme, lemon rind, and sugar. Bake for 1 hour or until well caramelized. Remove the baking sheet from the oven and let cool to room temperature. Leave the oven on.

In a food processor, combine the tomato mixture, bread, olives, butter, anchovies, and parsley. Process until well combined and granular.

In a bowl, toss the scallops with the olive oil, and salt and pepper to taste. Heat a large non-stick skillet over high heat and carefully add the scallops in a single layer. Cook them, without turning, for about 4 minutes or until they are golden brown on the undersides. Using tongs, transfer the scallops to a non-stick baking sheet, arranging them browned side up. Spoon a small amount of tomato-olive mixture onto each scallop, then bake for 8 minutes or until scallops are just translucent.

TO SERVE, using a spatula or an egg lifter, carefully remove the scallops from the baking sheet to a warm platter. Drizzle with the reserved oil from frying the eggplant. Spoon the caponata alongside the scallops.

AT HILLEBRAND WINERY, 1996

Barbecued Chicken with Honey-Apricot Glaze

The honey-apricot glaze is really a fancy way of saying apricot ketchup because the apricots cook down to a sauce-like consistency. But, marinating the chicken in the glaze first means the flavours reach deep into the succulent meat.

SERVES 8

1 cup (250 mL) dried apricots
2 Tbsp (30 mL) unsalted butter
¼ cup (60 mL) finely chopped shallots
⅔ cup (160 mL) white wine vinegar
½ cup (125 mL) honey

¼ cup (60 mL) Dijon mustard
1 tsp (5 mL) kosher salt
½ tsp (2 mL) white pepper
8 skinless, boneless chicken breasts

IN A SMALL SAUCEPAN over medium-high heat, combine the apricots and 1½ cups (375 mL) water. Bring to a boil, then reduce the heat to medium and simmer for 10 minutes or until the apricots are soft and plump and the water has reduced by half.

In a small skillet over medium heat, melt the butter and add the shallots. Sauté, stirring frequently, until the shallots are softened but not browned. Stir in the cooked apricots and their liquid. Remove the skillet from the heat.

In a food processor or blender, process the apricot mixture until smooth. Transfer the apricot mixture to a small saucepan and add the vinegar, honey, mustard, salt, and pepper. Bring to a simmer over medium heat, then simmer, stirring frequently, for 15 minutes or until thickened to the consistency of ketchup. Remove the saucepan from the heat and let cool completely.

Place the chicken breasts in a large non-reactive dish and pour enough of the honey-apricot glaze over the chicken breasts to coat them liberally, turning to coat on both sides (refrigerate the remaining honey-apricot glaze). Cover and refrigerate the chicken breasts for at least 2 hours or overnight.

Preheat the barbecue to medium. Remove the chicken breasts from the marinade, reserving the marinade in the dish. Grill the chicken for about 12 minutes, turning once and basting with the marinade from the dish halfway through cooking (discard any marinade that remains in the dish), until nicely browned and an instant-read thermometer inserted into the thickest part of the chicken breasts registers 160°F (71°C).

To serve, heat the refrigerated honey-apricot glaze in a small saucepan over low heat until hot. Arrange the chicken breasts on a warm platter and spoon the hot honey-apricot glaze over them.

I have already featured a recipe for peach tarte tatin in my other cook-book, Recipes from Wine Country. *My justification for including another one in this cookbook is twofold. First,*

Niagara Peach Tarte Tatin

this recipe is not typical, as the peaches are cooked in the tart shells; secondly, how could one ever get too much of such a good thing?!

SERVES 4

TART SHELLS

non-stick baking spray

1 cup (250 mL) all-purpose flour

½ cup (125 mL) unsalted butter, softened

1 Tbsp (15 mL) granulated sugar

¼ tsp (1 mL) table salt

SPRAY THE INSIDES of four 3-inch (8 cm) tart rings with baking spray and place on a baking sheet lined with parchment paper.

In the bowl of a stand mixer fitted with the dough hook, combine the remaining ingredients and mix on medium speed until the dough pulls away from the side of the bowl.

Turn the dough out onto a lightly floured surface and knead gently to form a smooth ball. Wrap in plastic wrap and refrigerate for 30 minutes.

Roll out the chilled dough on a lightly floured surface to ⅛-inch (3 mm) thickness. Cut out four 5-inch (12 cm) rounds and fit each round into a prepared tart ring. Trim the excess pastry from the lined rings with a sharp knife and refrigerate the lined rings while you make the filling.

PEACH TARTE TATINS

¼ cup (60 mL) granulated sugar

2 Tbsp (30 mL) unsalted butter

8 ripe peaches, blanched, peeled,
  pitted, and each cut into 8 wedges

¼ cup (60 mL) chopped almonds

4 tart shells

caramel sauce using hazelnut-caramel
  sauce recipe on page 18, but omit
  the hazelnuts

PREHEAT THE OVEN to 350°F (180°C).

In a large skillet over medium heat, combine the sugar and butter. Cook, stirring frequently, for 5 minutes or until light golden in colour. Add the peaches and almonds. Cook, stirring gently, for 10 minutes or until the peaches have caramelized slightly.

Remove the skillet from the heat and divide the peach mixture among the lined tart rings, pressing down firmly on the peaches with the back of a spoon so they fit snugly. Bake for 30 minutes or until the pastry has browned and the peaches are nicely caramelized and golden brown. Remove the tarts from the oven and let cool to room temperature.

TO SERVE, carefully remove the tartes from the rings and place each on a dessert plate. Spoon some caramel sauce over the top of each tart.

UNDER THE ORANGE MOON: SEPTEMBER
by Maria Giuliani

September begins with
Indian Summer heat
fiercely making up for lost days
for rain and clouds
cramming
and on its best behaviour
praying to stave off what is commonly acknowledged as
The Inevitable.

Nights out on the patio
drinking cheap red wine
from expensive crystal glasses
Feeling like kings
illuminated
in a citronella glow
The orange moon
The stars
They know

That by mid-month
ripe tomatoes will be canned
and everyone will be far too preoccupied
to linger
in languor
at farmers' market stalls
And so,
the skies will cry
the leaves will anger
then shrivel in denial

And this spider I see
weaving a silky thread
between this tree and that and the next
will move indoors
instead weaving woollens for my feet
and waiting
just like me
for the thaw.

September is the final prayer
before the sleep
It's rejoicing
over onyx-shelled oysters
sprinkled in a rain shower of lemon drops
or baked with a savoury zabaglione sauce
It's the final salute
The celebration
And then the curtains close
tight around my shoulders
a scarf around my neck
And taking its cues
From the orange moon
The stars
The masterpiece
regretfully
completes.

September I really enjoy my time spent in the kitchens in September. After my summer respite, I feel rejuvenated and find my creativity peaks this month. September is incredibly busy, both personally and professionally. With the children back at school, the pace of life picks up after the long, slow summer. In between rushing the kids to after-school programs and activities, weekends are full of harvest festivals and country fairs, fall weddings and barbecues.

From a culinary point of view, September is a festival of bounty. Personally, I think Thanksgiving should be moved from October to September since now is the time when I am most grateful for the harvest. The avalanche of availability starts in August and continues through September. It's easy to see the rhythm of the seasons by observing how, as the month progresses, we slide gently from the light and delicate vegetables and fruits of summer into the amazing colours and textures of the more robust fall varieties, like zucchini, squash, peppers, beets, and apples.

The anticipation of the grape harvest also adds to the simmering excitement of the season. Wineries in the Niagara region are beehives of activity as the grape growers deliver their precious cargo to anxiously waiting viniculturists and winemakers.

Wine Country Borscht

As early fall begins to chill the air, this comforting take on a classic borscht is the ideal way to warm up after a Sunday afternoon drive to see the changing colours of the season.

SERVES 4 TO 6

3 large beets
1 cup (250 mL) rock salt
¼ cup (60 mL) grapeseed oil
2 Tbsp (30 mL) unsalted butter
3 oz (90 g) prosciutto, finely chopped
1 small onion, finely chopped
1 carrot, finely chopped
¼ small Savoy cabbage, cored
    and cut into julienne strips
4 cups (1 L) chicken or vegetable
    stock (page 255)

4 ripe tomatoes, peeled,
    seeded, and chopped
1 cup (250 mL) dry white wine
1 large potato, peeled and chopped
4 sprigs thyme
4 sage leaves
1 bay leaf
1 cup (250 mL) apple cider
kosher salt and black pepper
    to taste
½ cup (125 mL) sour cream

PREHEAT THE OVEN to 350°F (180°C).

Trim the leafy tops from the beets, leaving 1 inch (2.5 cm) of stem on each. Make a "nest" of salt on a baking sheet and nestle the beets on top. Roast for 1½ to 2 hours (depending in the size of the beets) or until the beets feel tender when pierced with the tip of a sharp knife or a metal skewer. Remove the beets from the oven and discard the salt. When the beets are cool enough to handle but still warm, peel off the skins. Cut the beets into ½-inch (1 cm) cubes and set aside.

Meanwhile, heat a large pot over medium-high heat and add the grapeseed oil and butter. When the butter foams, add the prosciutto and sauté, stirring frequently, until the prosciutto is crisp. Using a slotted spoon, remove the prosciutto to a plate lined with paper towels and set aside.

Add the onion, carrot, and cabbage to the fat remaining in the pot. Sauté, stirring frequently, for 8 minutes or until the vegetables have wilted considerably and have coloured slightly. Stir in the stock, tomatoes, and wine and bring to a simmer, stirring frequently. Simmer for 3 minutes.

Stir in the roasted beets, potato, thyme, sage, and bay leaf. Bring back to a simmer and add the apple cider and season with salt and pepper to taste. Simmer for 10 minutes to meld the flavours. Discard the thyme, sage, and bay leaf.

To serve, ladle the soup into 4 to 6 warm soup bowls. Top each portion with a spoonful of sour cream and a sprinkling of crispy prosciutto.

I love taking a traditional recipe, perhaps something I grew up eating, and giving it a fresh twist. Sometimes I go over-the-top, taking a dish in a totally different direction so very little of the

Shrimp Minestrone

original recipe remains. This soup is a perfect example. In my family, minestrone was a staple that we ate once or twice a week. Adding Israeli couscous and shrimp gives it a totally new perspective that could make it one of your family's favourites.

SERVES 6

2 Tbsp (30 mL) unsalted butter

2 shallots, finely chopped

2 cloves garlic, finely chopped

1 carrot, cut into ½-inch (1 cm) dice

1 white turnip, cut into ½-inch (1 cm) dice

½ cup (125 mL) cooked, shelled fava beans, membranes peeled off (page 59)

pinch cayenne

kosher salt and black pepper to taste

3 cups (750 mL) vegetable stock (page 255)

¾ cup (185 mL) shrimp stock (made from shells) or fish stock (page 255)

½ cup (125 mL) cooked Israeli couscous

½ cup (125 mL) tomato concassé (page 257)

¼ cup (60 mL) olive oil

18 large black tiger shrimp, peeled and deveined

¼ cup (60 mL) shrimp butter (page 258)

20 lovage leaves

HEAT A LARGE SOUP POT over medium heat and add the butter. When the butter foams, add the shallots and garlic and cook, stirring frequently, until softened but not browned. Stir in the carrot, turnip, fava beans, cayenne, and salt and pepper to taste. Add the vegetable and shrimp stocks and simmer for about 5 minutes or until the vegetables are tender.

Stir in the couscous and tomato concassé. Return the soup to a simmer and keep warm until ready to serve.

Meanwhile, heat a large skillet over high heat and add the oil. When the oil begins to smoke slightly, add the shrimp. Sauté, stirring frequently, for 5 minutes or until the shrimp have cooked through and turned a nice pink colour. Season with more salt and pepper to taste.

Add the cooked shrimp, shrimp butter, and lovage leaves to the warm soup. Stir just until the butter has melted.

To serve, ladle the soup into 6 warm soup bowls.

Skate wing is a delicately flavoured fish with a light, meaty texture. It's wonderful with a variety of ingredients but goes particularly well with the acidity of wine, vinegar, or—as

Pan-Fried Skate with Mushroom, Corn, and Chardonnay Risotto

in this recipe—citrus. Skate wing should smell sweet and fresh; if you can smell ammonia, it means the skate is spoiled.

SERVES 6

SAUTÉED MUSHROOMS

2 Tbsp (30 mL) olive oil

2 Tbsp (30 mL) unsalted butter

8 oz (250 g) fresh wild mushrooms
 such as chanterelles or morels,
 coarsely chopped

1 clove garlic, finely chopped

kosher salt and black pepper
 to taste

2 Tbsp (30 mL) finely chopped
 Italian parsley

HEAT A LARGE SKILLET over medium-high heat and add the olive oil and butter. When the butter foams, add the mushrooms and sauté, stirring frequently, for 8 minutes or until the mushrooms have wilted and their liquid has evaporated. Add the garlic, and salt and pepper to taste and sauté, stirring frequently, for 5 more minutes. Remove the skillet from the heat and stir in the chopped parsley. Keep warm until ready to serve. (You will be using half for the risotto.)

MUSHROOM, CORN, AND CHARDONNAY RISOTTO

½ cup (125 mL) dried porcini
   mushrooms

6 cups (1.5 L) chicken or vegetable
   stock (page 255)

2 Tbsp (30 mL) olive oil

2 Tbsp (30 mL) unsalted butter

½ cup (125 mL) finely diced double-
   smoked bacon

½ cup (125 mL) finely chopped onion

1½ cups (375 mL) arborio, Vialone
   Nano, or Carnaroli rice

½ cup (125 mL) Chardonnay

½ cup (125 mL) fresh corn kernels
   (1 medium ear)

sautéed mushrooms (half)

kosher salt and black pepper to taste

⅓ cup (80 mL) freshly grated
   Parmesan cheese

IN A MEDIUM BOWL, pour 1 cup (250 mL) boiling water over the dried porcini and let stand for 30 minutes or until the water has cooled to room
temperature. Drain and rinse the mushrooms, reserving the soaking liquid
and mushrooms separately.

Bring the chicken stock to a simmer in a medium saucepan and keep
warm over low heat.

Heat a medium saucepan over medium heat and add the olive oil and
butter. When the butter foams, add the bacon and sauté, stirring frequently, until it crisps up slightly. Then add the onion and sauté, stirring
frequently, until the onion is softened but not browned. Add the rice and
sauté, stirring constantly, until the rice is coated with the oil.

Stir in the Chardonnay and simmer, stirring frequently, until the wine
has been absorbed. Stir in the mushroom soaking liquid and soaked
mushrooms and simmer, stirring frequently, until most of the liquid has
been absorbed.

Using a small ladle, gradually add the warm chicken stock to the rice
mixture, stirring continually and allowing the stock to be fully absorbed
by the rice before adding the next ladleful of hot stock. After 15 minutes,
add the corn and half of the sautéed mushrooms (reserving the remaining mushrooms). Continue adding the stock in small batches and stirring
for another 3 to 5 minutes or until the rice is al dente and has a creamy
consistency. You may or may not need more stock. Season with salt and
pepper to taste. Remove the saucepan from the heat, stir in the Parmesan,
and keep warm until ready to serve.

PAN-FRIED SKATE

1½ lb (750 g) fresh skate wing, cleaned
   and cut into 6 even-size pieces
kosher salt and white pepper
   to taste
1 cup (250 mL) all-purpose flour

¼ cup (60 mL) grapeseed oil
2 Tbsp (30 mL) unsalted butter
juice of 1 lemon
2 Tbsp (30 mL) finely chopped
   Italian parsley

PLACE THE PIECES of skate in a large bowl and season with salt and pepper to taste. Add the flour and toss to coat the skate completely.

Heat a large skillet over medium heat and add the grapeseed oil and butter. When the butter foams, add the prepared skate and fry for about 6 minutes, turning once, until golden brown on both sides. Do not crowd the skillet (the skate pieces shouldn't touch each other) so do this in batches if necessary. Sprinkle the lemon juice over the skate and remove to a warm platter. Sprinkle with the parsley.

TO SERVE, divide the mushroom, corn, and Chardonnay risotto among 6 warm dinner plates. Place a piece of skate on top of each portion of risotto. Top the skate with the reserved sautéed mushrooms.

The success of this pot roast depends on using a full-bodied Cabernet Sauvignon and fresh orange juice as the cooking liquid. A pot roast can be prepared from different cuts of beef, but I

Beef Pot Roast with Cabernet Sauvignon and Dried Fruit

like to use a chuck roast, as it seems to be more flavourful.

Keep on eye on the roast during cooking. If the liquid is evaporating too quickly and the casserole is in danger of becoming too dry, add a bit of water to keep the beef moist.

SERVES 6

1 boneless beef chuck–top blade or cross rib roast (about 3 lb/1.5 kg)
kosher salt and black pepper to taste
¼ cup (60 mL) olive oil
1½ cups (375 mL) finely diced red onions
2 tsp (10 mL) minced garlic
4 cups (1 L) fresh orange juice
1 cup (250 mL) Cabernet Sauvignon
1 cup (250 mL) chicken stock (page 255)
1 cup (250 mL) dried apple slices
1 cup (250 mL) dried figs or pitted prunes
3 Tbsp (45 mL) minced fresh ginger
2 tsp (10 mL) grated orange zest
1 tsp (5 mL) ground allspice
1 cinnamon stick

PREHEAT THE OVEN to 350°F (180°C).

Season the beef generously with salt and pepper. In a heavy flameproof casserole, heat 2 Tbsp (30 mL) of the olive oil over high heat and sear the beef for 2 minutes on each side or until well caramelized. Remove the meat from the casserole and set aside.

Heat the remaining olive oil in the casserole over medium heat and add the onions and garlic. Sauté, stirring frequently, until lightly coloured.

Return the meat to the casserole and add the orange juice, Cabernet Sauvignon, stock, dried apples, figs, ginger, orange zest, allspice, and cinnamon stick. Cover and bring to a simmer. Transfer the casserole to the oven and bake for 2½ to 3 hours or until the beef is very tender.

Using a slotted spoon, remove the beef to a cutting board and the fruit to a warm bowl. Discard the cinnamon stick from the cooking juices. Put the casserole over high heat and simmer the cooking juices until they are reduced by half. Season with more salt and pepper to taste.

To serve, slice the meat and arrange on a warm serving platter. Mound the fruit around the edge. Spoon the sauce over the beef and fruit.

This recipe underscores my current love of spicy broth-style sauces. For me they're a nice, light way to add flavour and depth to a dish. Don't get me wrong, I still love those heady

Grilled Pork Tenderloins with Wild Rice and Tomato-Chipotle Broth

wine reductions as well, but in this recipe the spicy tomato broth adds character, without heaviness, to the pork tenderloin.

SERVES 8

TOMATO-CHIPOTLE BROTH

6 ripe tomatoes, cut in half

⅓ cup (80 mL) olive oil, divided

kosher salt to taste

2 Tbsp (30 mL) unsalted butter

1 carrot, finely chopped

1 stalk celery, finely chopped

2 shallots, finely chopped

2 cloves garlic, minced

2 sprigs thyme

1 sprig rosemary

1 bay leaf

4 cups (1 L) chicken stock (page 255)

2 Tbsp (30 mL) minced canned
   chipotle chilis in adobo sauce

1 Tbsp (15 mL) tomato paste

black pepper to taste

PREHEAT THE OVEN to 400°F (200°C).

On a large rimmed baking sheet, toss the tomatoes with ¼ cup (60 mL) of the olive oil. Sprinkle with salt to taste. Roast for 35 to 40 minutes or until the tomatoes have lost most of their liquid and are slightly charred. Remove the baking sheet from the oven and let cool slightly.

Meanwhile, heat a large saucepan over medium heat and add the remaining olive oil and the butter. When the butter foams, add the carrot, celery, shallots, garlic, thyme, rosemary, and bay leaf. Sauté, stirring frequently, until the vegetables are soft and lightly coloured. Add the chicken stock, chipotles, and tomato paste and bring to a simmer.

Stir in the roast tomatoes and simmer until the liquid has reduced by half. Strain the tomato mixture through a fine-mesh sieve, discarding the solids. Return the broth to a clean saucepan and season with pepper and more salt to taste. Keep warm until ready to serve.

WILD RICE

2 cups (500 mL) Canadian wild rice

2 tsp (10 mL) kosher salt

4 green onions, finely chopped

2 Tbsp (30 mL) unsalted butter

IN A LARGE SAUCEPAN, combine the rice and salt with 8 cups (2 L) water and simmer, uncovered, for 1 hour or until the liquid has been completely absorbed by the rice.

Cover the saucepan and keep warm until ready to serve. Just before serving, add the green onions and butter, stirring until the butter melts.

GRILLED PORK TENDERLOINS

4 pork tenderloins, trimmed of any fat and each cut crosswise in half

¼ cup (60 mL) olive oil

kosher salt and black pepper to taste

PREHEAT THE OVEN to 400°F (200°C). Heat a large ridged ovenproof grill pan over high heat, or preheat the barbecue to high.

Rub the pork tenderloins with the oil and season to taste with salt and pepper. Sear the pork in the grill pan or on the barbecue until well marked on both sides with grill marks. Transfer the grill pan to the oven (if using the barbecue, transfer the pork tenderloins to an ovenproof dish large enough to hold them in a single layer). Roast for 15 to 20 minutes or until still slightly pink in the middle (an instant-read thermometer inserted into the thickest part of the tenderloins should register 140°F/60°C). Remove the tenderloins from the oven and let the meat rest for 5 minutes.

TO SERVE, slice the tenderloins. Divide the wild rice among 8 warm dinner plates and top with the slices of tenderloin. Spoon the tomato-chipotle broth around each plate.

Chicken Breasts with Mushroom and Goat Cheese Stuffing and Almond–Fig Vinaigrette

This very tasty dish is perfect for an autumn picnic as the chicken tastes great hot or cold. Dried figs lend a wonderful nuance to the mushroom and goat cheese flavours, and almonds provide a nice textural element.

SERVES 8

ALMOND-FIG VINAIGRETTE

¾ cup (185 mL) almond oil

½ cup (125 mL) olive oil

¼ cup (60 mL) aged balsamic vinegar

¼ cup (60 mL) dry red wine

2 Tbsp (30 mL) lemon juice

4 shallots, finely chopped

½ cup (125 mL) finely chopped
   dried figs

½ cup (125 mL) chopped
   toasted almonds

kosher salt and black pepper to taste

Tabasco sauce to taste

IN A MEDIUM non-reactive bowl, whisk together the almond and olive oils, vinegar, wine, and lemon juice until creamy. Stir in the shallots, figs, and almonds, and season with salt, pepper, and Tabasco sauce to taste. Cover and refrigerate. Let stand at room temperature. Whisk well before serving.

CHICKEN BREASTS WITH MUSHROOM AND GOAT CHEESE STUFFING

¼ cup (60 mL) olive oil

2 Tbsp (30 mL) unsalted butter

2 shallots, finely chopped

1 clove garlic, minced

3 cups (750 mL) assorted mushrooms
   (such as portobello, shiitake, and/or
   honey), chopped

¼ cup (60 mL) chicken stock (page 255)

½ cup (125 mL) chopped walnuts

½ cup (125 mL) soft goat cheese

1 egg

¼ cup (60 mL) freshly grated
   Parmesan cheese

2 Tbsp (30 mL) finely chopped
   Italian parsley

kosher salt and black pepper to taste

8 boneless chicken breasts with skin
   and wing bones attached

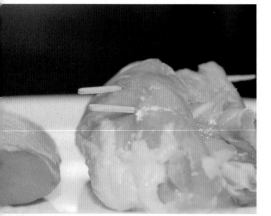

PREHEAT THE OVEN to 350°F (180°C).

Heat a medium skillet over medium-high heat and add the olive oil and butter. When the butter foams, add the shallots and garlic. Sauté, stirring frequently, until softened but not browned. Add the mushrooms and chicken stock and cook, stirring frequently, until the stock has all but evaporated. Remove the skillet from the heat and let cool to room temperature.

Stir the walnuts, goat cheese, egg, Parmesan, parsley, and salt and pepper to taste into the cooled mushroom mixture.

Place 1 chicken breast skin side down on a cutting board. Using a slim, sharp knife, cut a deep narrow pocket in the thickest part of the meat of the chicken breast, next to the wing bone. Using a small spoon, fill the cavity with some of the mushroom filling, securing the cavity shut with a toothpick. Repeat with the remaining chicken breasts and filling.

Place the stuffed chicken breasts on a large rimmed baking sheet. Bake for about 25 minutes or until an instant-read thermometer inserted in the thickest chicken breast registers 160°F (71°C).

TO SERVE, using a sharp knife, slice each chicken breast lengthwise into thirds and fan out the slices on each of 8 warm dinner plates. Either drizzle each portion with almond-fig vinaigrette or serve the vinaigrette in a small dish on the side.

Linguine with Late Harvest Vegetables and Broken Tomato Basil Sauce

In this rustic pasta dish, the tomato sauce is treated rather simply, so you'll need very ripe, full-flavoured tomatoes to get the best results. The goat cheese sprinkled over the top is optional but adds nice complexity.

SERVES 4

BROKEN TOMATO BASIL SAUCE

¼ cup (60 mL) olive oil

3 cloves garlic, finely chopped

4 lb (1.8 kg) Roma or field tomatoes, peeled, seeded, and chopped

6 basil leaves, cut into julienne strips

pinch granulated sugar

kosher salt and black pepper to taste

IN A LARGE SAUCEPAN, heat 1 Tbsp (15 mL) of the olive oil over medium heat. Add the garlic and sauté, stirring frequently, for about 1 minute. Add the tomatoes and cook for about 30 minutes, using a potato masher or a fork to break the tomatoes into chunks as they cook.

Remove the saucepan from the heat and stir in the remaining olive oil, the basil, sugar, and salt and pepper to taste. Keep warm until ready to serve.

LINGUINE WITH LATE HARVEST VEGETABLES

½ green zucchini, cut into ½-inch (1 cm) dice

½ yellow summer squash, cut into ½-inch (1 cm) dice

½ sweet red pepper, seeded and cut into ½-inch (1 cm) dice

½ sweet yellow pepper, seeded and cut into ½-inch (1 cm) dice

⅓ cup (80 mL) olive oil

2 shallots, finely chopped

8 cherry tomatoes, cut in half

2 cloves garlic, finely chopped

1 lb (500 g) linguine

6 basil leaves, cut into julienne strips

½ cup (125 mL) pitted black olives

freshly grated Parmesan cheese to taste

¼ cup (60 mL) crumbled goat cheese (optional)

PREHEAT THE OVEN to 350°F (180°C).

Sauté the zucchini, squash, and red and yellow peppers separately in 1 Tbsp (15 mL) of the olive oil each in a large skillet over medium-high heat, cooking each vegetable for 3 to 5 minutes or until tender, and transferring them to a baking sheet in the oven as each one cooks.

Heat the remaining oil in the skillet. Add the shallots, tomatoes, and garlic and sauté, stirring frequently, until the shallots are softened but not browned. Add the shallot mixture to rest of the vegetables on the baking sheet in the oven.

Bring a very large pot of water to a boil over high heat. Add the linguine and cook for 8 to 10 minutes or until al dente.

Drain the pasta in a colander and transfer to a large warm bowl. Remove the vegetables from the oven and add to the bowl with the noodles. Using kitchen tongs, combine the noodles with the vegetables. Add enough of the tomato basil sauce to just coat the noodles and mix just until combined.

TO SERVE, divide the pasta among 4 warm pasta bowls. Sprinkle each portion with basil, olives, Parmesan, and goat cheese (if using).

Roasted Autumn Apples Stuffed with Currants and Mascarpone

This simple fall dessert tastes good warm or cold. The mascarpone adds richness, and the maple syrup makes this a real Canadian treat.

SERVES 8

½ cup (125 mL) currants
½ cup (125 mL) brandy
1¼ cups (310 mL) granulated sugar
1 cup (250 mL) unsweetened 100% apple juice
1 cup (250 mL) mascarpone cheese
2 Tbsp (30 mL) packed brown sugar

2 tsp (10 mL) maple syrup
2 Tbsp (30 mL) unsalted butter, softened
8 small Northern Spy or Idared apples, cored but not peeled (roast with tops on if you like)
vanilla ice cream to serve

PREHEAT OVEN to 350°F (180°C).

In a small bowl, soak the currants in the brandy for 30 minutes or until soft. Drain well, discarding the brandy. Set the currants aside.

In a small saucepan, stir together the sugar and ⅓ cup (80 mL) water. Cook over medium heat, without stirring, for about 10 minutes or until light golden in colour. Remove the saucepan from the heat and, standing back in case the mixture spatters, carefully stir in the apple juice. Set aside and keep warm.

In a food processor, process the mascarpone cheese until smooth. With the motor running, add the brown sugar and maple syrup and process until well combined. Scrape the cheese into a small bowl and fold in the soaked currants until well combined.

Rub the butter over the base of shallow baking dish large enough to hold the apples snugly. Place the apples in the dish and spoon the mascarpone mixture into the cavity of each apple, dividing evenly. Pour the apple juice mixture over the apples and bake, uncovered and basting often with the cooking juices, for 15 minutes or until the apples are golden brown and tender.

To serve, carefully remove each apple to a warm dessert plate. Serve with vanilla ice cream.

October

October There's something special about October. As the nights grow cooler and the days get shorter, it's time to take out the sweaters and long pants and pack away the shorts and flip-flops. This is the month when our breath becomes visible and we tend to slow down a bit, maybe waiting a few extra minutes while the car warms up. It's a time when I like to spend my days off travelling round the region with my family, visiting Niagara's many fall fairs and harvest festivals, eating candy apples and riding Ferris wheels.

October also brings Thanksgiving, the perfect time to gather with family and be grateful for the many blessings in our lives. And, at the end of the month comes Halloween. Typically a slow night in the restaurant, I prefer to be at home handing out candy to little monsters. It's also a great month for the sports fan. With basketball, hockey, and football seasons getting under way, and the last of the year's baseball games to watch, it's fun to have friends over on brisk, chilly nights to enjoy some potluck get-togethers and cheer on our favourite teams.

October is the bridge between the last warm days of late September and November's more frigid temperatures. Now the landscape displays beautiful colours, and nature's palette is reflected in the foods we eat. Vibrant oranges, yellows, browns, and reds transform fall produce. It's the month for colourful gourds, pumpkins, Indian corn, and apples, and the earth tones of wild mushrooms. This is also the time of the year to enjoy perfectly ripe pears, the quintessential autumn fruit.

Signature Onion Tart

This lovely recipe is easy to prepare and very versatile. We often serve it as an amuse-bouche in the restaurant, but I've also paired it with simply dressed baby greens for a luncheon appetizer.

SERVES 6 AS AN APPETIZER

ONION FILLING

3 Tbsp (45 mL) unsalted butter
2 slices double-smoked bacon,
   cut into julienne strips
3 medium onions, cut crosswise
   into thin rings
1 cup (250 mL) 35% cream
1 cup (250 mL) milk

4 eggs
½ tsp (2 mL) kosher salt
black pepper and freshly grated
   nutmeg to taste
3 sprigs Italian parsley, stems
   discarded and leaves
   finely chopped

IN A LARGE SKILLET over low heat, melt the butter and sauté the bacon, stirring frequently, until browned. Add the onions and sauté, stirring frequently, until the onions are tender but not browned.

In a medium bowl, whisk together the cream, milk, eggs, salt, and pepper and nutmeg to taste. Add the onion mixture and parsley and stir well. Refrigerate until ready to use.

ONION TART

1½ cups (375 mL) all-purpose flour

½ cup (125 mL) unsalted butter, softened

pinch table salt

1 egg

additional unsalted butter for greasing

onion filling

PREHEAT THE OVEN to 325°F (160°C).

In a large bowl, combine the flour, butter, and salt and, using your fingertips, work the ingredients until the mixture resembles coarse meal. Add the egg and a touch of water and knead just until the dough comes together. Form into a disc, wrap in plastic wrap, and refrigerate for 1 hour.

Using a generously floured rolling pin, roll out the dough thinly to a 12-inch (30 cm) round. Fit the dough into a buttered 10-inch (25 cm) tart pan with a removable base and, using your fingers, gently push the dough up against the edges to fit well. Trim the edges with a sharp knife.

Prick the bottom of the tart shell all over with a fork. Cut a disc of aluminum foil to fit the base of the pan and press it on the dough. Bake the tart shell for 30 minutes or until only the edges of the tart shell begin to colour slightly.

Remove the tart shell from the oven and discard the aluminum foil. Spoon the onion filling into the tart shell, spreading the surface level. Return the tart to the oven and bake for 10 minutes. Turn off the oven and let the tart bake with the heat turned off and without opening the door for about 45 minutes or until just set. Remove the tart from the oven and let cool to room temperature.

TO SERVE, cut the tart into 1-inch (2.5 cm) wedges to serve as an *amuse-bouche*, or cut into large wedges and serve with simply dressed salad greens as an appetizer.

Wild mushrooms seem to sing the praises of the season in the fall. During October, we often prepare this soup to utilize the amazing variety of mushrooms coming into our kitchens.

Pumpkin Soup with Wild Mushrooms

Although not every grocery store carries the same extensive selection of mushrooms that we have access to at the restaurant, I highly recommend fresh mushrooms for this if you can find them, and sautéing some for a lovely garnish.

SERVES 8

½ cup (125 mL) dried porcini
   mushrooms or 2 cups (500 mL)
   fresh wild mushrooms, cleaned
   and chopped
2 Tbsp (30 mL) olive oil
2 Tbsp (30 mL) unsalted butter
2 leeks (white parts only), chopped
1 medium onion, sliced
3 cloves garlic, finely chopped
1 Tbsp (15 mL) honey

8 cups (2 L) coarsely chopped
   pumpkin (peeled and seeded)
6 cups (1.5 L) chicken or vegetable
   stock (page 255)
½ cup (125 mL) orange juice
½ cup (125 mL) 35% cream
5 sage leaves
6 whole cloves
kosher salt and black pepper
   to taste

IF USING DRIED MUSHROOMS, pour 1 cup (250 mL) boiling water over the dried porcini in a medium bowl and let stand for 30 minutes or until the water has cooled to room temperature. Drain and rinse the mushrooms, reserving the soaking liquid and mushrooms separately.

Heat a large saucepan over medium heat and add the olive oil and butter. When the butter foams, add the leeks, onion, garlic, and soaked or fresh mushrooms and sauté, stirring frequently, for 5 minutes or until the vegetables have softened. Stir in the honey.

Add the pumpkin, chicken stock, orange juice, and mushroom soaking liquid (if using dried mushrooms) and simmer for 30 minutes or until the pumpkin is soft. Stir in the cream, sage, and cloves and simmer for 5 minutes more.

Transfer the soup to a blender (not a food processor) and blend until smooth. Strain the soup through a fine-mesh sieve, discarding solids. Return to the rinsed-out saucepan.

To serve, bring back to a simmer and season with salt and pepper to taste. Ladle into 8 warm soup bowls.

Pasta need not always be served with a heavy cream–based or tomato sauce. In this version, which is perfect for fall, ravioli is stuffed with roasted sweet potatoes then topped with a brown

Sweet Potato Ravioli with Green Peppercorn and Brown Butter Sauce

butter sauce. The dish is rich yet will not leave you feeling too full. My family enjoys this as part of our Thanksgiving dinner.

SERVES 4

SWEET POTATO RAVIOLI

3 sweet potatoes	kosher salt and black pepper to taste
2 Tbsp (30 mL) unsalted butter	basic pasta (page 257)
2 Tbsp (30 mL) finely chopped chives	1 egg, lightly beaten

PRICK THE SWEET POTATOES all over with a fork. Place them on a microwaveable plate lined with paper towels and microwave on high power (100%) for 10 to 12 minutes, turning once, until the sweet potatoes feel tender when pierced with a slim knife. (Alternatively, bake in a 400°F/ 200°C oven for about 1 hour.)

When the sweet potatoes are cool enough to handle but still warm, peel them and pass them through a potato ricer or rub through a fine-mesh sieve into a medium bowl. Stir in the butter until it melts. Stir in the chives, and salt and pepper to taste. Let cool completely.

Prepare the basic pasta dough. Cut sixteen 3-inch (8 cm) squares from the sheets of dough. Brush each square with the beaten egg. Spoon 1 tsp (5 mL) of the sweet potato filling in the middle of the lower half of each pasta square. Fold the squares in half to enclose the filling, sealing the edges tightly with your fingers or the floured tines of a fork. Use a 1½-inch (4 cm) fluted cookie cutter to trim the edges and form round ravioli. Place the ravioli in a single layer on a well-floured baking sheet, cover with a kitchen towel and set aside at room temperature until ready to cook.

Just before serving, bring a large pot of salted water to a boil. Add the ravioli and cook for 2 minutes or until they float to the surface. Remove the ravioli from the pot with a slotted spoon.

GREEN PEPPERCORN AND BROWN BUTTER SAUCE

¾ cup (185 mL) chicken stock
  (page 255)
½ cup (125 mL) unsalted butter
¼ cup (60 mL) aged sherry vinegar

2 Tbsp (30 mL) finely chopped chervil,
  sage, rosemary, or thyme
1½ Tbsp (22.5 mL) drained pickled
  green peppercorns, chopped
kosher salt and black pepper to taste

IN A SMALL SAUCEPAN over medium heat, simmer the chicken stock until it is reduced to ¼ cup (60 mL).

In a separate small saucepan over medium heat, heat the butter until it is golden brown. Immediately remove the saucepan from the heat and stir in the vinegar, chervil, and peppercorns. Stir in the reduced chicken stock and season with salt and pepper to taste. Keep warm until ready to serve.

TO SERVE, divide the ravioli among 4 warm pasta bowls. Spoon the sauce over the top.

Peppercorn and Honey Roasted Pears with Candied Walnuts and Poppy Seed Yogurt Dressing

I love all pears, from Bartletts to Boscs, and they're particularly bountiful during early fall. Please select nice, ripe pears for this recipe. (A ripe pear smells sweeter and more floral than an unripe one.)

SERVES 8

CANDIED WALNUTS

2 cups (500 mL) simple syrup (page 23)

1 cup (250 mL) walnut halves

2 tsp (10 mL) dried chili flakes

½ tsp (2 mL) ground ginger

½ tsp (2 mL) cumin

kosher salt and black pepper to taste

PREHEAT THE OVEN to 300°F (150°C). Line a large baking sheet with parchment paper.

Bring the simple syrup to a simmer in small saucepan. Remove the saucepan from the heat and plunge the walnuts into the hot syrup.

Using a slotted spoon, lift out the walnuts and place in a large bowl. Add the remaining ingredients to the walnuts and toss well. Spread the walnut mixture out in a single layer on the prepared baking sheet and bake for 8 to 10 minutes, stirring occasionally, until the walnuts are golden brown. Let cool completely, then store in an airtight container until ready to serve.

POPPY SEED YOGURT DRESSING

1 cup (250 mL) plain yogurt

juice of 1 lemon

1 shallot, chopped

2 Tbsp (30 mL) poppy seeds

2 Tbsp (30 mL) honey

COMBINE all of the ingredients and ¼ cup (60 mL) water in a blender. Blend until smooth. Cover and refrigerate until ready to serve.

PEPPERCORN AND HONEY ROASTED PEARS

2 Tbsp (30 mL) grapeseed oil

2 Tbsp (30 mL) unsalted butter

8 ripe pears, peeled, cored, and each
    cut into 4 wedges

kosher salt to taste

2 Tbsp (30 mL) honey

2 Tbsp (30 mL) crushed pink
    peppercorns

1 Tbsp (15 mL) cracked black
    peppercorns

HEAT A VERY LARGE SKILLET over high heat and add the grapeseed oil and
butter (or use 2 large skillets and heat half of the oil and butter in each).
When the butter foams, add the pear wedges and cook, without turning,
for about 3 minutes or until golden brown on the undersides. Season the
pears with salt to taste.

Using tongs or a spatula, turn the pear wedges over. Stir in the honey
and pink and black peppercorns. Reduce the heat to low and continue
cooking for about 3 minutes or until the pears are cooked through.

TO SERVE

2 cups (500 mL) lightly packed baby
    greens, washed and dried

4 oz (125 g) crumbled blue cheese
    (such as roquefort) (optional)

DIVIDE THE PEARS among 8 salad plates. Drizzle each portion with the
poppy seed yogurt dressing and sprinkle with candied walnuts. Garnish
each plate with baby greens and blue cheese (if using).

I love the slightly bitter taste of radicchio, which I find stimulates the taste buds. Teamed with the smooth garlic purée, it's the perfect combo to go with seared scallops, but I wouldn't

Pan-Seared Scallops with Garlic Purée and Citrus-Glazed Radicchio

recommend cooking this full-flavoured dish for a first date!

SERVES 6

GARLIC PURÉE

1 cup (250 mL) garlic cloves, peeled
1 cup (250 mL) milk

2 sprigs thyme
1 bay leaf

COMBINE all the ingredients in a small saucepan and bring to a simmer over medium heat. Simmer for 25 minutes or until the garlic cloves are very tender.

Using a slotted spoon, transfer the garlic cloves to a blender with a bit of the hot milk. Blend until the garlic is smooth, adding more of the hot milk, if necessary, until the garlic purée has the consistency of pancake batter. Set aside and keep warm.

CITRUS-GLAZED RADICCHIO

3 heads radicchio di Treviso
2 Tbsp (30 mL) unsalted butter
1 cup (250 mL) orange juice
2 Tbsp (30 mL) honey

1 Tbsp (15 mL) crushed pink
   peppercorns
1 star anise

CUT each head of radicchio in half lengthwise. In a large skillet, melt the butter over medium-high heat. Add the radicchio, cut sides down, and cook for 4 minutes or until browned on the underside.

Turn the radicchio over and add the orange juice, honey, peppercorns, and star anise. Simmer, covered, until all the liquid has evaporated. Toss the radicchio to glaze it all over. Set aside and keep warm.

PAN-SEARED SCALLOPS

18 large fresh sea scallops

kosher salt and white pepper to taste

¼ cup (60 mL) grapeseed oil

3 Tbsp (45 mL) unsalted butter

PAT THE SCALLOPS DRY and season with salt and pepper to taste. Heat a large skillet over medium-high heat and add the grapeseed oil and 2 Tbsp (30 mL) of the butter. When the butter foams, add the scallops and sear them for about 2 minutes, without turning, until golden brown on the undersides.

Gently turn the scallops over and add the remaining butter to the skillet. Allow the butter to foam up and start to brown, then continue to cook the scallops, basting them often with the butter, for about 2 minutes or until the scallops are just cooked through. Drain the scallops on a plate lined with paper towels.

TO SERVE

3 oranges, peeled and cut into ½-inch
   (1 cm) slices (18 slices in total)

SPOON the garlic purée onto the centre of 6 warm dinner plates. Place 3 orange slices down the centre of the plate, the centre slice on top of the garlic. Arrange 3 scallops on top of the orange slices. Place a piece of citrus-glazed radicchio on the left-hand side of each plate. Spoon any of the glaze that has accumulated under the radicchio over the scallops.

Liver is a very popular luncheon item with my guests, particularly during the fall. I think this is because liver is one of those foods that you can enjoy a small portion of yet still feel nourished, and

Grilled Calf's Liver with White Bean Gratin and Hazelnut Dressing

it's not readily available everywhere. Here it's paired with a nutty dressing and a filling white bean gratin.

SERVES 6

HAZELNUT DRESSING

¾ cup (185 mL) grapeseed oil

⅓ cup (80 mL) dry sherry

⅓ cup (80 mL) hazelnut oil

2 shallots, coarsely chopped

1 Tbsp (15 mL) Dijon mustard

pinch granulated sugar

kosher salt and black pepper
   to taste

IN A BLENDER, blend all the ingredients until smooth. Cover and refrigerate. Let come to room temperature and whisk well before serving.

WHITE BEAN GRATIN

1 cup (250 mL) white beans, picked
   over, rinsed, and soaked in water
   overnight

non-stick baking spray

¼ cup (60 mL) olive oil

1 cup (250 mL) finely chopped onions

½ cup (125 mL) finely chopped carrot

4 cloves garlic, finely chopped

1 bay leaf

3 large tomatoes, seeded, cored,
   and chopped (they do not need
   to be peeled)

½ cup (125 mL) 35% cream

kosher salt and white pepper to taste

5 Tbsp (75 mL) freshly grated
   Parmesan cheese

truffle oil to taste

2 Tbsp (30 mL) finely chopped
   Italian parsley

IN A LARGE POT OF WATER, simmer the beans over medium-high heat for 1 to 1½ hours or until completely tender. Drain in a colander and set aside.

Preheat the oven to 350°F (180°C). Spray an 11- × 7-inch (2 L) baking dish with non-stick baking spray.

Heat the olive oil in a large pot over medium heat. Add the onions, carrot, garlic, and bay leaf and sauté, stirring frequently, until the carrots start to soften. Add the cooked beans and the tomatoes and sauté, stirring frequently, until the vegetables are soft. Stir in the cream and simmer, stirring frequently, until the cream has been absorbed. Season with salt and pepper to taste.

Transfer the bean mixture to a food processor and pulse until well combined but not entirely smooth. Pour the bean mixture into the prepared dish and sprinkle evenly with the Parmesan. Bake, uncovered, for 45 minutes or until bubbly and golden brown.

Keep warm until ready to serve. Just before serving, drizzle with truffle oil and sprinkle with parsley.

GRILLED CALF'S LIVER

6 pieces calf's liver (each 6 oz/175 g)	1 cup (250 mL) all-purpose flour
kosher salt and black pepper to taste	

PREHEAT the barbecue to high.

Pat the pieces of liver very dry with paper towel. Season on both sides with salt and pepper to taste.

Spread the flour out in a shallow dish and dip each piece of liver in the flour to coat completely. Shake off the excess.

Grill the liver for 1 minute on each side or until done to your taste.

TO SERVE, place a piece of liver on each of 6 warm dinner plates. Drizzle the liver with the hazelnut dressing. Spoon the white bean gratin alongside.

What could be more reassuring and tasty than a warm chocolate dessert? This is the recipe to make when winter's first chills creep in and you start thinking about turning on the furnace.

Soft Chocolate Cakes with Hazelnut-Icewine Sauce

Chocolate and hazelnuts seem to have an affinity for each other, and here the combo is made even more special with the addition of icewine.

SERVES 6

HAZELNUT-ICEWINE SAUCE

1 cup (250 mL) packed brown sugar

3 Tbsp (45 mL) all-purpose flour

¼ tsp (1 mL) table salt

¼ cup (60 mL) Niagara icewine

2 Tbsp (30 mL) unsalted butter

½ cup (125 mL) toasted hazelnuts (page 18), chopped

IN A SMALL SAUCEPAN, whisk together the sugar, flour, and salt. Whisk in ¼ cup (60 mL) water. Bring to a simmer over medium heat, whisking constantly, until smooth and thickened.

Whisk in the icewine and butter, whisking vigorously until smooth. Stir in the hazelnuts. Keep warm until ready to serve.

SOFT CHOCOLATE CAKES

non-stick baking spray

6 oz (175 g) bittersweet chocolate,
  chopped

⅔ cup (160 mL) unsalted butter

6 egg yolks

⅓ cup (80 mL) granulated sugar

3 egg whites

⅓ cup (80 mL) all-purpose flour

icing sugar for dusting

PREHEAT THE OVEN to 425°F (220°C). Spray six ½-cup (125 mL) ramekins with baking spray and place them on a baking sheet.

In a bowl set over a saucepan of simmering water, melt the chocolate and butter until smooth.

Meanwhile, in the bowl of a stand mixer fitted with the wire whisk attachment, whisk the egg yolks and sugar for 5 minutes or until light and fluffy. Slowly add the melted chocolate mixture to the egg yolk mixture and mix on low speed for about 8 minutes.

In a separate bowl, whisk the egg whites until they hold stiff peaks. Remove the bowl from the stand mixer and, using a spatula, gradually fold the egg whites into the chocolate mixture until no white streaks remain. Fold in the flour, one spoonful at a time, ensuring each spoonful is incorporated before adding the next.

Divide the batter among the ramekins. Bake for 7 minutes or until the edges look cooked but the centres are still jiggly. Allow to cool slightly then run a knife around the edges of the ramekins to loosen the cakes.

TO SERVE, remove the cakes from the ramekins and place each on a dessert plate. Dust the cakes with icing sugar. Pour the hazelnut-icewine sauce around each cake.

NOVEMBER
by Maria Giuliani

It's the crunch, crunch, crunch
That gets me.

Crackling leaves under my boots

—Boots!—

Refusing to rake,
Convincing myself that my garden also requires
The extra insulation.

And what can you say of a month
That begins with a No!
And ends with a brr

Like an infant that,
Assets aside,
Is destined for drear,
Eugene, Herman, Walter—
Never. Stood. A chance.

Sure,
I could talk about the oysters,
Cozy tummies of sauce-covered polenta,
Homemade spaghetti and veal parmigiana.

I could ponder
Slow-cooked stews with gravy and potatoes
So warm,
Like rediscovering that favourite sweater
In the cockles of my closet.

Sure,
I could contemplate cassoulet
And all things baked—

But it's the crunch, crunch, crunch,
Dropping temperatures
And turned-up thermostat
That seizes my imagination.

November In many ways, November seems to be the month when all we do is anticipate the coming winter. We put the snow tires on the car, we take out our heavy coats and put away the patio furniture. But, we also hang our Christmas lights and start getting regular reminders of how many shopping days are left before the holidays.

As November days get shorter and the nights bring with them the winter's first frost, we tend to embrace a slower pace and enjoy more family time. We linger over dinner or spend evenings by the fire, just chatting or playing a board game or two with the kids. Taking a long walk is one of my favourite ways to spend a November Sunday. Often my family and I will head to a conservation area to enjoy the outdoors riding our mountain bikes or simply strolling along the trails. There is something rejuvenating about a walk on a cool, sunny day.

The same rejuvenation goes on in the restaurant's kitchens. The subtle change in raw materials that began in October becomes more pronounced. With an abundance of wild mushrooms, hearty greens, and game meats, the recipes I gravitate to at this time of year are more comforting. I think less of salads and fruit and more about soups, braised dishes, and stews, and I enjoy the rituals of cooking longer, more involved recipes.

It's in November that Kaleen and I entertain more. I love spending the day in the kitchen trying out new ideas on my friends or treating them to old favourites. One of the regular November events Kaleen and I host is our annual paella party, usually scheduled for a chilly afternoon and eagerly anticipated by our friends. It's quite the spectacle.

I have an enormous, heavy stainless-steel pan that's three feet in diameter, which my friend Tim Gould had custom-made for me. We load it with piles of seafood, sausage, chicken, rice, and vegetables to make an enormous version of the great Spanish comfort food. We build a big fire (Tim's a woodworker and has copious amounts of scrap wood that he enjoys getting rid of at the paella party) and when it's hot enough, we put the pan on a stone platform over the fire and off we go. Everyone comes by for a look and to keep warm. We all take turns stirring the paella with a huge oar until it's ready. It takes two men to move the pan off the fire so we can dig in.

Butternut Squash and Goat Cheese Ravioli with Mushroom Butter Sauce

The spiced squash and goat cheese fill-ing for these ravioli can also be spread under the skin of chicken breasts before roasting. I've also used it to stuff a turkey—unconventional, I know, but tasty.

SERVES 4

MUSHROOM BUTTER SAUCE

¼ cup (60 mL) unsalted butter

½ lb (250 g) assorted wild mushrooms
   (such as chanterelles, honey, and
   porcini), cleaned and chopped

½ cup (125 mL) chicken stock
   (page 255)

2 shallots, chopped

½ cup (125 mL) dry white wine

2 Tbsp (30 mL) finely chopped chives

kosher salt and black pepper
   to taste

MELT THE BUTTER in a medium saucepan over medium heat. Add the mush-rooms and stir to coat well. Add the chicken stock, shallots, and wine and simmer until the liquid has reduced to ½ cup (125 mL). Stir in the chives and season with salt and pepper to taste. Keep warm until ready to serve.

BUTTERNUT SQUASH AND GOAT CHEESE RAVIOLI

1 cup (250 mL) cooked butternut
   squash purée

½ cup (125 mL) freshly grated
   Parmesan cheese

¼ cup (60 mL) soft goat cheese

2 Tbsp (30 mL) fresh, soft
   breadcrumbs

2 eggs, divided

pinch freshly grated nutmeg

pinch ground saffron

pinch ground cloves

pinch cinnamon

pinch cayenne

kosher salt and black pepper to taste

basic pasta (page 257)

¼ cup (60 mL) shaved Parmesan

IN A FOOD PROCESSOR, combine the butternut squash purée, Parmesan, goat cheese, breadcrumbs, 1 egg, nutmeg, saffron, cloves, cinnamon, cayenne, and salt and pepper to taste. Process until smooth.

Prepare the basic pasta dough. Beat the remaining egg in a small bowl. Cut 2-inch (5 cm) circles from the sheets of dough. Brush each circle with beaten egg. Spoon 1 tsp (5 mL) of the pumpkin filling in the centre of half of the pasta circles. Top with the remaining circles to enclose the filling, sealing the edges tightly with your fingers or the floured tines of a fork. Place the ravioli in a single layer on a well-floured baking sheet, cover with a kitchen towel and set aside at room temperature until ready to cook.

Just before serving, bring a large pot of salted water to a boil. Add the ravioli and cook for 2 minutes or until the ravioli float to the surface.

TO SERVE, with a slotted spoon remove the ravioli and divide them among 4 warm pasta bowls. Spoon the sauce over the ravioli. Garnish with shaved Parmesan.

With so many types of squash available in the fall, I designed this appetizer to highlight the various characteristics of the different varieties. Use kabocha, butternut, acorn, blue banana, blue

Squash Ragout with Curried Carrot Butter Sauce

hubbard, and/or spaghetti squash, or any other type you can find.

SERVES 6

SQUASH RAGOUT

2 lb (1 kg) assorted squash, peeled, seeded, and coarsely chopped

¼ cup (60 mL) olive oil

kosher salt and black pepper to taste

3 Tbsp (45 mL) unsalted butter

12 cloves garlic

3 shallots, cut into quarters

3 sprigs thyme

PREHEAT THE OVEN to 375°F (190°C).

In a large roasting pan, toss the squash with the olive oil and salt and pepper to taste. Roast for 30 to 40 minutes or until golden brown and cooked through, stirring every so often to prevent burning. Remove the roasting pan from the oven and set aside.

Heat a large skillet over medium heat and add the butter. When the butter foams, add the garlic, shallots, and thyme and reduce the heat to low. Sauté, stirring frequently, until the shallots and garlic are golden brown and tender.

Discard the thyme and add the roasted squash to the skillet, tossing until combined and heated through. Keep warm until ready to serve.

CURRIED CARROT BUTTER SAUCE

3 Tbsp (45 mL) unsalted butter, softened

1 Tbsp (15 mL) curry powder

2 cups (500 mL) carrot juice

½ cup (125 mL) late-harvest Vidal (or other dessert wine)

2 Tbsp (30 mL) finely chopped chives

IN A SMALL BOWL, stir together the butter and curry powder until well combined. Set aside.

In a small saucepan, combine the carrot juice and Vidal and simmer over medium heat until the liquid has reduced to ½ cup (125 mL). Remove the saucepan from the heat and whisk in the curry butter.

TO SERVE, divide the squash ragout among 6 warm salad plates. Spoon the curried carrot butter sauce over the ragout. Garnish with chives.

This recipe is a good example of my belief that, when it comes to cooking, all fresh seasonal produce is fair game for us to use in whatever manner we like. Creating a soup from apples may

Apple Harvest Soup with Herbs and Blue Cheese

seem unusual, but during apple season, I love using the fruit in as many ways as possible.

SERVES 6 TO 8

2 Tbsp (30 mL) olive oil

2 Tbsp (30 mL) unsalted butter

1½ cups (375 mL) chopped leeks
   (white parts only)

½ cup (125 mL) chopped onion

½ cup (125 mL) chopped celery

4 cups (1 L) chicken or vegetable
   stock (page 255)

3 medium apples, peeled, cored,
   and chopped

2 cups (500 mL) peeled and
   chopped potatoes

½ cup (125 mL) dry white wine

½ cup (125 mL) 35% cream

kosher salt and black pepper
   to taste

¼ cup (60 mL) Calvados

2 Tbsp (30 mL) finely chopped
   herbs (such as tarragon, chives,
   or chervil)

½ lb (250 g) blue cheese (such
   as roquefort), cut into 6 to
   8 even-size slices

HEAT A LARGE POT over medium heat and add the olive oil and butter. When the butter foams, add the leeks, onion, and celery and sauté, stirring frequently, until softened but not browned. Add the chicken stock, apples, potatoes, and wine and bring to a simmer. Cook, stirring occasionally, until the vegetables are tender.

Transfer the soup to a blender (not a food processor) and blend until smooth. Return the soup to the rinsed-out pot and stir in the cream. Heat through over low heat and season with salt and pepper to taste. Remove the pot from the heat and stir in the Calvados.

To serve, ladle the soup into 6 to 8 large warm soup bowls and sprinkle each portion with herbs. Float a slice of blue cheese in each bowl.

This very festive stew is nice with a side dish of wild rice or even spooned over buttered noodles. Of course, the Brussels sprouts are optional, but since they are one of my favourite vegetables,

Turkey Stew in Grainy Mustard Sauce with Glazed Brussels Sprouts

I've included a recipe for them that I learned while working at the Hotel Wilder Mann in Passau, Germany.

SERVES 6

TURKEY STEW IN GRAINY MUSTARD SAUCE

2 lb (1 kg) skinless, boneless turkey, cut into 1-inch (2.5 cm) pieces

½ cup (125 mL) olive oil, divided

5 sprigs thyme, divided

4 sprigs sage, divided

2 cups (500 mL) chicken stock (page 255)

½ cup (125 mL) dry white wine

¼ cup (60 mL) aged sherry vinegar

2 shallots, finely chopped

2 cloves garlic, minced

½ cup (125 mL) 35% cream

1 Tbsp (15 mL) veal jus (page 254)

2 cups (500 mL) chopped Swiss chard leaves

2 Tbsp (30 mL) Kozlik's mustard (or any grainy mustard)

1 Tbsp (15 mL) unsalted butter

kosher salt and black pepper to taste

IN A LARGE BOWL, toss the turkey with ¼ cup (60 mL) of the olive oil, 3 sprigs of the thyme, and 2 sprigs of the sage. Cover and refrigerate for at least 1 hour or overnight.

Combine the chicken stock, wine, vinegar, shallots, garlic, and the remaining thyme and sage sprigs in a large saucepan and bring to a simmer over medium heat. Add the cream and veal jus and simmer until the liquid has reduced to 1½ cups (375 mL).

Heat a large skillet over medium-high heat and add the remaining olive oil. When the oil is hot, add the turkey and sauté, stirring frequently, for 10 minutes or until the turkey is lightly browned and no longer pink inside.

Strain the shallots and garlic and the herb sprigs out of the sauce, and reheat it over medium heat. With a slotted spoon, transfer the cooked turkey meat to the sauce, along with the Swiss chard and mustard. Cook, stirring, over low heat just until the Swiss chard wilts. Add the butter and stir until the butter melts. Season with salt and pepper to taste. Keep warm until ready to serve.

THE OLD WINERY RESTAURANT, 2008

GLAZED BRUSSELS SPROUTS

⅓ cup (80 mL) diced pancetta

2 cups (500 mL) trimmed and halved
   small Brussels sprouts

1 shallot, finely chopped

1 cup (250 mL) chicken stock (page 255)

2 Tbsp (30 mL) unsalted butter

kosher salt and black pepper
   to taste

IN A LARGE NON-STICK SKILLET over medium heat, cook the pancetta, stirring frequently, until it has rendered all its fat and is browned and crispy. Add the Brussels sprouts and sauté, stirring frequently, until the sprouts have browned slightly. Stir in the shallot and sauté, stirring frequently, for 2 minutes or until shallot is softened.

Add the chicken stock and simmer, stirring frequently, until the stock has reduced to a glaze. Add the butter and stir until it melts. Season with salt and pepper to taste.

TO SERVE, ladle the stew into a large serving bowl or soup tureen. Serve at the table in large warm soup bowls, along with the glazed Brussels sprouts.

Rustic Seafood Stew with Rouille

Use as many different types of fish and seafood as you like to make this hearty soup. Loosely based on traditional European recipes, my version is served with spicy rouille-topped baguette to help sop up the broth.

SERVES 8

ROUILLE

⅓ cup (80 mL) cooked mashed potato

4 cloves garlic, coarsely chopped

2 tsp (10 mL) tomato paste

kosher salt and black pepper to taste

1 cup (250 mL) olive oil

juice of 1 lemon

¼ tsp (1 mL) cayenne

IN A FOOD PROCESSOR (not a blender), combine the mashed potato, garlic, tomato paste, and salt and pepper to taste. Process until smooth. With the motor running, gradually add the olive oil in a slow, steady stream until the mixture is smooth and creamy. Add the lemon juice and cayenne and process briefly.

Scrape into a small bowl, cover and refrigerate until ready to serve.

SEAFOOD STEW

¼ cup (60 mL) olive oil

½ cup (125 mL) chopped onion

½ cup (125 mL) finely chopped carrot

½ cup (125 mL) finely chopped leek
(white part only)

½ cup (125 mL) finely chopped fennel

2 cloves garlic, minced

1 Tbsp (15 mL) tomato paste

2 cups (500 mL) dry white wine

2 cups (500 mL) fish stock (page 255)

2 Tbsp (30 mL) lemon juice

2 generous pinches saffron

16 tightly closed fresh littleneck
clams, scrubbed

16 tightly closed fresh mussels,
scrubbed

8 black tiger shrimp, peeled
and deveined

¼ lb (125 g) squid, cut into strips

1 cup (250 mL) tomato concassé
(page 257)

½ lb (250 g) cooked crabmeat

¼ cup (60 mL) finely chopped
Italian parsley

kosher salt and black pepper
to taste

8 slices baguette, toasted

HEAT A LARGE HEAVY POT over medium heat and add the olive oil. When the oil is hot, add the onion, carrot, leek, fennel, and garlic and sauté, stirring frequently, for about 10 minutes or until the vegetables are softened but not browned. Add the tomato paste and cook, stirring, for 2 minutes. Stir in the wine, fish stock, lemon juice, and saffron and simmer for 10 minutes until the liquid has reduced slightly.

Add the clams and mussels. Reduce the heat to low and simmer, tightly covered, for about 10 minutes or until the clams and mussels have opened (discard any that don't open). Add the shrimp and squid and simmer for a few more minutes, until the shrimp are pink and firm.

Stir in the tomato concassé, crabmeat, and parsley. Remove the pot from the heat and season the stew with salt and pepper to taste.

TO SERVE, ladle the stew into 8 warm soup bowls, making sure to divide the seafood evenly among the bowls. Spread the rouille on the toasted baguette slices and serve them on the side.

November is the time when truffles, both black and white, are at their peak. While I acknowledge they are very expensive and sometimes difficult to find, they are worth the price and the

Potato and Truffle Frittata

legwork involved in finding them and are, in fact, one of my favourite gastronomic ingredients. Here I marry the majestic earthiness of the black truffle with the simplicity of an open-face omelette to serve as a sophisticated dinner entrée or a lunch.

SERVES 4

¼ cup (60 mL) olive oil
½ cup (125 mL) chopped red onion
2 cups (500 mL) diced peeled potatoes
8 eggs, lightly beaten
2 Tbsp (30 mL) milk

2 small black truffles, chopped
additional olive oil for drizzling
4 slices crispy pancetta (page 10)
1 cup (250 mL) lightly packed baby
    greens, washed and dried

PREHEAT THE OVEN to 400°F (200°C).

In a large non-stick ovenproof skillet, heat the olive oil over medium-low heat. Add the onion and sauté, stirring frequently, until slightly softened. Add the potato and continue to sauté, stirring frequently, until the vegetables are tender and slightly browned.

In a medium bowl, whisk together the eggs and milk then pour into the skillet. Transfer the skillet to the oven and bake for about 10 minutes or until the frittata is lightly browned around the edges and firm.

Remove the skillet from the oven and turn the frittata out onto a large round platter. Sprinkle with the black truffles and drizzle with a little olive oil.

To serve, cut the frittata into quarters and place each quarter on a warm dinner plate. Garnish each plate with a slice of crispy pancetta and small bouquet of salad greens.

This innovative recipe serves up a carrot cake like none you've ever had before. The carrots are glazed with butter and brandy before they go into the cake and, instead of the traditional cream cheese

Brandy Caramelized Carrot Cake with Cream Cheese Ice Cream and Caramel Sauce

frosting, I've created a cream cheese ice cream that you scoop on top of the cake. Finally, the caramel sauce brings it all together in a slice of gooey goodness.

SERVES 9 OR 10

CREAM CHEESE ICE CREAM

1 lemon

1½ cups (375 mL) 35% cream

1 cup (250 mL) packed brown sugar

4 oz (125 g) cream cheese, softened

1 egg

½ tsp (2 mL) vanilla

¾ cup (185 mL) buttermilk

PARE THE ZEST from the lemon, avoiding the white pith. In a small saucepan, bring the cream to a simmer over medium heat. Add the lemon rind. Remove the saucepan from the heat and let steep for 5 minutes.

Meanwhile, in the bowl of a stand mixer fitted with the wire whisk attachment, combine the sugar and cream cheese and whisk on medium speed for about 8 minutes or until light and fluffy. Whisk in the egg until well combined. Whisk in the vanilla.

Discard the lemon rind from the cream. With the motor on low speed, add the hot cream to the cream cheese mixture, 1 Tbsp (15 mL) at a time at first, then in a steady stream, mixing until well combined.

Transfer the contents of the food mixer to a medium saucepan and stir in the buttermilk. Cook the custard over low heat, stirring frequently, until thick enough to coat the back of a spoon (do not allow to boil).

Remove the saucepan from the heat. Strain the custard through a fine-mesh sieve. Cover and refrigerate until chilled.

Freeze in an ice cream maker following the manufacturer's instructions. (Or, pour the mixture into a shallow container, cover and freeze for 2 to 3 hours or until a 1-inch/2.5 cm frozen border has formed around the edge. Scrape the ice cream into a bowl and beat until smooth. Scrape the ice cream back into the container. Repeat freezing and beating process once more, then cover and freeze until firm.)

BRANDY CARAMELIZED CARROT CAKE

1 lb (500 g) carrots, chopped

1 cup (250 mL) brandy

2 Tbsp (30 mL) granulated sugar

non-stick baking spray

1½ cups (375 mL) all-purpose flour

1½ tsp (7.5 mL) baking powder

1 tsp (5 mL) baking soda

1 tsp (5 mL) freshly grated nutmeg

½ tsp (2 mL) ground cardamom

pinch cinnamon

pinch table salt

2 eggs

¼ cup (60 mL) corn syrup

¼ cup (60 mL) molasses

1 Tbsp (15 mL) finely grated
fresh ginger

½ cup (125 mL) packed brown sugar

½ cup (125 mL) unsalted butter,
softened

caramel sauce using hazelnut-caramel
sauce recipe on page 18, but omit
the hazelnuts

IN A MEDIUM SAUCEPAN, combine the carrots, brandy, granulated sugar, and ½ cup (125 mL) water. Simmer over high heat until the liquid has reduced by half and the carrots are tender. Transfer the carrot mixture to a blender (not a food processor) and blend until smooth. Set aside.

Preheat the oven to 300°F (150°C). Spray a 9-inch (1.5 L) round or square cake pan with baking spray.

In a medium bowl, whisk together the flour, baking powder, baking soda, nutmeg, cardamom, cinnamon, and salt. Set aside. In a pitcher, whisk together the eggs, corn syrup, molasses, and ginger. Set aside.

In the bowl of a stand mixer fitted with the wire whisk attachment, combine the brown sugar and butter and whisk on medium speed for about 8 minutes or until light and fluffy.

With the motor on low speed, carefully add the corn syrup mixture to the creamed butter and sugar, mixing until well combined. Still with the motor on low speed, slowly add the flour mixture to the batter a spoonful at a time, mixing until all the dry ingredients have been thoroughly incorporated. Add the carrot purée and mix just until combined.

Pour the batter into the prepared cake pan. Bake for 15 to 20 minutes or until cooked around the edges but still jiggly in the centre. Remove from the oven and let the cake cool completely in the pan on a wire rack.

TO SERVE, remove the cake from the pan and cut it into 10 even-size wedges or 9 squares. Place each piece on a dessert plate and spoon caramel sauce over the top. Finish each piece of cake with a scoop of cream cheese ice cream.

ember

December is a special month I absolutely adore. This is my favourite part of the winter, despite the fact that we're faced with craziness at work from all the holiday parties we cater, and a hectic time at home as well. It has always been that way.

One of my earliest memories of Italy was all the baking the village ladies would do during the holiday season and, of course, the presents. I remember the last Christmas we ever celebrated in Italy. I was just four years old and my dad, who was working as a mason in Switzerland, sent me a long air gun, which my mother hid under the bed. Back then, we opened our one gift after Mass on Christmas Eve. I don't know what my dad was thinking giving a weapon to a small child but he was away from home and no doubt missing us.

I also recall being very mischievous around Christmas and sabotaging some of the holiday baking by stealing pies left by an open window to cool. I'd take a pie, run to a hiding place, devour the whole thing, then run back for another. It's no wonder I was so naughty with all that sugar pulsing through my veins.

I think the most compelling part of the Christmas season is how family ties are reinforced round the celebratory table. My family were all avid cooks when I was growing up—well, not the men, but the women.

Families would gather at one another's houses, and each woman would bring her specialty, something she was particularly proud of. My mom was famous for her Christmas Eve fish feast, and I think that's why I am such an avid lover of fish and seafood today.

When I joined the hospitality business, the holidays invariably meant lots of work. Rarely do restaurant and hotel employees get to enjoy Christmas the way someone in a more conventional business would. This meant we would have to fit celebrating around our work schedules. We might skip midnight mass on Christmas Eve and go on Christmas Day or vice versa. Or, we opened our gifts on the 24th instead of Christmas morning. I hated that. If you surveyed every cook and waiter in the restaurant business and asked them what's the worst shift of all, they will overwhelmingly say it's the Christmas Day breakfast shift.

But, cooking during the holiday season can be very pleasurable. Christmas is a time to focus on special ingredients and bring out some of the finer foods we love to cook. There's no better time to spoil yourself and your family and friends by using such premium ingredients as foie gras, oysters, lobster, and beef tenderloin. December is a slow crescendo of food with the climax coming at New Year's Eve when we pull out all the stops and truly indulge.

Cubes of luscious foie gras fried in a crisp breadcrumb coating make remarkable little treats that will amaze your taste buds. Serve them as canapés or as an accompaniment to roast wild

Molten Foie Gras Fritters

game. Just be sure to warn your guests to be careful of the hot liquid centre.

Look for truffle juice in specialty grocery stores.

SERVES 6 TO 8

FOIE GRAS FILLING

2 cups (500 mL) port

24 sheets gelatin or 6 Tbsp (90 mL) unflavoured powdered gelatin

¾ lb (375 g) foie gras, large veins removed

3 cups (750 mL) 35% cream

¼ cup (60 mL) truffle juice

kosher salt and black pepper to taste

IN A SMALL NON-REACTIVE SAUCEPAN, simmer the port over low heat until it is reduced by half.

Meanwhile, in a large bowl, soak the gelatin sheets in enough cold water just to cover them for about 5 minutes or until softened. Remove the gelatin from the bowl, squeezing the sheets to remove the excess water. Set aside. (If you are using powdered gelatin, sprinkle the gelatin over ⅓ cup/ 80 mL cold water in a small bowl and let stand for 5 minutes or until puffy. Set the bowl in a small saucepan of simmering water and stir gently until melted.)

In a medium saucepan over high heat, cook the foie gras for about 5 minutes on each side until browned and softened. Stir in the reduced port, the cream, and truffle juice. Simmer for a few minutes then remove the saucepan from the heat and stir in the gelatin and salt and pepper to taste. Keep stirring until the gelatin has completely melted into the foie gras mixture.

Transfer the foie gras mixture to a food processor or blender and process until smooth. Strain through a fine-mesh sieve into a shallow non-reactive dish. Cover and refrigerate until set. Remove from the fridge and cut the foie gras mixture into 1-inch (2.5 cm) cubes. Arrange the cubes on a baking sheet lined with parchment paper and freeze overnight.

FRITTERS

3 cups (750 mL) all-purpose flour
6 eggs
¼ cup (60 mL) milk

4 cups (1 L) dry breadcrumbs
foie gras filling
vegetable oil for deep-frying

PLACE the flour in a large bowl. Whisk together the eggs and milk in a second large bowl. Place breadcrumbs in a third large bowl.

Working with a few pieces at a time, dredge the frozen cubes of foie gras filling first in the flour then the egg mixture, then the breadcrumbs, ensuring the entire surface is coated with breadcrumbs. As soon as the cubes are coated, return them to the freezer to prevent them from melting.

When all the pieces are coated, repeat the process to double-coat each piece with flour, eggs, and breadcrumbs.

Heat the oil in a deep pot until a candy thermometer registers 370°F (187°C), or use a deep fat fryer and follow the manufacturer's instructions. Working with a few pieces at a time, drop the coated pieces of foie gras into the hot oil. Cook for 1 to 2 minutes or until golden brown and crisp. Remove the foie gras fritters from the pot with a slotted spoon and let drain on a plate lined with paper towels.

TO SERVE, pile on a serving platter and serve at once.

DE LUCA'S WINE COUNTRY
RESTAURANT, 2009

The Perfect Cheese Soufflé

SERVES 6

⅓ cup (80 mL) unsalted butter, softened, divided
¼ cup (60 mL) fresh, soft breadcrumbs
1½ Tbsp (22.5 mL) all-purpose flour
1 cup (250 mL) 35% cream

pinch each freshly grated nutmeg, kosher salt, and white pepper
1 cup (250 mL) shredded Gruyère or aged cheddar cheese, or freshly grated Parmesan cheese
6 egg yolks
8 egg whites

PREHEAT THE OVEN to 400°F (200°C) for at least 20 minutes. Rub six ½-cup (125 mL) individual soufflé dishes or ramekins with 2 Tbsp (30 mL) of the butter. Sprinkle with the breadcrumbs, shaking out any excess. Put the dishes on a large baking sheet.

In a medium saucepan over low heat, cook the remaining butter and the flour for 10 minutes, stirring frequently, until the mixture looks dry but has not coloured. Slowly whisk in the cream and cook, whisking constantly, until the sauce is smooth and glossy. Stir in the nutmeg, salt, and pepper. Fold in the cheese.

Meanwhile, in a small bowl, beat the egg yolks lightly. In a large bowl, whisk the egg whites until they hold stiff peaks.

Fold the egg yolk mixture into the cheese mixture by quarters, blending throughly after each addition. Gradually fold in the egg whites until no white streaks remain. Divide the mixture among the prepared dishes. Bake for 40 minutes or until golden brown and tall.

To serve, place each soufflé dish on a round plate with a vine leaf under the dish so it does not shift on the plate. Serve at once.

Pan-Seared Foie Gras with Cornbread Muffins, Applesauce, and Armagnac Honey

This playful recipe is a study in contrasts. Here, I've combined the extravagant richness of foie gras with rustic cornbread muffins, comforting applesauce, and decadent Armagnac-flavoured honey.

SERVES 6

CORNBREAD MUFFINS

1 cup (250 mL) all-purpose flour

½ cup (125 mL) cornmeal

2 tsp (10 mL) baking powder

½ tsp (2 mL) table salt

¼ cup (60 mL) granulated sugar

2 Tbsp (30 mL) unsalted butter, softened

1 egg

2 tsp (10 mL) maple syrup

2 tsp (10 mL) honey

1 cup (250 mL) milk

non-stick baking spray

PREHEAT THE OVEN to 375°F (190°C).

Whisk together the flour, cornmeal, baking powder, and salt in a medium bowl.

In a separate bowl, beat together the sugar and butter until creamy. Beat in the egg, maple syrup, and honey. Stir in the flour mixture alternately with the milk, starting and ending with flour, until no dry spots remain. (Batter will be runny.)

Spray a 24-cup mini muffin pan with baking spray. Divide the batter evenly among the cups. Bake for 10 to 12 minutes or until a toothpick inserted in the centre of one of the muffins comes out clean. Let the muffins cool in the pan for 5 minutes, then remove and let cool completely on a wire rack.

APPLESAUCE

2 Granny Smith apples, peeled, cored, and chopped

½ cup (125 mL) granulated sugar

½ cup (125 mL) dry white wine

IN A MEDIUM non-reactive saucepan, combine all the ingredients with 1 cup (250 mL) water. Bring to a simmer over medium heat. Reduce the heat to low and simmer, covered, for 12 minutes or until the apples are very soft. Strain the apples through a fine-mesh sieve, reserving the cooking liquid. Transfer the apples to a blender or a food processor and blend until smooth. Add a little of the reserved cooking liquid and blend again until the purée is the consistency of thick pancake batter. Discard the remaining cooking liquid. Keep the applesauce warm until ready to serve.

ARMAGNAC HONEY

½ cup (125 mL) honey   3 Tbsp (45 mL) Armagnac

IN A SMALL SAUCEPAN, combine the honey and Armagnac and simmer over low heat for about 10 minutes or until caramelized. Remove the saucepan from the heat and keep warm until ready to serve.

PAN-SEARED FOIE GRAS

1 lb (500 g) foie gras, large veins   kosher salt and black pepper
   removed and cut into 6 even-size   to taste
   medallions   frisée for garnish

SEASON the pieces of foie gras on both sides with salt and pepper. Preheat a large, good-quality non-stick skillet over very high heat. Place the foie gras in the skillet and cook without moving for 1 minute or until golden brown on the underside. Foie gras yields a lot of fat so don't be surprised to see it "swimming" in its own fat at this point. Spoon out the excess as the foie gras sears to prevent it from poaching in the fat.

Using a spatula or an egg lifter, carefully turn the foie gras over and continue cooking for 1 minute. Carefully touch the top of the foie gras with your index finger. The foie gras is done when you feel no resistance in the centre. It should be crispy on the outside and molten on the inside. Carefully remove the foie gras from the skillet and transfer to a plate lined with paper towels to absorb the excess fat.

TO SERVE, spoon the applesauce onto the centre of 6 warm salad plates. Cut the tops off 6 muffins (reserve the remaining muffins to serve another time) and place 1 muffin base on each portion of applesauce. Place a few frisée leaves on each muffin base, then top the frisée with foie gras. Place the muffin tops on the foie gras. Drizzle the Armagnac honey over the muffin tops.

Oyster and Lobster Vichyssoise

While I acknowledge that vichyssoise is usually the name for a chilled soup, this warm seafood version of the classic leek and potato soup is so smooth, I thought it deserved the same moniker.

SERVES 6

2 Tbsp (30 mL) unsalted butter
1 leek (white part only), chopped
1 Tbsp (15 mL) grated fresh ginger
lobster stock (page 256)
2 potatoes, peeled and chopped
½ cup (125 mL) 35% cream
3 sprigs Italian parsley
2 sprigs tarragon

1 sprig thyme
1 bay leaf
12 oysters, shucked, meat and
    juice reserved separately
cooked meat from 2 lobsters
    (page 36), diced
juice of 1 lemon

HEAT A LARGE POT over medium heat and add the butter. When the butter foams, add the leek and ginger and sauté, stirring frequently, for a few minutes. Add the lobster stock and potatoes and bring to a boil.

Reduce the heat and simmer until the potatoes are cooked through. Add the cream, parsley, tarragon, thyme, and bay leaf and simmer for 5 more minutes. Discard the thyme and bay leaf.

Add the meat from 6 of the oysters to the soup and then transfer the soup to a blender (not a food processor) and blend until smooth. Strain the soup through a fine-mesh sieve into a clean saucepan. Stir in the lobster meat, lemon juice, and reserved oyster juice and heat through over low heat.

To serve, ladle the soup into 6 warm soup bowls and garnish each portion with one of the remaining oysters.

One of my dearest possessions is a selection of menus given to me by my great-uncle that he collected from Mediterranean cruise ships in the '40s, '50s, and '60s. Without the modern

Beef Tenderloin with Double-Smoked Bacon and Potato Hash and Bordelaise Sauce

technology we use today, I'm sure the conditions in those floating kitchens must have been terrible. Bordelaise sauce appears often on those old menus and it amazes me that we still enjoy classic recipes like this today. Here's my 21st century version, teamed with moist beef tenderloin.

Beef marrow is available from any reputable butcher. Soak it overnight in lightly salted water before using.

SERVES 4

BORDELAISE SAUCE

2 sprigs Italian parsley

1 sprig thyme

1 bay leaf

1 green leek leaf

2 cups (500 mL) Cabernet Sauvignon

⅓ cup (80 mL) finely chopped shallots

2 tsp (10 mL) cracked black peppercorns

1 cup (250 mL) veal stock (page 254)

½ lb (250 g) beef marrow, diced

2 Tbsp (30 mL) cold unsalted butter, cubed

kosher salt and black pepper to taste

ENCLOSE the parsley, thyme, and bay leaf in the leek leaf and tie with a small piece of kitchen twine to make a bundle. Set aside.

In a small non-reactive saucepan, simmer the Cabernet Sauvignon, shallots, and peppercorns over high heat until the wine has reduced by half. Add the veal stock and the herb bundle and simmer until the liquid has reduced by one-third and has thickened enough to coat the back of a spoon. Add the beef marrow and simmer for 1 minute. Discard the herb bundle.

Transfer the sauce to a blender (not a food processor) and blend until bone marrow has emulsified into the sauce. Strain the sauce through a fine-mesh sieve into a clean saucepan. Whisk in the butter and salt and pepper to taste. Keep warm until ready to serve.

DOUBLE-SMOKED BACON AND POTATO HASH

4 slices double-smoked bacon,
 finely diced
2 large potatoes, peeled and cut into
 ½-inch (1 cm) dice
¼ cup (60 mL) olive oil
¼ cup (60 mL) finely diced sweet
 red pepper

¼ cup (60 mL) finely diced rutabaga
¼ cup (60 mL) finely diced butternut
 squash
2 shallots, finely diced
1 clove garlic, finely chopped
kosher salt and black pepper
 to taste

IN A LARGE SKILLET over low heat, sauté the bacon gently for a few minutes to release its fat. Add the potato and stir to coat it in the rendered bacon fat. Stir in the olive oil, sweet red pepper, rutabaga, squash, shallots, and garlic and continue to cook, stirring frequently, until the potatoes are cooked through and the vegetables are tender. Season with salt and pepper to taste. Keep warm until ready to serve.

BEEF TENDERLOIN

1 lb (500 g) beef tenderloin, cut
 crosswise into 4 even-size
 medallions
kosher salt and black pepper to taste
1 Tbsp (15 mL) unsalted butter

1 tsp (5 mL) olive oil
2 Tbsp (30 mL) finely chopped
 Italian parsley
additional olive oil for drizzling

PREHEAT THE OVEN to 400°F (200°C).

Season the pieces of beef tenderloin with salt and pepper to taste. Heat a large ovenproof skillet over medium-high heat and add the butter and oil. When the butter foams, add the beef tenderloin pieces and sear for 1 to 2 minutes on each side or until browned. Transfer the skillet to the oven and cook for 4 to 5 minutes for medium-rare beef.

TO SERVE, divide the hash among 4 warm dinner plates and sprinkle with parsley. (If desired, you may place sautéed Swiss chard in the centre of the plates as a base for the beef.) Top each portion of hash with a piece of beef tenderloin. Spoon the bordelaise sauce around the edge of the plates and drizzle the beef with olive oil to taste.

This one-pot meal is perfect for a chilly weekend afternoon. I often make this dish when my buddies and I gather to watch Sunday afternoon football. Check the ribs often during cooking to

Beef Short Ribs and Pancetta Braised in Red Wine

ensure there's always enough liquid in the casserole.

SERVES 4

3 lb (1.5 kg) beef short ribs, cut into
   2-inch (5 cm) pieces and fat trimmed

1 bottle (750 mL) dry red wine,
   such as Cabernet Sauvignon

1 Tbsp (15 mL) chili paste (or to taste)

6 sprigs Italian parsley

3 sprigs thyme

6 black peppercorns

1 bay leaf

¼ cup (60 mL) olive oil

2 Tbsp (30 mL) unsalted butter

1 cup (250 mL) chopped onions

¼ lb (125 g) pancetta, chopped

2 lb (1 kg) potatoes, scrubbed and cut
   into 1-inch (2.5 cm) pieces

kosher salt and black pepper to taste

IN A LARGE NON-REACTIVE BOWL, combine the short ribs, wine, chili paste, parsley, thyme, peppercorns, and bay leaf, making sure the beef ribs are completely submerged. Cover and refrigerate overnight.

Preheat the oven to 325°F (160°C).

Heat a large flameproof casserole over medium-high heat and add the olive oil and butter. When the butter foams, add the onions and pancetta and sauté, stirring frequently, until the onions have browned slightly and the pancetta has crisped up.

Add the marinated beef ribs, the marinade, and the potatoes. Bring to a boil, cover with a lid, and transfer to the oven. Cook for 2 to 3 hours or until the meat is fork tender and the potatoes are cooked. Remove the casserole from the oven and season with salt and pepper to taste.

To serve, discard the thyme and bay leaf and spoon the ribs and potatoes into a warm shallow serving dish.

Chocolate Cappuccino Cheesecake

A festive dessert for a festive month, this is the ideal treat for a New Year's Eve bash.

SERVES 8 TO 10

CHOCOLATE CRUST

1 cup (250 mL) chocolate cookie
   crumbs
¼ cup (60 mL) unsalted butter,
   softened

2 Tbsp (30 mL) granulated sugar
¼ tsp (1 mL) cinnamon

COMBINE all the ingredients until crumbly. Press the crust evenly over the base of a well-greased 9-inch (2.5 L) springform pan. Set aside.

FILLING

8 oz (250 g) semi-sweet chocolate,
   coarsely chopped

2 Tbsp (30 mL) 35% cream

2 tsp (10 mL) instant coffee granules

8 oz (250 g) cream cheese, softened

1 cup (250 mL) granulated sugar

3 eggs

1 cup (250 mL) sour cream

2 tsp (10 mL) vanilla

¼ tsp (1 mL) table salt

icing sugar for dusting

PREHEAT THE OVEN to 350°F (180°C).

In a medium bowl set over a saucepan of simmering water, melt the chocolate with the cream until it is smooth. Remove the bowl from the heat and let cool slightly. In a small bowl, dissolve the coffee granules in ¼ cup (60 mL) hot water. Set aside.

In the bowl of a stand mixer fitted with the paddle attachment, beat the cream cheese until smooth. Gradually beat in the sugar until smooth. Beat in the eggs, one at a time, beating well after each one is added.

Beat in the chocolate mixture. Add the sour cream, dissolved coffee, vanilla, and salt and beat until smooth.

TO ASSEMBLE, pour the chocolate mixture into the prepared crust. Bake for 45 minutes. The centre of the cheesecake should still be quite runny. Turn off the oven and leave the cheesecake in the oven for another 30 minutes or until jelly-like in the centre. Remove the cheesecake from the oven and let cool to room temperature. Cover and refrigerate overnight.

To serve, release the sides of the pan and place the cheesecake on a serving platter. (Alternatively, you may use a cookie cutter dipped in warm water to cut out 8 to 10 portions.) Dust the top with icing sugar and cut into wedges.

Basic Recipes

VEAL STOCK

This stock is the foundation of most of my meat-based dishes. While I have come a long way since my early culinary days when I believed that every dish needed a sauce, I do acknowledge that a properly made sauce, one based on exceptional ingredients, can raise a dish from mundane to outstanding.

Ask your butcher to cut the veal bones into pieces for you.

MAKES ABOUT 4 CUPS (1 L)

5 lb (2.2 kg) veal bones, chopped into 2-inch (5 cm) pieces

2 carrots, cut into 1-inch (2.5 cm) pieces

1 large onion, chopped

1 cup (250 mL) dry white wine

6 tomatoes, seeded and chopped

2 cups (500 mL) chopped button mushrooms

1 stalk celery, chopped

2 cloves garlic, crushed

1 bouquet garni (one 4-inch/10 cm piece of leek leaf wrapped round 2 sprigs parsley, 2 sprigs thyme, and 1 bay leaf, and tied with kitchen twine)

PREHEAT THE OVEN to 400°F (200°C).

Spread the veal bones out in a large shallow roasting pan and roast, uncovered, for about 20 minutes, stirring occasionally, until the bones are nicely browned. Add the carrots and onion to the veal bones and stir well. Roast for a further 5 minutes.

Transfer the veal bones, carrots, and onion to a large stockpot. Discard any fat from the roasting pan and add the wine to the pan. Place the roasting pan over high heat and bring to a boil, stirring to scrape up any browned bits from the bottom of the roasting pan. Simmer over high heat until the wine has reduced by half.

Add the reduced wine to the stockpot, along with 12 cups (3 L) water. Bring to a boil over high heat. Reduce the heat until the liquid is barely simmering and simmer for 10 minutes, skimming off any impurities that rise to the surface.

Add the tomatoes, mushrooms, celery, garlic, and bouquet garni and simmer, uncovered, for about 2½ hours, skimming as necessary, until the

VEAL JUS

Simmer veal stock until it is reduced by one-third.

VEAL REDUCTION

Simmer veal stock until it is reduced by half and thick enough to coat the back of a spoon.

liquid has reduced and is just covering the bones and vegetables. Remove the pot from the heat and let stand for 20 minutes.

Strain the stock through a fine-mesh sieve, discarding the solids. Let cool slightly then cover and refrigerate for up to 3 days or freeze for up to 3 months.

CHICKEN STOCK

MAKES ABOUT 12 CUPS (3 L)

6 lb (2.7 kg) chicken bones
2 stalks celery, chopped
1 onion, chopped
1 carrot, chopped
6 cloves garlic, crushed
4 sprigs thyme
4 sprigs Italian parsley
2 bay leaves
12 black peppercorns

PLACE the chicken bones in a large stockpot and add enough water to come 2 inches (5 cm) above the bones. Bring to a boil over high heat. Reduce the heat until the liquid is barely simmering and simmer for 10 minutes, skimming off any impurities that rise to the surface.

Add the remaining ingredients and simmer, uncovered, for about 1½ hours, skimming as necessary, until the liquid has reduced and is just covering the bones and vegetables. Remove the pot from the heat and let stand for 20 minutes.

Strain the stock through a fine-mesh sieve, discarding the solids. Let cool slightly then cover and refrigerate for up to 3 days or freeze for up to 3 months.

VEGETABLE STOCK

MAKES ABOUT 8 CUPS (2 L)

2 Tbsp (30 mL) olive oil
6 tomatoes, chopped
3 leeks (white and pale green parts only), chopped
2 stalks celery, chopped
1 large onion, chopped
1½ cups (375 mL) chopped fennel
1½ cups (375 mL) chopped button mushrooms
6 cloves garlic, crushed
¾ cup (185 mL) dry white wine
1 Tbsp (15 mL) black peppercorns
2 bay leaves
4 sprigs thyme
3 sprigs Italian parsley

HEAT A LARGE STOCKPOT over medium heat and add the olive oil. When the oil is hot, add the tomatoes, leeks, celery, onion, fennel, mushrooms, and garlic. Sauté, stirring frequently, for about 20 minutes or until the vegetables are very soft but not brown.

Add the wine, peppercorns, bay leaves, and 10 cups (2.5 L) water. Bring to a boil over high heat. Reduce the heat until the liquid is barely simmering and simmer, uncovered, for about 40 minutes or until the liquid has reduced slightly. Remove the pot from the heat, add the thyme and parsley, and let stand for 10 minutes.

Strain the stock through a fine-mesh sieve, discarding the solids. Let cool slightly then cover and refrigerate for up to 3 days or freeze for up to 3 months.

FISH STOCK

MAKES ABOUT 8 CUPS (2 L)

4 lb (1.8 kg) fish bones (from white fish only)
2 leeks (white parts only), chopped
2 cups (500 mL) chopped white button mushrooms
2 cups (500 mL) dry white wine
2 stalks celery, chopped
¼ fennel bulb, trimmed and chopped
1 lemon, sliced
1 Tbsp (15 mL) puréed canned chipotle chilis in adobo sauce
3 sprigs thyme
2 bay leaves
8 white peppercorns

PLACE the fish bones in a colander set in the sink. Run cold water over the bones for 2 hours to remove any blood.

In a large stockpot, combine the bones and all the remaining ingredients. Add enough cold water to cover the ingredients. Bring the stock to a simmer over low heat, then simmer, uncovered, for 1 hour or until the liquid has reduced slightly.

Stain the stock through a fine-mesh sieve, discarding the solids. Let cool slightly then cover and refrigerate for up to 3 days or freeze for up to 3 months.

LOBSTER STOCK

MAKES ABOUT 4 CUPS (1 L)

1 Tbsp (15 mL) vegetable oil
½ cup (125 mL) finely chopped onion
½ cup (125 mL) finely chopped carrot
½ cup (125 mL) finely chopped celery
1 clove garlic, crushed
½ cup (125 mL) dry white wine
2 lobster carcasses
1-inch (2.5 cm) piece fresh ginger
1 sprig Italian parsley
1 sprig tarragon
1 sprig thyme
4 black peppercorns
1 bay leaf

HEAT A LARGE STOCKPOT over medium heat and add the vegetable oil. When the oil is hot, add the onion, carrot, celery, and garlic and sauté, stirring frequently, for about 5 minutes or until the vegetables are softened but not browned. Add the wine and simmer until it has almost all evaporated.

Add the lobster carcasses and 8 cups (2 L) water, adding more water if necessary so that the ingredients are just covered. Bring to a simmer and, using a large spoon, skim off any impurities that float to the surface.

Add the ginger, parsley, tarragon, thyme, peppercorns, and bay leaf. Reduce the heat to medium-low and simmer until the liquid has reduced by half. Remove the saucepan from the heat and set aside at room temperature for 20 minutes.

Strain the stock through a fine-mesh sieve, discarding the solids. There should be 4 cups (1 L) of stock. If not, top up the stock with a bit of water. Let cool slightly then cover and refrigerate for up to 3 days or freeze for up to 3 months.

LOBSTER COURT BOUILLON

MAKES ABOUT 10 CUPS (2.5 L)

1 cup (250 mL) finely chopped carrots
1 stalk celery, finely chopped
1 leek (white part only), finely chopped
½ cup (125 mL) finely chopped onion
2 shallots, finely chopped
pared rind and juice of 1 lemon
2 Tbsp (30 mL) kosher salt
2 cloves garlic, crushed
25 drained pickled green peppercorns
6 sprigs Italian parsley
2 sprigs thyme
1 clove
1 bay leaf
2 cups (500 mL) dry white wine

IN A LARGE STOCKPOT, combine all of the ingredients except the wine. Add 8 cups (2 L) water. Bring to a simmer over medium heat. Reduce the heat to low and simmer for about 30 minutes. Add the wine and simmer for another 5 minutes.

Stain the court bouillon through a fine-mesh sieve, discarding the solids. Let cool slightly then cover and refrigerate for up to 3 days or freeze for up to 3 months.

When ready to cook lobsters, bring the court bouillon to a rapid boil in a large stockpot.

BASIC PASTA

MAKES 1 LB (500 G) DOUGH

2½ cups (625 mL) all-purpose flour
3 eggs
1 Tbsp (15 mL) olive oil
1 tsp (5 mL) table salt
all-purpose flour for dusting

IN THE BOWL of a stand mixer fitted with the dough hook, combine the flour, eggs, olive oil, salt, and 1 Tbsp (15 mL) lukewarm water. Mix until the dough forms a dry, spongy (not sticky or wet) ball, adding up to 1 Tbsp (15 mL) more lukewarm water, if necessary.

Remove the bowl from the food mixer and cover it with plastic wrap. Let the dough rest for 1 hour at room temperature.

Using a pasta machine and following the manufacturer's instructions, roll out the dough to ⅛-inch (3 mm) thickness. Dust the sheets of dough liberally with flour and set aside.

GARLIC CONFIT

MAKES ABOUT ½ CUP (125 ML) (20 CLOVES)

2 whole heads garlic, separated into individual cloves
    and peeled
1 cup (250 mL) olive oil
1 tsp (5 mL) granulated sugar
1 sprig rosemary
1 sprig thyme
1 bay leaf
6 black or white peppercorns

PREHEAT THE OVEN to 300°F (150°C).

Combine all the ingredients in a small ovenproof dish, making sure the garlic is completely submerged in the oil (add more oil if necessary). Cover and bake for about 3 hours or until the garlic is very soft.

Remove the dish from the oven and cool to room temperature. Refrigerate, covered, for up to 5 days.

ROASTED GARLIC

MAKES ABOUT 2 TBSP (30 ML)

1 whole head garlic
⅓ cup (80 mL) grapeseed oil, divided

PREHEAT THE OVEN to 375°F (190°C).

Cut the head of garlic in half horizontally and place, cut sides up, in a shallow ovenproof dish. Drizzle 2 Tbsp (30 mL) of the oil over the cut side of each half of the garlic head.

Cover the dish and roast for 1 hour or until the garlic is very tender. Remove the dish from the oven and let the garlic cool to room temperature.

With your fingers, break the garlic into individual cloves, squeezing each clove out of its skin into an airtight container. Pour the remaining oil over the surface of the garlic. Cover and refrigerate for up to 5 days.

TOMATO CONCASSÉ

MAKES ABOUT 1 CUP (250 ML)

2 very ripe medium tomatoes

BRING A LARGE POT of water to a rapid boil over high heat and have ready a large bowl of ice water. With a small, sharp knife, make an X in the skin of the smooth end of each tomato. Add the tomatoes to the pot of boiling water and blanch for 5 seconds. Using a strainer or a slotted spoon, transfer the tomatoes to the bowl of ice water.

Drain the tomatoes. Using a small, sharp knife, peel away the skin from where the incision was made. Cut each tomato into quarters and discard the seeds and tough stem ends. Dice the tomatoes. Cover and refrigerate for up to 5 days.

SHRIMP BUTTER

You only need ¼ cup (60 mL) of this delectable shrimp butter for the Shrimp Minestrone recipe (page 183), so spread the remainder on slices of toasted baguette to serve alongside the soup. Any leftover butter can be stored in an airtight container in the freezer for up to one month.

MAKES ABOUT 1½ CUPS (375 ML)

2 Tbsp (30 mL) cold unsalted butter

½ small onion, finely diced

½ small carrot, finely diced

½ tsp (2 mL) minced garlic

5 large black tiger shrimp, peeled and deveined

2 Tbsp (30 mL) Armagnac, Cognac, or brandy

¼ cup (60 mL) dry white wine

¾ cup (185 mL) unsalted butter, softened

1½ tsp (7.5 mL) finely chopped tarragon

kosher salt, white pepper, and cayenne to taste

HEAT A SMALL SKILLET over medium heat and add the cold butter. When the butter foams, add the onion, carrot, and garlic and sauté, stirring frequently, until the vegetables are softened but not browned.

Stir in the shrimp. Add the Armagnac and, standing well back, ignite carefully. When the flames die away, add the wine and simmer for about 5 minutes or until the shrimp are pink and firm. Remove the skillet from the heat and let cool slightly.

Transfer the shrimp mixture to a food processor (not a blender) and process until the mixture is quite smooth. With the motor running, add the softened butter, tarragon, and salt, pepper, and cayenne to taste. Process until very smooth.

Scrape the shrimp butter into an airtight container and refrigerate for up to 3 days. Let soften slightly before serving.

I WOULD LIKE TO TAKE THIS OPPORTUNITY to acknowledge some of the people who have entered my life—a very rewarding and fulfilling life.

First and foremost is my family, beginning with my wife, Kaleen, and my sons, Matthew and Nicholas. They are the centre of my universe, and without their love, support, and understanding (especially), there would be no chance for success and happiness. Secondly, my parents, who continue

Acknowledgements

to be my biggest fans and take an active interest in both of my restaurants. Their deep sincerity continues to inspire and move me.

To my brother, Dan, my best friend and hero, and to Ashleigh, my sister-in-law, who both always says nice things when I cook for them (even when I cheat and order in, but pass it off as my own creation). Thanks, guys—you're too kind.

To Monique and Robert Glatt, my business partners at the Old Winery Restaurant, who indulge me in my absent-minded-professor antics and keep our business on the straight and narrow. Rob, with his insightful business acumen, is a true mentor to me, and Monique's acute wine palate and fresh approach provide inspiration without fail.

To Geoffrey Bray-Cotton and his partner, Janice Bartley, who run the Niagara-on-the-Lake Culinary School—one of the best in Canada at putting out ready-to-hire chefs, and making our frequent labour shortages easier to bear. Thanks for all your support over the years.

To John and Liz Hawley, for making the dream of de Luca's Wine Country Restaurant become a reality. For Liz's amazing restaurant design and John's constant encouragement, business advice, and vision. Truly, deeply: thank you.

To Anna D'Agrosa, my high-school friend, who returned to my life as a talented photographer and still a wonderful person. Thank you for the delicious photography. We were constantly at odds with each other as to whether it was the food or the photographs that made this book so special. I maintain it's the photography, and since it's my book, I get the last word. So, there!

A special heartfelt thank you to Maria Giuliani, my cousin from Montreal, who by contributing her special poetry to this book has elevated it as I never could have dreamed. Her word-smithing, particularly in the September poem, is magical. I keep a printed copy of it hanging in my office so I can reread it often. I know she worked on the poems with sincerity and passion.

To the staff of both my restaurants, the Old Winery and de Luca's, who put up with my style of management. You continue to help move my culinary vision forward, and you graciously bear with me in times of extreme stress and adversity. I especially want to thank Lynn Kuta, who has faithfully worked with me since 2001. Thank you for making me look good, Lynn, and for keeping it all together.

To the guests who frequent my restaurants, come to my cooking classes, and buy my cookbooks: thank you for being so enthusiastic, for sending me your insightful suggestions, words of praise, and words of inspiration, and for allowing me to tell my stories (they're all true, I swear!).

To the staff of Whitecap Books, especially Taryn Boyd, who pushed me along and was the cause of many sleepless nights as another deadline loomed. Also, to my editor Julia Aitken, who was an absolute joy to work with. Really great suggestions and an ability to take what I had in my head and on little scraps of paper and make them into good, usable recipes. To designer Mauve Pagé, who put it all together and made it truly spectacular. And, of course, to publisher Robert McCullough, who has believed in this project since the early days of *Recipes from Wine Country*.

There are a lot of other people who should be thanked. Those of you who've also come into my life in one way or another, and who enrich my day-to-day experiences, thank you all. Thank you to those of you who inspire me, and perhaps you don't even know you do. You may not know this, but I'm not the most communicative guy in the world. I will try harder.

Finally, I would like to express gratitude to the profession itself. It has entered me and fused itself to the very fibre of who I am, and never will I be able to excise it from my bones. That is why every high is so intense and every low so devastating. I have laboured in this business for over 32 years, and I still find every day a crazy mix of emotions, some of joy, some of fear and anxiety. But in the end, when I look out into a full dining room and see the joy people are sharing over the food and service we've provided, then it all becomes crystal clear. It's what we do, not who we are, that really matters—and to me that is perfect.